PUBLICATIONS ON THE NEAR EAST

The Martyrs of Karbala

SHI'I SYMBOLS AND RITUALS IN MODERN IRAN

KAMRAN SCOT AGHAIE

UNIVERSITY OF WASHINGTON PRESS

SEATTLE & LONDON

This publication was supported in part by the Donald R. Ellegood
International Publications Endowment.

University of Washington Press
PO Box 50096, Seattle, WA 98145
www.washington.edu/uwpress

Library of Congress Cataloging-in-Publication Data
Aghaie, Kamran Scot.
  The martyrs of Karbala : Shi'i symbols & rituals in modern Iran /
Kamran Scot Aghaie.— 1st ed.
     p.   cm.
  Includes bibliographical references and index.
  ISBN 0-295-98448-1 (hardback : alk. paper)
  ISBN 0-295-98455-4 (pbk. : alk. paper)
  1. Shâi'ah—Iran—History.   2. Shâi'ah—Iran—Tehran—Case
studies.   3. Muslim martyrs—Iraq—Karbalâa'.   4. Shâi'ah—Customs
and practices.   5. Islam and politics—Iran.   I. Title.
  BP192.7.I68A37 2004
  297.8'2'0955—dc22   2004010766

THIS BOOK IS DEDICATED TO MY PARENTS.

꙳ To my father, Reza Aghaie, whose life and laughter were cut short while he was far too young. I was ten when he was killed in a car accident, and he was barely older than I am now.

꙳ To my mother, Edna Boyce Aghaie, who has always been such a wonderful and nurturing parent. She is an amazing and unique woman who has overcome a great deal of hardship while remaining compassionate, generous, self-sacrificing, and ethical to a fault. When I was growing up, nobody influenced me more than my mother. As an adult I realize more and more every day how much my values, ethics, and character are the result of her influence.

Contents

Preface

This book explores the significant transformation of Iranian Shi'i rituals and symbols of *Moharram*, which center on the seventh-century Battle of Karbala. Patterns of change are traced from the mid nineteenth century to the close of the twentieth century, in an effort to demonstrate the diverse ways in which the processes of modernization have affected the broader society, political dynamics, and religious culture of Iran. It is hoped that by looking at the popular religious rituals of *Moharram* it is possible to shed light on how selected aspects of popular culture, politics, and society have either changed or resisted change in relation to the broader transformations brought on by state-led modernization and international influence. This study argues that the modern Iranian state was unable fully to control, transform, or marginalize these rituals and symbols. Rather, *Moharram* symbols and rituals evolved both in response to state-initiated changes and independently of state actions. Often other forces of change were more important factors than the modernization trends led by the state.

Historical studies of developing countries like Iran have generally been concerned with issues primarily related to the "modernity" debate. This debate focuses attention on such topics as imperialism, the development of nation-states, economic modernization, efforts by governments to promote their own legitimacy, and the spread of modern ideologies like nationalism, democracy, and secularism. These issues are generally analyzed either within the context of colonial and postcolonial relationships between Western imperialist states and developing countries or within the context of state-centered politics.

As a result of the economic, political, and cultural influences brought on by modern international forces, the governments of these countries have implemented modernization programs that inevitably incorporate at least some Western ideas, institutions, and values. This process of modernization has led to very rapid, and at times traumatic, change in the societies and cultures of developing countries. Historians who analyze the modern history of these societies are often interested in better understanding the process of rapid change underway in developing countries during the modern era.

The first task of the historian is to find evidence with which to analyze changes in the society under study. Because of the scarcity of certain types of primary resources available to historians of Iran, many have been forced to deal with this problem by studying modernization programs supported both by the state and by the modernizing elites. This is done partly because the state and the ruling elites provided a great deal of evidence upon which to draw. It is a simple historical fact that the state and the educated elites have left far more detailed records than have farmers, butchers, children, laborers, and women. It therefore stands to reason that the state and elites should be the starting point of any scholarly study on modern Iran. This book is not an exception to this general rule. However, this book tries to expand the analysis as far beyond the state as the sources will allow. This approach is intended to ascribe or attribute greater agency to groups and individuals outside the circles of government and power in Iran.

A state-centered approach runs the risk of forcing the historian to postulate that there existed a traditional culture within a social, economic, and political order that is either static or in decline. The traditional order may then be characterized as having been progressively supplanted by the process of modernization promoted in society by the state and the modernizing elites. This has often caused proponents of traditional social and cultural norms, as well as newly emerging political opposition groups, to reject and criticize these modernization programs. One of the main difficulties posed by this approach is that it usually focuses primarily upon politics, the state, and the modernizing elites, often ignoring broader social and cultural processes of transformation taking place in the society. The challenge facing historians who want to examine traditionally unexplored areas of society is the difficulty of finding evidence with which to analyze alternative dimensions of social and cultural change.

In the case of Iran, there is an excellent vehicle for analyzing both the state and broader changes in society, namely, the Karbala Paradigm.[1] The symbols derived from interpretations of the seventh-century Battle of Karbala have historically been used by Shi'is to articulate a wide range of political, ethical, and cultural values. Hoseyn and Yazid represent a spectrum. At one end of this spectrum, Hoseyn symbolizes goodness, truth, justice, piety, courage, self-sacrifice, honor, and devotion to God. At the other end of the spectrum, Yazid symbolizes evil, moral corruption, injustice, cruelty, pride, obsession with the material world, and so forth. This set of religious symbols and rituals constitutes the single most pervasive expression of social, political, and cultural ideals throughout the past century and a half in Iran. Other ideologies, symbols, and rituals, such as those associated with nationalism or imported from Western cultural practices, are also very important. However, during the past century and a half, Shi'i symbols and rituals have cut much more thoroughly across ethnic, regional, class, political, economic, and social categories.

The policies and agendas of the various regimes ruling Iran have influenced manifestations of Karbala. However, these symbols and rituals have proven to be substantially independent of the control of the state. The state's ability to make use of the Karbala Paradigm has been an important factor in the state's ability to maintain its legitimacy and at least some degree of connection or integration with the broader society. The state's failure to incorporate these symbols and rituals adequately into its program and ideology, as was the case with the Pahlavis, contributed in part to the state's crisis of legitimacy. This shortcoming allowed opposition groups to make effective use of these symbols and rituals in overthrowing the regime. The government of the Islamic Republic, in comparison, has used these symbols and rituals effectively to articulate the state's ideology and policies. This course of action has made it difficult for anyone critical of the Islamic regime to use these same symbols and rituals to denounce or oppose the state. However, this state versus the opposition dynamic is only part of the story.

Karbala symbols and rituals have been one of the most significant forces in modern Iranian society, culture, and politics. While they exercised a considerable influence upon the fortunes of the state, the state itself was usually not the most important factor in the evolution of Karbala symbols and rituals. Rather than a "trickle-down" effect, according to which the state's policies eventually determined the nature of these diverse forms of religious expression, the relationship between the state and society was complex, inconsistent, and, above all, a "two-way street." In other words, religious symbols and rituals were produced through a complex process of interaction between the state and society. Furthermore, much of the evolution one sees in religious expression in Iran was the product of factors that had little or nothing to do with the state.

Karbala symbols and rituals have been one of the primary means for expressing social and political ideals on a broad societal level. In some cases this process took the form of direct opposition to the state. In other cases these rituals served as a means for maintaining social bonds, ideals, and identities independently of the agendas and policies of the state. Changing economic and demographic forces transformed preexisting and newly emerging political relationships. Other important factors include changes in ethics, aesthetics, class dynamics, social institutions, groupings, and identities. Discourses on contemporary social and political crises have also found expression in Karbala symbols and rituals. By studying these symbols and rituals it is possible to understand how Iranian society has changed over the past century and a half both in response to and independently of state-led modernization and social transformation programs.

This study uses manifestations of Karbala symbols and rituals in an attempt to expand the focus of analysis beyond the state and the ruling elites. However, it must be admitted at the outset that, given the scarcity of the evidence available, there are limits to how far this process can successfully be carried out. Given this constraint, this study attempts to push the analysis as far as the source materials allow. Four thematic foci are analyzed: (1) changing patterns of state patronage of Karbala rituals, (2) religious oppositional discourse, (3) expression and reinforcement of a wide variety of social relationships and identities, and (4) an emerging discourse on gender in Iranian society.

First, the patterns of state patronage and use of Shi'i symbols and rituals have been radically discontinuous over the past century and a half. The Qajars were enthusiastic patrons of these rituals, which they used to reinforce their relationships (characterized by mediation) with their subjects. Reza Shah, after consolidating his power and authority, aggressively suppressed these symbols and rituals. His son, Mohammad Reza Shah, followed an inconsistent pattern of sometimes patronizing and more often suppressing them. The revolutionaries used these symbols and rituals quite effectively to overthrow the Pahlavi regime and to develop and maintain an Islamic state.

Second, while the state and the elites associated with it have been able to influence these symbols and rituals, they generally have not been able to control or dominate them. The Karbala Paradigm has proven to be a very flexible and dynamic set of symbols and rituals. It has been a powerful tool in the hands of the government, opposition elements, and society as a whole. The state's use of the Karbala Paradigm has not always secured its authority and legitimacy. However, ignoring this powerful tool has been a risky proposition for any regime intent on staying in power. The patterns of interaction between the state and society have been both complex and mutual.

Third, the patterns of evolution of these symbols and rituals on a much broader social and cultural level have been relatively continuous, although certainly not static. Throughout the past century and a half, Karbala symbols and rituals have continued to serve a variety of functions, including personal, spiritual, soteriological, social, cultural, or political functions. Transformations in technology, economics, social structures, aesthetics, and demographics, to name only a few factors, have been the driving forces behind much of the change that one sees in relation to *Moharram* symbols and rituals.

Fourth, gender dynamics have played an important part in religious culture in Iran. Both men and women have been active participants in *Moharram* rituals, and religious symbols have been gender coded in various ways. Religious symbols and rituals, therefore, have served as vehicles and sites for contentious gender discourses. This book attempts to include gender analysis in an integrated fashion, by looking at the roles of men and women throughout the discussion and by examining gender discourses that define the roles of both men and women.

Acknowledgments

I am indebted to Nosrat Hemmatiyan and Kamal Hosayni for their friendship, hospitality, and help when I was in Tehran conducting research. Hushang Dabbagh and his family were similarly supportive and welcoming when I was doing research in Isfahan and Shahreza. These two families included my father's closest friends, and I view them as my family in Iran.

I want to extend my gratitude to Dr. Asghar Karimi in Tehran, who, from his great understanding of Iranian popular culture, generously consulted and gave advice. He was a wonderful colleague, and I benefited greatly from his vast knowledge and experience. I would also like to acknowledge Faegheh Shirazi for being such a wonderful colleague and friend. She often served as the "guinea pig" so that the rest of us junior faculty could follow in her footsteps. Abraham Marcus, Harold Liebowitz, Ian Mourners, and Richard Lariviere helped me complete this project by providing a supportive and nurturing environment at the University of Texas at Austin. Moh Ghanoonparvar was also very supportive and helpful in giving advice about practical matters related to publishing.

I would like to thank everyone who helped me in completing and preparing my manuscript for publication. Diane Watts did a wonderful job of digitizing and cleaning up the photographs for this manuscript. Elisabeth Sheiffer helped me format and edit the final manuscript. I am also indebted to Mehrnoosh Massah for her assistance with my research in Iran, and to Annes McCann-Baker for her advice on the "ins and outs" of academic publishing.

Nikki R. Keddie, James Gelvin, Michael Morony, Edward Berenson, and Jean-Laurent Rosenthal at UCLA trained me as a historian and guided me through the process of completing my dissertation, revised portions of which are included in this book. My thanks to them.

I would like to express my gratitude to the reviewers of this manuscript for their valuable comments and suggestions. I also thank Michael Duckworth, executive editor of the University of Washington Press, for his dedication, efficiency, and professionalism toward authors.

Very special thanks go to Jackie for putting up with me when I was in the crazy final stages of completing this book, and also to my mother and my sister, Laila, for their help over the years. They have encouraged me to pursue my career goals and helped by reviewing and editing my work at various stages.

Many grants and fellowships made this book possible, and I am most grateful for them. The Vice President of Research at the University of Texas at Austin provided financial support in the form of the Faculty Research Grant, the URI Summer Research Assignment, and the University Coop Subvention Grant. Richard Lariviere, Dean of the College of Liberal Arts, was generous in appointing me to be the Dean's Fellow for Spring 2003, which allowed me to complete this book. I was happy to receive the Religious Studies Forum-Research Award from the Religious Studies program at UT Austin. The UCLA History department supported my earlier research in graduate school, which is what started me on the path to writing this book.

The Martyrs of Karbala

SHI'I SYMBOLS AND RITUALS IN MODERN IRAN

1 ༀ

A Brief Historical Background
of Shiʿism and Moharram

$\mathcal{T}$he two main sects or branches of Islam are Shiʿism and Sunnism. Today, Shiʿis make up between ten and fifteen percent of the world's Muslim population, with approximately half of this number residing in Iran. Other major concentrations of Shiʿis are in Lebanon, Iraq, Bahrain, Yemen, Eastern Arabia, and parts of South Asia. The majority of these Shiʿis belong to the "Twelver" branch, which is discussed below. While Iran is arguably the most influential Shiʿi nation today, this has not always been the case. In fact, the population of the Iranian plateau was predominantly Sunni until after the establishment of the Safavid Empire in 1501. It was only at this time that the dynasty's founder, Shah Esmaʿil (r. 1501–24), initiated policies that eventually led to the conversion of nearly the entire Iranian population to Twelver Shiʿism. Equally significant were the efforts of the prominent religious scholar Baqer Majlesi (d. 1699) in popularizing Twelver Shiʿism throughout the Safavid territories.

While Shiʿism has often been treated as an "Iranian" variant of Islam, its history is far more complex. A survey of the origins and early development of Shiʿism takes one not to medieval Iran but to Arabia, the Levant, and even North Africa. The specific details of the early development of the Sunni-Shiʿi schism, along with the complex evolution of Twelver Shiʿism out of the diverse heterodox strains of early Shiʿism, have been the subject of intense debate, both today and in the past. Without being drawn into these debates, which are far beyond the scope of this book, it can be said that the roots of this schism lie in the crisis of succession that occurred upon the death of the Prophet Mohammad in 632 CE. However, this sectarian division took two to three centuries to develop fully. Additionally, the particular strain of Shiʿism with which this study is concerned, Twelver Shiʿism, also developed slowly over several centuries.

The discussion turns now to the very beginning of this long process of division or schism. During the lifetime of the Prophet, whatever differences or conflicts there may have been between individuals and groups were overshadowed by the unifying effect of his presence and personality. Upon his death in 632, there was a crisis of succession. The main challenges facing the young Muslim community were who should succeed the Prophet and in what capacity. Also unclear was who had the right to select a successor. The ruling institution that evolved out of this crisis was called the "caliphate," in which one man, the caliph, held both temporal and religious authority. The caliph did not, however, possess any of the supernatural or metaphysical qualities of the Prophet, such as infallibility, supernatural knowledge and ability, or the power to receive revelation.

While some Muslims supported the ruling caliphs, others believed that the Prophet's son-in-law and cousin Ali Ebn-e Abi Taleb should have succeeded the Prophet, and later they believed that Ali's descendants should be his successors, beginning with his two sons, Hasan (d. 669) and Hoseyn (d. 680). They believed that the Prophet, before his death, selected Ali as his successor on more than one occasion. For example, they believed that shortly before his death the Prophet gave a speech, at a place called Ghadir Khom, in which he raised Ali's hand and stated as follows:

> We were with the Apostle of God in his journey and we stopped at Ghadir Khum. We performed the obligatory prayer together and a place was swept for the Apostle under two trees and he performed the midday prayer. And then he took 'Ali by the hand and said to the people: "Do you not acknowledge that I have greater claim on each of the believers than they have on themselves?" And they replied: "Yes!" And he took 'Ali's hand and said: "Of whomsoever I am Lord [*Mawla*], then 'Ali is also his Lord. O God! Be thou the supporter of whoever supports 'Ali and the enemy of whoever opposes him." And 'Umar met him ['Ali] after this and said to him: "Congratulations, O son of Abu Talib! Now morning and evening [i.e., forever] you are the master of every believing man and woman."[1]

The institution of leadership that eventually evolved out of this view was called the "imamate," which differed from the caliphate in that the imam had to be a descendant of the Prophet and was usually considered to have supernatural qualities and abilities, such as infallibility and special (or supernatural) religious knowledge. Also, according to most Shi'is, he had to be appointed by either the Prophet or the previous imam in an unbroken chain of succession leading back to the Prophet. They believe that the Prophet endorsed this idea before his death in 632. For example, they attribute the following statement to the Prophet: "My family among you is like Noah's Ark. He who sails on it will be safe, but he who holds back from it will perish."[2] Needless to say, Sunnis and Shi'is have passionately disagreed about the authenticity of some of these accounts. Furthermore, while both sides have accepted many of these accounts as authentic, their interpretations of them have been in conflict.

It is out of the crisis of succession after the Prophet's death, along with a series of political events that unfolded during the first two to three centuries of Islamic history, that the roots of the division between Sunnis and Shi'is are to be found. The term *Shi'i* derives from the phrase *"Shi'at Ali,"* or "partisans of Ali." The term *Sunni* takes its meaning from the phrase *"Ahl al-Sunnah wa al-Jama'ah,"* or "those who follow the [prophetic] traditions and the [official/orthodox] consensus." As it implies, the term Shi'i originates from the partisans' support of the Prophet Mohammad's progeny as his successors, beginning with Ali. Sunni orthodoxy, which was in part a reaction to Shi'i ideological and political challenges, rejected this notion in favor of the caliphs, who in fact did succeed the Prophet and who actually ruled during these early centuries.

While the disputes and schisms may have begun with the crisis of succession, they evolved in accordance with later political and theological trends. For example, regional, ethnic, or tribal loyalties frequently sparked political rebellions. Sectarian rhetoric often accompanied such rebellions. Proto-Shi'i sentiments were often the most effective way to challenge the legitimacy of the ruling caliphs. The Shi'i imams, who were descendants of the Prophet and who had varying degrees of popular support among the masses, were rivals of the Sunni caliphs, who actually ruled the empire. For much of their early history, Sunnis have been associated with the state and the ruling elites, while Shi'is were more often associated with political opposition to the Sunni rulers and elites. While there were several Shi'i states, particularly in the tenth century, their long-term political influence was at its greatest when it took the form of opposition movements that challenged the legitimacy of the ruling caliphs.

It is helpful to keep in mind the basic political chronology of the Muslim empire during this period (i.e., 632–1258). Following the death of the Prophet in 632, there were three successive caliphates: the Rashedin (r. 632–61), the Umayyads (r. 661–750), and the Abbasids (r. 750–1258). All three ruled in succession over nearly the entire Muslim empire, which stretched at it zenith from North Africa (and later Spain) to Central Asia. Sunnis refer to the immediate successors to the Prophet Mohammad as the Rashedin (righteous) caliphs, who included Abu Bakr (r. 632–34), Omar Ebn al-Khattab (r. 634–44), Othman Ebn-e Affan (r. 644–656), and Ali Ebn-e Abi Taleb (r. 556–661). Unlike later caliphs, all four of the Rashedin caliphs were close companions or relatives of the Prophet and have generally been viewed by Sunnis as being highly pious and of impeccable moral character. The Rashedin caliphs were succeeded by the Umayyad caliphate (661–750), which essentially took the form of a hereditary monarchy and has always been characterized by Shi'is as religiously corrupt and politically oppressive. During the Umayyad period, the rivalry between the rulers and opposition groups with popular Shi'i leanings was bitter. It is also during this period that the Battle of Karbala occurred. This battle is the focus of the discussion below.

In 749–50, the Umayyads were overthrown by the Abbasids, who assumed the caliphate and ruled the empire as a dynasty from Iraq until 1258, when the Mongols sacked Baghdad. One significant development for the purposes here was that the Abbasids made fairly extensive use of popular Shi'i sentiments in mobilizing opposition to the Umayyads. For example, they claimed descent from the Prophet's uncle, Abbas. However, after assuming power, they mostly viewed the Shi'is as a threat to their legitimacy. Also important to note is that several Shi'i dynasties rose to power during the Abbasid period, including the Fatimids of Egypt, the Hamdanids of Syria and northern Iraq, and the Buyids of Iran and Iraq.

Throughout this early period, political and religious divisions constituted an endemic crisis for the ruling caliphs. Beginning with the death of the Prophet Mohammad, political divisions began to manifest themselves right away. During the Ridda Wars of 632–33, Abu Bakr prevented some Arabs from seceding from the Muslim empire and community. During the reign of the third Rashedin caliph, Othman, discontent with his policies escalated until he was killed by an angry mob in 656. However, the conflicts that had the greatest impact on sectarian divisions were a series of challenges to Ali's authority between 656 and 661. These included the Battle of the Camel in 656, led by the Prophet's widow A'esheh, and the Battle of Seffin in 657, in which Ali was forced to agree to arbitration with the powerful general Mo'aviyeh, who later established the Umayyad caliphate in 661 after Ali was assassinated by a radical political opposition group called the Khavarej. These divisions and conflicts intensified during the Umayyad period, culminating in 680 in the Battle of Karbala in which the Prophet's grandson Hoseyn, along with seventy of his family members and associates, was massacred by the troops of the second Umayyad caliph, Yazid. The discussion returns to the Battle of Karbala shortly.

During the Umayyad and early Abbasid periods, Shi'ism was in its formative stage, which meant that it was tremendously diverse or heterodox. Many branches of Shi'ism emerged and disappeared, such as the Ghulat (the so-called extremists), who were deemed to be heretics both by Sunnis and by most later Shi'is. The main branches that have continued to be influential to the present day are the Zaydis, the Isma'ilis, and the *Ithna Asharis* (or Twelvers). This book is concerned only with the last of these three, the Twelvers. The differences among these branches of Shi'ism consisted mainly of their varying beliefs and practices, along with disagreements over succession within the chain of imams. For example, the Isma'ilis and the Twelvers disagreed on who was appointed as the seventh imam, with the Isma'ilis following one son named Isma'il, while the Twelvers followed a different son named Musa Kazem. The Zaydis, in turn, have had a more flexible definition of who could be an imam, which has resulted in numerous descendants of the Prophet being recognized as imams throughout history.

During the Abbasid period, in particular the tenth century, numerous Shi'i states emerged, such as the Fatimids and the Qarmatians, both of which were Isma'ili Shi'i dynasties. The Fatimids took control of Egypt in 969, while the Qarmatians rose to prominence in Arabia beginning in the 880s and eventually became a major power in the Levant. There have also been numerous Zaydi rulers and regional powers in the Yemen. Of particular interest for the discussion here are the Buyids, who rose to power in the Iranian plateau and eventually took control of the Abbasid capital, Baghdad, in 945. The Buyids were a Shi'i dynasty that, while allowing the Abbasids to remain the nominal rulers of the empire, wielded power themselves. Although early on the Buyids had some Zaydi tendencies, they subscribed to the Twelver branch of Shi'ism. They were also quite active in popularizing Shi'i mourning rituals and the celebrations of the imamate. The rise to power of the Buyids was a watershed event, because for the first time it was possible for Shi'is to worship publicly and to take part in religious debates without as much fear of persecution. However, Sunni-Shi'i rivalries have continued to the present day.

As previously stated, one of the most consistent and significant trends throughout this early period was that Shi'i imams, who were descendants of the Prophet and who had varying degrees of popular support among the masses, were rivals of the Sunni caliphs, who actually ruled the empire. This rivalry was particularly intense during the Umayyad period and came to a head with the Battle of Karbala in 680 during the reign of the second Umayyad caliph, Yazid. This brings the discussion to the Battle of Karbala (680), and the resulting "Karbala Paradigm," which is the focus of this study.[3]

The story of Karbala begins with the "Battle of Karbala," which occurred in 680 in a desert region of southern Iraq. Many different accounts of this important battle have been written by such prominent historians as the classical Arab scholar al-Tabari (d. 923). However, the concern is not with the historical accuracy of the narratives that purport to recount the details of this battle. For the purposes here, it is only necessary to keep in mind what Shi'is have historically considered to be the "correct" representations of this event. Like many other famous historical events, the tale of the Battle of Karbala has been told and retold over the centuries without a single authoritative version emerging to supplant completely all others.

The most commonly accepted narratives of the Battle of Karbala begin with an account of the discontent of Muslims (especially in southern Iraq) under the rule of the second Umayyad caliph, Yazid (r. 680–83). Yazid is portrayed as having been politically oppressive and morally corrupt. The Prophet Mohammad's grandson Hoseyn (in Medina) received several letters from the caliph's subjects in southern Iraq asking him to travel to Iraq in order to lead them in an uprising against Yazid. After sending scouts to assess the situation in southern Iraq, Hoseyn and a number of his close relatives left the Hijaz, in Western Arabia, and began the trip to Iraq.

In southern Iraq in a desert named Karbala, located near the

Euphrates river, the caravan was surrounded by an overwhelmingly large army sent by Yazid. A standoff ensued because Hoseyn refused to give an oath of allegiance (bey'at) to Yazid. At the end of ten days of waiting, negotiating, and occasionally fighting, a final battle took place, in which Hoseyn and all of his adult male relatives and supporters were killed in a brutal fashion. The survivors, consisting of women and children, together with Hoseyn's son Ali Zeyn al-Abedin (d. 712–13), who was too ill to take part in the fighting, were then taken captive and transported, along with the heads of the martyrs, which had been placed on spears, to Yazid's court in Damascus. Along the way they were exhibited in chains in the public markets of the cities through which they passed and a series of unpleasant incidents occurred, as a result of which Hoseyn's relatives, especially his sister Zeynab and his son Zeyn al-Abedin, publicly condemned Yazid for his cruelty toward the descendants of the Prophet Mohammad.

In this story, Yazid represents the ultimate impious, tyrannical villain. His supporters, like Shemr, the soldier represented as being the one who actually killed Hoseyn, are also portrayed mostly as being immoral, worldly, and cruel. Hoseyn and his supporters, such as Abbas, his sons Ali Asghar and Ali Akbar, the young bridegroom Qasem, to name just a few, are represented by Shi'is as symbols of courage, piety, and truth. These men are depicted as courageous warriors who fought for the sake of God and divine justice and willingly gave up their lives as martyrs. The women and girls, in particular Zeynab, serve as symbols of the ideal of women supporting their male relative, suffering the indignation of captivity with dignity, educating and preparing their sons to follow the path of Hoseyn, willingly sacrificing their male loved ones to martyrdom, and serving as spokespersons for the cause after the men were martyred.

For Shi'is, this event has become the root metaphor upon which many of their religious beliefs and practices are based. It has served as a vindication of the Shi'i cause in the face of Sunni criticism, as well as constituting the central event in their understanding of human history. At the same time, the rituals associated with the battle have historically served as a vehicle for expressing and strengthening a variety of political and social relationships, associations, and identities. The Karbala Paradigm has also provided an opportunity for spiritual redemption for Shi'is. By mourning the fate of the family of the Prophet Mohammad (the *ahl al-beyt*) generally, and his grandson

Hoseyn specifically, Shi'is hope to gain salvation and admission to paradise.

Mourning for Hoseyn and his fallen supporters at Karbala began almost immediately after the massacre when Hoseyn's surviving relatives and supporters lamented the tragedy. As part of the long-term trend toward the development of popular mourning rituals based on commemoration of Karbala, popular elegies of the martyrs were composed during the remainder of the Umayyad period (680–750) and the first two centuries of Abbasid rule (roughly 750–930). Karbala symbolism was important in many rebellions throughout this period, including the political overthrow of the Umayyads by the Abbasids in 749–50. The most famous propagandist for the Abbasid political uprising, Abu Moslem, made use of popular sentiments against the Umayyad rulers by appealing to popular support for the family of the Prophet. For example, the Abbasids claimed to be descendants of Mohammad's uncle, Abbas.

The political uses of Karbala symbols and simple mourning practices date almost as far back as the Battle of Karbala itself (680). However, the more elaborate Shi'i ritual, commonly referred to as the "*Moharram* procession," was not documented until the tenth century. These three centuries were also an important period in the development of relatively distinct Shi'i identities and doctrines. The earliest reliable account of the performance of public mourning rituals that in any way resembles what are now called *Moharram* processions (especially with a political connotation) concerns an event that took place in 963 during the reign of Mo'ezz al-Dowleh, the Buyid ruler of southern Iran and Iraq. The Buyid rulers, who were Shi'is themselves, promoted this practice, along with a celebration of the Ghadir Khom incident, in order to promote their religious legitimacy and to strengthen the sense of Shi'i identity in and around Baghdad. It should be noted, however, that during this period popular sentiment for the family of the Prophet was not restricted exclusively to the Shi'is. The famous fourteenth-century Arab historian Ibn al-Kathir states that,

> On the tenth of *Moharram* of this year [AH 352], Mu'izz ad-Dawla Ibn Buwayh, may God disgrace him, ordered that the markets be closed, and that the women should wear coarse woolen hair cloth, and that they should go into the markets with their faces uncovered/unveiled and their hair disheveled, beating their faces and wail-

ing over Hussein Ibn Abi Talib. The people of the *Sunna* could not prevent this spectacle because of the *Shi'a*'s large numbers and their increasing power (*zuhur*), and because the sultan was on their side.[4]

During the following centuries historians continued to record the details of the Battle of Karbala in historical texts and popular commemorative elegies, and mourning processions were common throughout the Muslim world. For example, Saheb Ebn-e Abbad, a famous poet of the Buyid era, wrote many elegies for the *ahl al-beyt*, including the following:

The blood of the friends of the Prophet Mohammad is flowing; Our tears rain plentifully. Let there be infinite curses and blame upon his enemies in the past and the future. Distress yourselves about what befell the children. Now listen to the story of the martyrdom and how they deprived Hussein of water; and when he was fighting on the plain of Kerbela how they behaved meanly and unjustly. They cut off the head of a descendant of the Prophet in that fiery land! But the Imam lives, his foot in the stirrup and mounted upon his horse! He will not be killed! Then the sinners and the merciless attacked the Prophet's Family. Fly to salvation while there is still the chance, hurry! Shemr [the soldier who is represented as the one who actually killed Hoseyn] the bastard of Ibn al-Baghi struck his sword on the ground while laughing. This is a kindness to the Prophet and is pleasing! Then the soldiers of the Banu Hind moved out with the heads of the descendants of the Chosen Prophet fixed to the points of their lances. The angels in heaven bewailed their deaths and have wept so copiously that water was flowing from the leaves of the trees and plants. Then you must weep for a while; for after this tragedy of Taff, laughter is unlawful.[5]

A major development in Shi'i rituals occurred with the establishment of the Safavid state in 1501 in a territory largely encompassing the modern state of Iran. The Safavids were originally a Sufi order, but the founder of the dynasty, Shah Esma'il, decreed that the official state religion would be orthodox Twelver Shi'ism. Shi'i symbols and rituals were important to the self-definition of the Safavid dynasty. The rulers made fairly liberal use of Shi'i symbols and rituals (such as the *Moharram* procession) to promote their legitimacy vis-à-vis their Sunni rival to the east (the Uzbeks) and their more dangerous rival to the west (the Ottomans).

Shi'i rituals took on new meanings and new forms during the Safavid era. The fact that the rulers themselves were Shi'is meant that these rituals could be used to bolster their legitimacy. It also meant that public rituals could be performed without any regard for Sunni attitudes toward these rituals. Shi'is could publicly express their sense of community identity and their negative sentiments toward Sunnis. For example, they could openly condemn with impunity the first three caliphs, Abu Bakr, Omar, and Othman. These seventh-century caliphs have historically been highly regarded as "righteous caliphs" by the Sunnis. Shi'is, however, have historically condemned them as usurpers of Ali's right to be the successor to the Prophet. Earlier rituals had been performed within a society in which the Sunnis made up the majority, but the Safavid period created a new environment that was relatively more isolated from Sunnis. This also meant that the Sunni "other" was now more of a symbolic reality than a practical reality, because very few Iranians remained Sunni in the centuries to follow. Because of the large numbers of Shi'is living under Safavid rule, rituals became more elaborate and the demand for talented authors of elegies dramatically increased.[6]

One of the most significant developments in the sixteenth century was the emergence of a new practice called *rowzeh khani,* a ritual sermon recounting and mourning the tragedy of Karbala. The primary catalyst in the creation of this ritual was the appearance of Hoseyn Va'ez Kashefi's 1502 composition titled *Rowzat al-shohada* (*The Garden of Martyrs*). Kashefi's text was a synthesis of a long line of historical accounts of Karbala by religious scholars. He drew material from such famous texts as Sa'id al-Din's *Rowzat al-Eslam* (*The Garden of Islam*), and al-Khwarazmi's *Maqtal nur al-'a'emmeh* (*The Site of the Murder of the Light of the Imams*). *Rowzat al-shohada* became one of the main sources for a series of "Karbala narratives" and is one of the most often quoted sources in later narratives and histories retelling the story of the battle and its aftermath. Excerpts from Kashefi's work also served as the basis for scripts that were used in the *rowzeh khani* sermons, which eventually became one of the primary rituals of Shi'is around the world and which bear the same name as Kashefi's book.[7]

The *rowzeh khani* is a ritual in which a sermon is given based on a text like *Rowzat al-shohada,* with a great deal of improvisation on the part of a specially trained speaker. The objective of the speaker is to move the audience to tears through his recitation of the tragic details of the Battle of Karbala.[8] This type of mourning ritual has been viewed by Shi'is as a means of achieving salvation, as is illustrated by the often-repeated quotation, "Anyone who cries for Hoseyn or causes someone to cry for Hoseyn shall go directly to paradise."[9]

By the Qajar period (1796–1925) the *rowzeh khani* had evolved into a much more elaborate ritual called *shabih khani* or *ta'ziyeh khani*. The *ta'ziyeh* was an elaborate ritual drama or theatrical performance of the Karbala story based on the same narratives used in the *rowzeh khani*. The *ta'ziyeh* involved a large cast of professional and amateur actors, a director, a staging area, elaborate costumes, and props. This ritual reached its greatest level of popularity during the late Qajar period, after which it began a slow, relative decline, until it became much less common in the large cities in the 1930s and 1940s. However, *ta'ziyeh*s continued to exist in Iran on a smaller scale throughout the twentieth century, especially in traditional neighborhoods in cities and in rural areas.[10]

Because of the grand scale of the urban *ta'ziyeh*, it serves as one of the best examples of patronage of Shi'i rituals by the state and by the wealthy elite. Its fortunes have been greatly affected over the years by changes in both state policies and elite culture. One of the reasons for the relative decline of *ta'ziyeh*s in the twentieth century was that they were banned, off and on, by both Pahlavi rulers. More important, Iranian elites became less interested in sponsoring such ritual events. Scholars of literature and drama attempted to revive this theatrical tradition in the 1970s, and again in the 1980s and 1990s. Since 1979, the Ministry of Culture of the Islamic Republic, as well as other religious and community organizations, have also tried to preserve this tradition by televising performances and by establishing cultural preservation centers that regularly sponsor *ta'ziyeh*s. However, these governmental and scholarly efforts have been focused more strongly upon the preservation of *ta'ziyeh*s as cultural artifacts than upon promotion of a living tradition that has broad appeal and popular participation. Unlike the Qajar period, which was the heyday of the *ta'ziyeh* ritual, the dominant public rituals since the 1930s have been the *Moharram* procession and the *rowzeh khani*.

One should be careful not to overstate the so-called decline of *ta'ziyeh*s, which are still performed regularly in Iran and have a strong following in many sectors of society. The decline discussed above applies only in relation to the trends in the Qajar period. It is also important not to attribute this relative decline entirely to the reduction in patronage by the state and elites associated with the state. A case in point is the more dramatic decline in the mid-twentieth century of the practice of *pardeh khani*, in which a professional narrator told the story of Karbala while using an elaborate painting containing many different scenes (almost like a collage) as a visual aid. This trend is important in that, while it followed a similar (although far more dramatic) pattern of decline as did the *ta'ziyeh* tradition, it was not an expensive ritual practice sponsored by wealthy elites. Its decline was due to various factors, including the waning significance of coffeehouses (the most common site of this type of performance) in many urban centers of Iran, as well as changing aesthetics and the emergence of new forms of entertainment and religious performance such as television, theater, film, print media, and, more recently, computer technology.

As a footnote to the discussion of the evolution of Karbala rituals, it should be noted that, while *Moharram* rituals were more prevalent in areas where Shi'is were concentrated, some Sunnis (especially those oriented more toward popular culture and Sufism) also commemorated Karbala in similar observances. In some areas, such as South Asia, Sunnis can also be enthusiastic participants in Shi'i rituals. In the modern era, the rituals of Sunnis and Shi'is have become more distinct from one another. However, throughout much of Islamic history the differences between them based on ideological constructs were less prevalent. This was particularly true of popular practice, which could often be at variance with the views of the elite ulama. By the end of the twentieth century, commemoration of Karbala has declined among Sunnis, whereas among Shi'is it has continued to evolve and change as it did in previous centuries.[11]

2

The Qajar Elites and Religious Patronage (1796–1925)

*B*etween 1796 and 1925, the Qajar dynasty ruled over a territory that roughly corresponds to the boundaries of modern Iran. This period marked the first time since the fall of the Safavids in 1722 that Iran was ruled by a relatively centralized monarchy. By the early nineteenth century, Qajar rule became more decentralized as Western imperialist powers progressively encroached upon the shah's authority. Military defeat at the hands of Russia, along with economic pressures from the West, resulted in a variety of unequal treaties that required Iran to grant both land and economic concessions to various European states. For example, after being defeated in two wars with Russia in 1804–12 and 1826–28, the shah was compelled to sign two humiliating treaties: the Treaty of Golestan in 1813 and the Treaty of Turkomanchai in 1828. In accordance with the terms of these treaties, portions of the Caucasus and Azerbaijan were ceded to Russia. Furthermore, European powers imposed terms of free trade upon Iran at a time when Iranian merchants increasingly called for government protection against Western goods, which were increasingly being imported on a large scale.[1]

The effects of the increase in trade with the West, both beneficial and harmful, were unevenly distributed in Iranian society. Some economic concessions ensured European merchants and traders low tariffs and exemptions from internal duties that their Iranian counterparts were forced to pay. Efforts at economic and political restructuring in the Qajar empire remained limited, with the notable exception of the initiatives undertaken by Abbas Mirza, the crown prince and the governor of the large province of Azerbaijan. He gave his troops Western-style military training and even sent a few to study in Europe as early as the 1820s. During most of the empire's span there was little real reform of the system of administration or the economy until the reign of Reza Shah Pahlavi, who took power in the 1920s.

The Qajars continued many Safavid traditions of rule. For example, they used Shi'i religious symbolism to promote their political legitimacy. Qajar elites were enthusiastic patrons of Shi'i rituals, most notably both the *rowzeh khani* (the ritualized sermon) and the public *Moharram* processions. However, unlike the Safavids, the Qajars were also enthusiastic supporters of the *ta'ziyeh*. As a result of this high level of patronage, large *takyeh*s (amphitheaters) were built during this period in most major cities and towns for the performance of *ta'ziyeh*s. In addition, those professionals whose job it was to act out the narrative of Karbala onstage or in an open area were financially supported by the court, wealthy elites, guilds, and a variety of community associations centered around neighborhoods and other social or family institutions. The Qajar elites occupied the top-ranking position in a hierarchy of patrons that extended downward to the lowest strata of society. In this way, these rituals served to strengthen the bonds of loyalty between the state and its subjects, thus ensuring the Qajar elites a certain degree of religious and political legitimacy. However, there were limits to the degree of religious legitimacy to which the Qajars could lay claim.

It has been argued that, according to nineteenth-century Twelver Shi'ism, no ruler was considered to be "truly" legitimate except for the twelfth imam, who was believed to be living in occultation. Nevertheless, the ulama did not always challenge the temporal authority of the Qajar rulers. While the ulama did not necessarily endorse the legitimacy of these rulers, they generally accepted their rule as a practical necessity. Furthermore, the ulama often tacitly endorsed the religious mandate of the Qajars. Said Amir Arjomand paraphrases the eminent nineteenth-century *mojtahed* (a religious scholar whose religious rulings are given the highest degree of authority) Mirza Abu al-Qasem Qomi (d. 1817–18), who described the inherent congruence between political and religious authority in the following way:

> God has made the king His Lieutenant (*janishin*) on earth (not the *janishin* of the Hidden Imam, as the Safavids had claimed to be). . . . The king's rule is a trial; he is not absolved from performing his ethical duties by virtue of being king, and will be punished by God for all evil doing. . . . [Qummi stresses] the interdependence of kingship and religion . . . kings were needed for the preservation of order, the *'ulama* for the protection of religion.[2]

The ulama had ambivalent attitudes toward both the rulers and some of the more extreme Shi'i rituals, which they did not always officially endorse (particularly *ta'ziyeh*s). Some ulama viewed them as popular innovations that were not based on proper religious foundations either in the Qur'an or in the documented example set by the Prophet and the imams. The main issues raised by most of these religious scholars were that acting onstage and representing other people (particularly women) are religiously forbidden practices and that Islam forbids hurting or injuring oneself, as many did while participating in the popular processions. However, there has not been unanimity of opinion among the ulama. Mirza Abu al-Qasem Qomi discussed the lawfulness of *shabih khani* and *ta'ziyeh* (reenactments of the events of Karbala) in his highly influential work on Shi'i law, *Jame' al-shetat* (published in 1818–19). He argued the following:

Question: Is it lawful on the days of Ashura to play the roles of the Imam or the enemies of the Family of the Prophet in order to induce the people to weeping? Is it lawful that men wearing the clothing of the Family of the Prophet or others should play their roles for the same purpose, or is it not?

Answer: We say that there is no reason to prohibit the representations of the innocent and pure one and the generality of the excellence of weeping, causing weeping, and pretending to weep for the Lord of Martyrs and his followers. . . . However, [as to] the representation of the enemies of the Family of the Prophet: There is no proof for the view that it is prohibited as might be imagined. . . .

[In 1903–4, a prominent scholar, Sayyid Ali Yazdi, paraphrased the remainder of Qomi's ruling.] Fadel Qummi says: dressing up as women is forbidden if the impersonation is done for a private purpose in order to appear as a woman and of their sex. It is evident that the custom in the plays [*ta'ziyeh*s] is not of this kind and it is plain that a man playing Zainab Khatun, for example, is not dressed as a woman simply for the purpose of appearing as a woman; rather his intention is to portray her form and figure in order to induce weeping [for the family of the Prophet Muhammad]. . . .[3]

Other respected scholars disagreed with Qomi's view, especially in the twentieth century. For example, on this matter the opinion of Ha'eri Yazdi (1897–1976), grand ayatollah and *marja' al-taqlid* (the highest clerical rank in Shiʿism), was that *taʿziyeh* and *shabih khani* were not permissible. Similar views were also evident in the nineteenth century. For example, during the month of *Safar* in 1886, during a *rowzeh khani* sermon given in the *Dang Masjed* of the Udlajan quarter in Tehran, Mirza Mohammad Ali Mohtaj criticized *taʿziyeh* and expressed his desire to have a royal decree outlawing this practice.[4] These examples notwithstanding, the practice of performing *taʿziyeh* was not usually challenged openly by the ulama living under Qajar rule. All this being said, the dominant view promoted by Iranian Shiʿi ulama during the Qajar period did not challenge the acceptability of *taʿziyeh,* as a religious ritual.

Many prominent ulama sponsored rituals in their homes. For example, Ayatollah Fazlollah Nuri, one of the highest-ranking ulama in Tehran at the turn of the twentieth century, sponsored rituals in his home in the Mahalleh-e Bagh-e Sangalaj every year. He was also active in supporting the Constitutional Revolution of 1905–6 and was hanged for sedition. People from all classes of society attended, including notables, ulama, and visitors from Najaf and Samarra.[5] Another prominent scholar, Ayatollah Mohammad Hasan Ashtiyani, who was active in opposition to the tobacco concessions in the 1890s, also had a tradition of sponsoring *Moharram* rituals in his home.[6] This tradition was carried on by his descendents after he died in 1901. For example, his son, Ayatollah Mirza Ashtiyani, who was active in the Constitutional Revolution, established a *hoseyniyeh* (a religious building devoted primarily to rituals associated with *Ashura*) in Galubandak and built two other ritual sites that were later destroyed as a result of modern city renovations.[7] In some rare cases, these ayatollahs climbed the *menbar* (pulpit) and gave sermons themselves. For example, during the reign of Naser al-Din Shah, Ayatollah Sayyed Mohammad Behbahani, who held rituals in his home every year, occasionally gave sermons during the *majles* and even gave *rowzeh khani* sermons.[8]

Many ulama attended *Moharram* rituals, but the elite members of the ulama attended the more controversial rituals less often than did those from the lower ranks. Furthermore, when they did participate in these rituals, their roles were often distinct. The Qajar notable Abdollah Mostowfi commented in his memoirs:

The clergy who were asked to take the pulpit in these ceremonies were divided into two groups. First, there were those who were strictly preachers [more respected ulama]. They opened the day's session with a homily and a verse from the Koran, then analyzed it in depth. They proceeded with examples, rules, and interesting stories, discussing any particular ethical or religious aspect that they had in mind. Finally, they concluded with a brief mention of the hardship of the leaders of Islam in reaching sainthood and a prayer, blessing the shah of Islam.

The second group of clergy [common preachers] chanted the summary story of the martyrdom. They started the minute they reached the pulpit, and continued for ten minutes, chanting a combination of related poetry and prose, with the customary blessing as a finale. The first group required education, and the second a good voice. As yet, the profession had not been invaded by a third group, who could neither sing, nor give any intelligent speech![9]

Many ulama participated in their own variants of the *rowzeh khani* ritual in which they abstained from what they considered to be the more objectionable practices such as theatrical performances, striking the body with metal chains, piercing the body with sharp hooks, or striking one's head with a sword. Sven Hedin, a Western resident in a smaller city at the turn of the nineteenth century, reported that "Tebbes has two tekkiehs. One is that of the Mollahs or priests; it is more dignified and religiously orthodox, and is more confined to the recitation and intoning of sacred legends, without any *tamashuh* or theatrical plays. The day is commenced at the mollahs' tekkieh and is continued in ours, which belongs to the *hokumet* or government; that is under the supervision of Emad-ul-Mulk."[10]

These theological disputes about the legitimacy of the Qajars and the legality of certain ritual practices are important as examples of elite attitudes. They also constitute law. However, they did not necessarily represent attitudes of Iranians from the middle and lower strata of society. This was true even when religious authorities debated very practical aspects of temporal rule, such as a particular shah's sense of justice or overall effectiveness as a leader. What is of primary importance here is the extent to which the Qajars used specifically Shi'i concepts and practices in the nineteenth and early twentieth centuries to legitimize their rule on a broader, popular level.

By studying patterns of ritual patronage by both the state and elites who were not actually ruling, it is possible to analyze political and social

dynamics on a broader societal level. Studying the patterns of participation by the masses of average Iranians in these rituals allows for a
more inclusive approach to understanding the importance of these rituals in Iranian society during the period under study. The main concerns here are the various uses of Karbala symbols and rituals in
promoting the religious legitimacy of both Qajar rulers and other elites
under their rule in the nineteenth and early twentieth centuries. Patronage by the state and by the elite was important in reinforcing the political order. The debates and contestations surrounding the use of
ta'ziyeh as a means of representing and even defining the state to its
subjects and to foreigners, and the socialization effects of these rituals, were equally important.

The Qajars were fairly aggressive in representing themselves as
patrons of *Moharram* rituals. Not only did they attend public mourning rituals such as the *rowzeh khani, ta'ziyeh,* and *shabih khani,* but they
were also avid financial supporters of such ritual observances. The
wealthy elites in the capital and in the provinces generally behaved in
a similar manner. Patronage of this sort was one of the more important means utilized by individuals and groups in Qajar society to raise
their social status. Hence, wealthy individuals and organizations often
competed for prestige by sponsoring elaborate rituals attended by their
clients and associates. However, such financial support was not
restricted to the elites. People from all segments of society contributed
in their own way, either financially or by donating their possessions
or services. Consequently, every ritual became a massive cooperative
project in which a variety of social relationships, such as those between
elites and their various subordinates, were expressed and strengthened.

Basic economic factors ensured the central importance of wealthy
patrons within the cooperative venture of organizing rituals. The
expenses associated simply with feeding the spectators at such ritual
events could be enormous. Many European visitors to Iran were
impressed by the lavish provisions, "The crowds are often regaled with
sherbets by the personage at whose cost the tazzia is given, also pipes,
and even coffee; and the amount expended in pipes, coffee, tea, etc.,
for the numerous guests is very considerable indeed."[11] Eugene Abin,
the French ambassador to Iran in 1907, estimated that the annual cost
to the shah of financially supporting the *ta'ziyeh* performances held in
Naser al-Din Shah's *Takyeh Dowlat* to be 30,000 *tumans.*[12] Another

account estimated the cost of even a small *ta'ziyeh* for the ruler to be 1,500 *tumans*.[13] The *takyeh* itself could also be extremely expensive to build. For example, the cost of the construction of the *Takyeh Dowlat* by Naser al-Din Shah has been estimated at between 150,000 and 300,000 *tumans*.[14] Just as the rituals were dependent upon the patronage of wealthy elites, many lower- and middle-strata individuals and groups were often similarly dependent upon individuals or families from among the elites. Thus, patterns of status within rituals often reflected both realities and ideals within the broader society.

The high degree of patronage was critically important to the development of *ta'ziyeh* rituals because of the high costs involved in paying for equipment and costumes, providing a site for the performances, and hiring professional actors and *rowzeh khans* (who would deliver these specialized performances and sermons). While many people participated without pay in *Moharram* rituals, there were usually professionals to be hired, especially for the most elaborate ritual of all, the *ta'ziyeh* (the theatrical performance). These actors, who often came from families with a long history in the profession, were hired by the patron of the *ta'ziyeh*, who might be the shah, a governor, another wealthy individual, or an organization such as a guild or a neighborhood association.[15] One particularly elaborate account below describes how a talented young actor could achieve a great deal of wealth and fame by pursuing this profession, thus becoming "a star":

> The Mirza told me that he [the young actor] came from Ispahan, where the people are most graceful and animated. He had begun by being trained when quite small by his father, the chief of a company of dancers, who wished to make of him a singing dancer. His voice was so melodious, and his elocution so perfect, that he abandoned the profane profession for the sacred art, and came to Teheran, where he obtained large salaries—he was supposed to be paid four hundred *tomans* for the representations of the first ten days of Moharrem. This constitutes affluence for a Persian of the lower class, who live on a pound a month handsomely. During the remainder of the year he led a life of a man of means, singing only from time to time at the houses of grandees. . . . Like every self-respecting star, he was capricious, exigent, and disagreeable, and was a thorn in the side of his director and his colleagues.[16]

While *ta'ziyeh* performances were not exactly the most common ritual events in Qajar Iran, they were closely related to other simpler rituals that were performed on a more popular level in society. *Ta'ziyeh* performances, therefore, serve as a good indicator of a comprehensive set of symbols and rituals that helped to connect the state and wealthy elites to lower- and middle-strata social groups. *Ta'ziyeh* performances were based on scripts composed from historical accounts embellished with tragically graphic detail. While variants of the *ta'ziyeh* rituals were also performed in popular processions, in which case they were usually referred to by the more general term *shabih khani*, they were best suited to being performed in a *takyeh*, which was dedicated almost exclusively to this purpose. However, any open space could also be used, such as a mosque, home, *bagh* (orchard or yard), *madreseh* (seminary), caravanserai, or an open area in a neighborhood or marketplace.

Because of the resources available to the court, the shah was the greatest patron of all. The most elaborate example of court patronage of Shi'i rituals was the *Takyeh Dowlat*, which was completed in 1873 by the order of Naser al-Din Shah following his trip to Europe. This *takyeh* was built on a grand scale. Nevertheless, it was in most ways a typical *takyeh*, in that it consisted of a large circular amphitheater with several entrances surrounding a sizable open area and a tent that was used as a roof. Its primary purpose was to provide a staging area for the most elaborate *ta'ziyeh* performances. The status of the shah and his high officials was enhanced by his patronage of *ta'ziyeh*s. Many European residents in Iran attested to the fact that "the shah and most of his grandees have their own private tekkyehs, which are fitted up with considerable splendour."[17] In Tehran the shah built a large *takyeh* that could hold several thousand people.[18]

There are many accounts of the *ta'ziyeh* performances of the *Takyeh Dowlat* both by foreign diplomats stationed in or visiting Tehran and by local inhabitants of Tehran. The accounts of Western visitors to Tehran are useful to historians because they provide clues to patterns of participation and reinforcement of social status in Tehran during this period. Lady Sheil, a European traveler resident in Tehran in the 1850s, gave the following brief account of the *ta'ziyeh* performance in the *Takyeh Dowlat*:

> The shah's box was at the top, facing the performers; on his right were the boxes of his uncles, the prime minister, the English minis-

ter as senior, the Russian minister, &c. On his left were the boxes of his mother . . . and his wives; then that of the prime minister's wife, then mine, and next the Russian minister's wife. . . . Part of the pit was appropriated for women of humble condition, who were in great numbers, all however carefully veiled, and all seating on the bare ground. Before the Curtain drew up, it was ludicrous to witness the contention among these dames for places, which was not always limited to cries and execrations. They often proceed to blows, striking each other heartily on the head with the iron heel of their slippers, dexterously snatched off the foot for the purpose; and, worse still, tearing off each other's veils; several ferrashes were present to keep the peace, armed with long sticks, with which they unmercifully belaboured these pugnacious devotees.

It would be tedious to describe a drama of ten days' duration. Everything was done to make the scene as real as possible. Hoossein, his family, and attendants, were in the costume of the time. They make their appearance, traveling to Cufa, in the desert of Kerbella. Camels, led horses caparisoned, kejawas, are conducted round the platform; trumpets, kettledrums resound far and near. Yazeed's army appears, his general makes a speech, Imam Hoossein laments his pathetic fate; he then goes out to fight, and returns, himself and his horse covered with arrows. The scene proceeds; they are cut off from the Euphrates; more lamentations over their impending fate, more fighting.

The fierce Shimr and his cavaliers, all in mail, come forward, mounted on their war-horses; Shimr makes speeches in character; Imam Hoossein replies with dignity and with grief for the distress of his family. His young sons Ali Akbar and Ali Asghar go out to fight, and are brought back dead. Sekkeena and Rookheeya, his little daughters, are slain amid the loud and unfeigned weeping of the audience. The angel Gabriel descends from the skies, attended by his ministering angels, all radiant in spangled wings, and deprecates the hard lot of the prophet's offspring; the King of the Gins, or Genii, with his army, appears, and follows the angelic example. Moses, Jesus Christ, and Mahoomed, revisit the earth, and are stricken with the general contagion of grief. At length Shimr does his work, amidst a universal outburst of sorrow and indignation; and next day, the tenth, the interment of Imam Hoossein and his family takes place at Kerbella.

It is a sight in no small degree curious to witness an assemblage of several thousand persons plunged in deep sorrow, giving vent to their grief in a style of school boys and girls. . . . The events are indeed affecting, and many of the parts are acted with great spirit and judgment.[19]

Even a short description like Lady Sheil's account can provide useful information regarding patterns of participation, authority, and social status. The status of the shah and his associates was reinforced by the seating plan of the *takyeh*. The *Takyeh Dowlat* had three floors, in addition to "the pit," with the shah himself occupying a central box on the top floor. Because seating was determined by status, seating reinforced status in a very public way. Many accounts describe how the processions saluted the shah (or the governor, if it was being performed elsewhere), after which they either left or stayed to perform in the *ta'ziyeh*. While it was considered far too demeaning for the shah and his family to participate in the actual processions, sometimes a similar effect was created by having the servants of the shah lead the procession.[20] Lady Sheil's account also serves as a rare example of how Iranian women participated in public life. The topic of women's involvement in these rituals is returned to shortly.

The influence of the rituals was not directed exclusively toward the local Iranian population. By sponsoring *ta'ziyeh* performances the shah also displayed his power and glory to foreign diplomats, who were usually invited to attend. While the presence of non-Muslims at these performances may have been somewhat controversial from the perspective of many ulama, the Qajars considered it to be good diplomacy. This attitude progressively changed as the government was increasingly criticized in the second half of the nineteenth and in the early twentieth centuries by both the ulama and other elite members of society. According to a royal edict issued in 1855, Westerners were officially excluded from attending *Moharram* performances, although many of them continued to attend them in private homes. Others managed to attend the performances, such as those of the *Takyeh Dowlat*, by wearing disguises.[21] It was not until this time that a combination of factors, including rising political hostility toward Western imperial powers, became a major consideration in this debate.

Some Iranians, notably the merchants and their close associates the ulama, were becoming increasingly hostile to the economic influence of Western imperialist nations. Concessions to the British throughout the nineteenth century put Iranian merchants at a competitive disadvantage. For example, the massive concession given to the British subject Baron Julius de Reuter in 1872 gave him "exclusive rights for railroad and streetcar construction, all mineral-extraction rights except for a few already being exploited, all unexploited irrigation works, a national bank, and all sorts of industrial and agricultural projects, in return for a modest royalty and initial sum. Lord Curzon, himself a firm economic and political imperialist, later called it the most complete and extraordinary surrender of the entire industrial resources of a kingdom into foreign hands that had probably ever been dreamed of."[22]

Another concession giving a complete monopoly over tobacco trade in Iran was granted to a British subject in 1890. Many Iranians made a profit from producing, selling, or transporting tobacco, and even more spent their income on tobacco products. In the spring of 1891, mass protests broke out across the empire, and by fall of 1891 a nationwide boycott of tobacco was in place. As a result of this opposition and pressure from Russia, the shah was forced to cancel the concession by the spring of 1892. Many segments of the Iranian population took part in these protests, most notably the bazaar merchants and some ulama. This growing hostility toward Westerners was one of the reasons they were no longer invited to attend *Moharram* rituals. *Moharram* rituals were no longer used as an important strategy for promoting a positive image of Iran among foreign diplomats.

A government concern about the rising discontent on the part of Iranian merchants was not the only factor in the progressive exclusion of Westerners from *Moharram* rituals. Many of the new modernizing elites, who considered *ta'ziyeh* and other *Moharram* rituals to be a "backward" and "lower-class" affair, were not anxious to have Westerners view the "Iranian nation" portrayed in such a manner. This was the beginning of a general trend that did not gain full force until the Pahlavi era and according to which many elite intellectuals became more and more disassociated from religious rituals. The famous Iranian intellectual and historian Ahmad Kasravi (d. 1946), for example, was very hostile to Shi'i rituals. In his 1943 publication *Shi'ehgari* he describes how, following the Constitutional Revolution, which began in 1905, groups that he identifies as "the enemies of freedom, comprised mostly of professional religious mourners, clerics and their followers, who were disappointed after much resistance and fighting and began to despair . . . , the clerics and professional religious mourners and many of the people were moved and began to fight the liberals who were trying to eliminate religious mourning ceremonies . . . They gathered, performed religious mourning ceremonies, fabricated lies and attacked the constitutional movement."[23]

While Kasravi's account is a good example of this emerging trend, he himself even better represents a more mature phase in this general trend, which more properly belongs to the Pahlavi era. He, like some other educated elites, was hostile to all forms of *Moharram* ceremonies, considering them to be backward, barbaric, and unpatriotic. This trend marks the beginning of a shift in discourse among some intellectuals, most of whom either were educated in the West or were heavily influenced by Western ideas. The newly emerging nationalist discourse promoted by these new elites gained greater acceptance during the Pahlavi era, as Islamic referents were almost completely abandoned by the state and many members of the new modernizing elites. There was no place for Shi'i symbols and rituals within this new discourse. This negative attitude toward "traditional" social practices combined with the economic and political criticisms of the rising influence of imperialist powers in Iran discouraged the Qajar rulers from inviting foreign diplomats to Shi'i rituals.

Social status and social bonds were reinforced by these rituals in many other ways. For example, *sayyed*s and religious scholars were commonly the "guests of honor" in these rituals. Ivar Lassy, a European traveler to Iran in 1913–15, gave a detailed account of such practices.[24] Patrons frequently gave cash gifts to young religious scholars, or *tollab*. Also a general practice was to give cash gifts to women participants, the poor, and the needy. These acts of charity often reached the amount of 1,000–2,000 *dinar*s.[25] The most common charitable act was giving food (*nazr*) to guests and to the needy. This might include any number of food items, but the most common were tea, tobacco (*qelyan*), water, sweets, and, of course, dinner, which sometimes involved ritually slaughtering a sheep.

Patron-client relationships were further strengthened through the reversal of patronage patterns. A common practice was for the patron to ask other participants to make financial contributions, and this request was generally limited to the patron's immediate subordinates. This practice allowed other sub-elites present at the ritual to be distinguished from regular participants, who were accorded lower status. It also allowed them to share in the praise lavished on the shah or the patron. Dorothy De Warzee, a Western observer of the royal *taʿziyeh* performance, states, "The shah nominally pays the expenses, but the strain on his purse cannot have been very great, as when he attended the performance, he visited the important merchants present, who each made him a contribution."[26] There are many similar accounts of the public act of soliciting donations during the rituals themselves, which suggests a method by which status and social bonds were reinforced during these rituals. In the case of the shah, the act of reversing the patterns of patronage during the performance allowed for a strengthening of relations between the shah and his immediate subordinates, such as wealthy landowners, merchants, and government officials. Participants from many different levels of society contributed in their own way, but status was proportional to the participant's ability to contribute.

The status of the shah or the patron was also promoted in more direct ways. The performers usually prayed for the patron following a prayer for Hoseyn and his descendants. Heinrich Brugsch, the German ambassador to Iran, described how "after praising the family of the prophet and the Prince of Martyrs he [the giver of the sermon] said a prayer [*doʿa*] for Naser al-Din Shah and for Iran."[27] In another account describing a sermon given at a *rowzeh khani* in the Sepahsalar Mosque in Tehran in 1887, the prayer for the shah was followed by affirmation of the justice of his rule.[28] This pattern was duplicated in other rituals such as performances and competitions in the *zurkhaneh* (buildings devoted to traditional Iranian wrestling and acrobatics), in which the competitors interrupted their competition and athletic performance to shout out praises to the generous sponsors attending the event.

It is clear that the shah and other elites used these rituals in several ways to promote their legitimacy and the social bonds with their subordinates. These patterns of patronage were not limited to the court or the shah. The pattern of court patronage was also not restricted to Tehran. The shah's appointed representatives in the provinces duplicated this pattern of patronage, extending all the way to small towns and villages in far-off provinces.[29] Nor was this patronage pattern restricted only to state officials. C. J. Wills, an English medical officer stationed in Shiraz, states that "almost all of the wealthy did some public act or other in the Mohurrim, . . . [the *taʿziyeh*] was given by the Zil-is-Sultan, the Governor, in the garden of his place, on a very large scale indeed, and in a smaller way by the Muschir and the Kawam and others."[30] He goes on to describe how government troops were used to assist professionals in erecting the large tent used for the occasion.[31]

Government officials, elites, and non-elites all made contributions. This provided a sense of common purpose among elites and non-elites. There are many accounts of people from all classes contributing to these ritual performances. According to one report: "They are performed in the courtyards of the houses of the rich, who consider it a meritorious act to lend them for the purpose without charge. . . . The neighbours as a meritorious act had lent all their pictures, carpets, curtains, mirrors, lusteres, and lamps to ornament the *Tekieh*. Even the poor had participated in these offerings, by lending small things without value."[32]

The poor were usually the ones who volunteered to serve and prepare food or play the roles of "extras" in the performances. They were often joined by the children of elites who were offered for service by their parents. In fact, the mixing of classes and the role reversals involved in the rituals were important. Many accounts attest to the high regard many people, especially the poor, had for this practice. By having their children serve food and drinks to the poor, elite families could perform an act of humility without risking humiliation, as they would if they were to serve the poor themselves (as adults). As the Qajar notable Abdollah Mostowfi states, this process was mutually beneficial for both elites and their clients:

> To assemble the learned and the common, the aristocracy, the middle class, and the poor under one roof, for one sole purpose, brought reality to life. The wealthy became aware of the existence of the poor. The different classes of society came in contact with each other, which was an education in itself. The wealthy promoted good deeds and spread culture among the less fortunate people. General discussions about the topic that the preacher had chosen for the day would continue among the crowd. . . . The son of this same nobleman at the door would welcome the modest store keeper, serve him tea, and extend his gratitude for the storekeeper having come to his house.[33]

Another important example of using *Moharram* rituals for reinforcing the authority of the state and elites was the practice of allowing the populace to request of the governor that a prisoner be released. "Every band has the right to ask the governor for the freedom of some one prisoner, and these requests are always granted, no matter what the crime of the imprisoned."[34] This practice allowed an opportunity for benevolence on the part of the ruler and his local representatives. While it would be a mistake to take accounts like this one entirely at face value, they do nevertheless indicate a cultural or social ideal that had currency in late nineteenth-century Iran (in this case, in Urumia, Azerbaijan). Ella Sykes gives a similar account of a *Moharram* procession in the southwestern city of Ahvaz.[35]

These patterns of patronage are important aspects of Qajar politics. By performing pious acts the rulers and the elites promoted their legitimacy, as well as their social stature. Ritual patronage allowed for a greater degree of integration or mediation between the rulers and the ruled in Qajar society. The state was, therefore, incorporated into a much broader social and cultural dynamic, which often stretched beyond the scope of its military authority. These patterns of patronage were not, however, limited to the state, or to the ruling elites. Rather, they reflected trends within the broader Iranian society and culture during this period. These broader trends tell a great deal about Qajar society and culture during the nineteenth and early twentieth centuries.

3 ⸗

Qajar Society and Religious Culture

TEHRAN AS A CASE STUDY

The focus of the discussion now shifts away from the Qajar court and rural government. Many of the patterns of court patronage of *Moharram* rituals were reflected not only in rural government but also in other sectors of society in both Tehran and the provinces. This study, for purely practical reasons, focuses mainly upon the capital city of Tehran. This decision is not because Tehran is typical of other cities and provinces, or because Tehran is more significant than other cities and regions. It is simply a compromise between the desire to be inclusive and comprehensive, on the one hand, and concern about the logistical difficulties posed by the incredible regional diversity of religious culture one encounters all over Iran, on the other hand. While the focus is Tehran, the approach taken here is to place Tehran within a broader context, in order to give indications of how trends in Tehran are similar to, or different from, those in other parts of Iran. It is important that future studies focus on areas other than Tehran, in order to compare the trends in these regions to those in Tehran and other areas. Transnational trends are also not included in this analysis, for the same reasons.

Tehran provides an excellent example of the patterns of ritual patronage and participation on a broader societal level. In Tehran, the *Takyeh Dowlat* is a rather dramatic example of the court's use of *Moharram* rituals to enhance its religious legitimacy. However, it would not be as historically significant if it were the exception to the rule rather than being representative of more "typical" *takyeh*s in Qajar society. While some members of the population attended the performances at the *Takyeh Dowlat,* it would be a mistake to assume that all segments of society were highly represented in these performances. According to some accounts, the *Takyeh Dowlat* was capable of seating as many as 20,000 spectators. This is a large number for a city with a population of approximately 147,000, but it still does not represent the entire population.[1]

Moharram rituals were among the largest and most heavily attended public events at all levels of society. According to official surveys of Tehran conducted by Qajar officials, there were totals of 54 *takyeh*s in 1852 and 43 in 1899.[2] These are large numbers for a single city, especially considering the fact that this survey included only permanent *takyeh*s, which were by no means the only sites devoted to ritual performances. Public processions, sometimes including the mobile variant of the *taʿziyeh* referred to by the more general term *shabih khani*, were conducted in city streets and alleys. *Taʿziyeh*s and *rowzeh khani*s were often performed in homes, mosques, and yards; under temporary tents in the streets; and sometimes simply in an open space in the market or in an alley. Comparing the numbers of *masjed*s and *madreseh*s (mosques and Islamic seminaries) to *takyeh*s is another indication of the broad appeal of these rituals. The significance of the *takyeh* is that, while mosques and *madreseh*s were often used for these rituals, the *takyeh*s were usually used primarily for ritual performances. In 1852 there were 54 registered *takyeh*s and 121 *madreseh*s/mosques, while in 1899 there were 43 registered *takyeh*s and 85 *madreseh*s/mosques. So there was roughly one *takyeh* for every two mosques/*madreseh*s during the last half of the nineteenth century. These numbers, which include all the *mahalleh*s of Tehran, indicate that these rituals were among the most important and most widely attended public events in Qajar society. More important, they were attended by extremely diverse segments of society including representatives from virtually all communities and status groups (the most significant exception, of course, being religious minorities).

Another useful indication of the prevalence of these rituals is provided by the police reports from this period. On a typical night in the month of *Moharram* in 1886, an average of fifty rituals was reported in the city of Tehran.[3] These reports list only ritual events that either were very large or included participants or hosts who were politically or economically significant, such as wealthy merchants, ulama, military officers, notables, leaders of guilds, court officials, and so forth. If all rituals are counted, including small ones by average members of the society, the number of rituals performed on an average night in Tehran would certainly have been much higher, at least one or two hundred each night, and probably more. In fact, Abdollah Mostowfi claimed that there were as many as two thousand *Moharram* preachers active in Tehran alone.[4]

In order to understand the role of *Moharram* rituals in Tehran, it is important first to know how Tehran functioned as a social space in the second half of the nineteenth century. In the center of the city was the royal quarter (*Arg* or *Dowlat*) containing the citadel, where military personnel and court officials were concentrated. Immediately south was the bazaar quarter (*Bazar*). To the east were two residential quarters (Udlajan and Chalmeydan), and to the west was another residential quarter (Sangalaj). The bazaar was the center of most commercial and social activities, while the royal quarter was the center of court politics, and these two quarters were closely interrelated. Unlike in the later twentieth century, the bazaar quarter was the center of urban life in Qajar society.

Despite the primacy of the bazaar quarter as the center of social and cultural activities, and the royal quarter as the center of political activities, religious life was not restricted to the bazaar or the royal quarter. The distribution of *takyeh*s in Tehran, according to the 1852 survey, were 17 in the bazaar quarter; 3 in the royal quarter (citadel); 12 and 10, respectively, in the eastern quarters of Udlajan and Chalmeydan; and, finally, 12 in the western quarter of Sangalaj. It is clear from .these numbers that *takyeh*s were widely distributed throughout the city, in all sorts of quarters and neighborhoods. A comparison of these numbers to the distribution of residences and stores shows that in the three residential quarters to the east and west there was roughly a two-to-one ratio of residences to stores, while in the bazaar and royal quarters the ratio was approximately one-to-one. The bazaar was the second least populous quarter (except for the royal quarter), yet it had the largest number of both *takyeh*s and mosques/*madreseh*s (17 and 35, respectively). Hence, while *takyeh*s were broadly distributed in Tehran, the bazaar was the center of both commercial and religious activities.

Moharram rituals were not restricted to upper-class elites or to wealthier neighborhoods. It is particularly instructive to compare the two eastern residential *mahalleh*s of Udlajan and Chalmeydan. According to the 1869 census, they both had roughly the same population size (34,000–36,000). However, Udlajan had a larger concentration of wealthy elites. The vast majority of Udlajan's population owned their own homes (about 80 percent), as compared to less than half of Chalmeydan's population being homeowners. Udlajan had the largest concentration of Qajar residents (1,268 Qajars, or approximately two-thirds of the city's total), whereas Chalmeydan had only 358 Qajar residents (or roughly one-sixth of the city's total). Thus, while Chalmeydan had a larger percentage of less prosperous residents, it still contained 10 takyehs.[5] Udlajan, which contained a large percentage of the wealthiest and most powerful elites in the city, not to mention the largest concentration of Qajars (not all of whom were members of the ruling class), had only 12 takyehs. It seems clear that ritual performances constituted a broad-based social phenomenon involving both the rich and the poor.

Before continuing, it is important to understand how these takyehs were established, funded, and run. Religious institutions were usually self-sustaining, either with pious endowments or with community support. However, they also required a great deal of ongoing supervision. Abdollah Mostowfi again gives an instructive account of the financing of these religious institutions. "Almost every neighborhood in the city of Tehran had a market place [takyeh], which was built and donated by a philanthropist. A few of these properties had one or two locations attached to them to provide rental income for expenses, as the case may be. But the majority had no funds. With the coming [of] the mourning months, it was up to the neighborhoods to see that a performance or sermon sessions got under way."[6]

The religious institutions also needed to be recognized by the state in order to function efficiently. Many takyehs were endowments established by court officials or other wealthy individuals and families, often remaining in use long after their deaths (e.g., endowments by Mo'tamed al-Dowleh, Agha Bahram Khajeh, Haji Mohammad Ja'far Khabbaz, Mirza Aghasi, the Khalaj family, etc., all of whom were associated with the Qajar elites). The takyeh was often endowed with several stores, the profits from which would help to defray the cost of maintaining the takyeh. There are many examples of such stores in the bazaar. According to the 1899 survey, three stores were registered as belonging to the vaqf (pious endowment) of the Takyeh-e Khalajha. Three more are listed under Takyeh-e Abbasabad, two for Takyeh-e Haft Tan, two for the Takyeh-e Zargarha, and five for the Takyeh-e Kheshti. Other takyehs were supported by economic and social associations based on ethnicity or regional affiliations (Arabs, Turks, Afghans, Caucasians, Kermanis, Qomis), occupation (goldsmiths, muleteers, cloth dealers, bread bakers), or location (*Darb-e Hammam, Darb-e Masjed-e Howz, Zamburak Khaneh*).

The next important questions that need to be addressed are: who were the patrons of the *takyeh*s spread out across the city; who participated in rituals performed in various quarters; and what sorts of community institutions and identities were associated with them? The answers to these questions shed light on how a wide variety of identities and social bonds were expressed and reinforced through these ritual performances.

While small family-sponsored ritual events were quite common, the patrons of the largest rituals included wealthy merchants, landowners, government officials, religious leaders, military men, heads of guilds, and community leaders. These rituals were often held in the homes of these elites, who also provided for most of the financial expenses of the rituals. Often a patron might offer rituals in his or her home every night during the first ten days of *Ashura*. However, most of the rituals were in commemoration of some significant event, such as the birth or death of an imam, or some other important event in Shi'i history, or the death, or the anniversary of the death, of a community leader. Those in attendance included the clients or servants of these elites, members of various guilds, religious scholars or students, the poor, *sayyed*s, aristocrats and royalty, merchants, craftsmen, soldiers from particular units, ethnic groups, Tehrani residents from other regions such as Qom or Isfahan, or simply neighbors from the local quarter.

The convergence of identities with those formed by quarter and neighborhood affiliations was important in determining who participated in ritual performances. Among the most important neighborhood affiliations were ethnic and regional identities. The ethnic and regional groups and groups with non-Tehrani affiliations tended to converge in particular neighborhoods and build *takyeh*s there. For example, the Arab quarter in the northeastern region of the city just outside the citadel walls contained a large percentage of the Arab population, which necessitated the construction of the *Takyeh-e Arabha* within the quarter. There was also another Arab *takyeh* just inside the southeastern *Abd al-Azim* gate. Similarly, the Qomis had a *takyeh* in the southwestern Qomi quarter. The Kermanis had a *takyeh* in the Kermani quarter. The *Takyeh-e Afsharha* was located in the *Afshar* (Afghan) quarter in the east of the city. The bazaar contained the Caucasian *takyeh* (*Takyeh-e Qafqaziha*). The Azerbaijanis were also concentrated in the bazaar (9,485, or approximately two-thirds of the city's Azerbaijani population, were registered as living in the bazaar quarter). Many of these non-Tehrani *takyeh*s were located in the western *mahalleh* of Sangalaj, one of the fastest growing *mahalleh*s in the second half of the nineteenth century. Sangalaj was therefore the site of immigration of many non-Tehranis (25,248 non-Tehranis, as compared to only 1,884 Tehranis).

Corporatist associations were also important as a basis for various urban identities. Occupations and craft guilds (*asnaf*) provided a sense of community identity through ritual patronage, the goldsmiths guild (*zargarha*) being one of the more famous institutional patrons. They had a well-endowed *takyeh* in the bazaar, as did the muleteers guild (*qaterchiha*) in the south of the bazaar. Because the bazaar itself was organized according to specialization, any subset of the bazaar, called a *bazarcheh* (minibazaar), could serve as the locus for a *takyeh*. Occupational affiliations, therefore, served as an important basis of urban identity during this period.

A wide variety of societal affiliations existed that served as focal points for neighborhood identities. Personal relationships, family ties, and patron-client relationships were important bases of urban identities. Many *takyeh*s were associated with specific individuals and their families (e.g., Agha Bahram Khajeh or the Khalaj family). Major buildings or sites, such as the *Masjed-e Howz*, also served as the focal points for neighborhoods. These neighborhoods almost always contained *takyeh*s for ritual performances.

The planning and financing of *Moharram* rituals was carried out by a variety of social groups and reinforced a sense of cohesion among its members. When they performed rituals, they acted out various forms of neighborhood identity. In a similar way, if a wealthy patron was the primary supporter of such rituals, the bonds between that individual and his or her family, on the one hand, and the rest of the participants from the neighborhood, on the other hand, were strengthened and reinforced. While there was tremendous similarity in the ritual practices of these different groups, in some cases distinctive practices or dress were associated with specific groups. However, in most cases, they were not defining the basic characteristics of their group as much as they were reinforcing the cohesion and sense of community within an already existing social group. It should also be pointed out that there were many subcategories of these identities, which were usually expressed through *Moharram* processions rather than *ta'ziyeh*s.

While the *ta'ziyeh*s were important as large social events, the most common form of ritual performance was the *Moharram* procession. There were many more processions (*dasteh*) than there were *takyeh*s because they were far cheaper to fund. Organizations and community associations that could not afford to build and maintain *takyeh*s could still organize processions. A procession did not require a permanent *takyeh*, and thus participants could meet in a temporary ritual site, such as someone's home or a tent in an alley, and then travel around their neighborhood and into other neighborhoods.[7] In addition, each *takyeh* usually had a corresponding procession that moved through the streets and visited other *takyeh*s or other ritual sites before returning to its own quarter. Processions did not require large numbers of professional actors, nor did they require much in the way of expensive costumes or equipment. So while there may have been only one Qomi *takyeh* in a given city, there were likely to be many Qomi processions in different neighborhoods. Similar to the large *takyeh*s, there was a strong sense of community identity associated with these less permanent ritual practices. Because these processions were essentially mobile, a sense of community identity could be reinforced by visiting other quarters in processions. Abdollah Mostowfi gives the following brief account of this practice in his memoirs:

> The beginning of constitutional democracy renewed friendships among the local processions and wailing groups. They went to the extent of making prior arrangements to visit each other's neighborhoods in full regalia, and were received by the host leaders at the boundaries of each neighborhood. Then they were accompanied to the gathering place, where they were welcomed with respect, at times even having the banners showered with flowers. The host group chanted words of praise about the faith of the visitors. Containers of rose water were circulated. The leaders of each group sat in their designated boxes. The popular slogan of Islam, "There is one god and Mohammed is his prophet," echoed through the area. Once more a new area of competition became established. Each year, the host or the visiting group added to their respective pomp, reception, and performance in order to attract a greater audience.[8]

While community identities were more fluid and dynamic, they could also be quite rigid and exclusive at times. The practice of neighborhood processions visiting each other could reinforce amicable relations between two different groups. They also had the potential to promote hostilities and rivalries between these groups. There are many accounts of violence breaking out among processions from different quarters. There are also accounts of rival groups deliberately confronting or challenging each other when traveling in processions. While sometimes these conflicts were caused by neighborhood rivalries, at other times they were caused by personal rivalries or arguments.[9] According to one police report:

> Six hours after dark, on the night of [commemorating] the murder of the Commander of the faithful [i.e., imam Ali] peace be upon him, several vulgar ruffians from among the residents of the area of the citadel went to the royal street of *shams al-emareh* with the excuse of performing *sineh zani*; due to pre-existing hostilities they got into a fight with a local ruffian of that area; in the dark the head of Ebrahim, the son of Heydar the straw merchant, was injured. As soon as the police arrived, everyone scattered to escape. Ebrahim and Hashem, who were the cause of the conflict, were captured and detained. They are being investigated so that with their help, the others can be identified, captured and punished appropriately.[10]

Both the government and the procession organizers tried hard to plan the path of the procession well in advance in order to avoid two processions accidentally crossing each other's path, because in the heat of the ritual performance fights could break out between members of two different processions. This planning sometimes led to conflicts between authorities and participants. For example, one report documented the following:

> For practical reasons processions were forbidden from going with their standards from one quarter to another on the day commemorating imam Hasan's murder [Quarter leaders and their agents enforced this regulation] . . . the residents of *gozar-e hayat shahi* wanted to carry their banner, which is associated with Mohammad Jan Larijani, in a procession around the city [but were prevented from doing so]. . . . Rahim Aqa Qajar came with a group of his friends and associates, and they shouted profanities and disrespectful comments at the representative of the police, and intended to beat him up.[11]

This pattern was common not only throughout the Qajar period, but it also continued to be prevalent throughout the twentieth century. While the state was often able to influence the rituals, or even to use them for its political benefit, it was rarely able to control the rituals or the participants completely. These rituals were within the realm of the state's influence but were outside the scope of its control. The reason for this position was that the organizers of these rituals were represented in all segments of society. Some were large and prominent, while most were small and less organized. It stands to reason, therefore, that the organizers represented more popular, or even populist, strains within Iranian society.

Another important dimension of *Moharram* rituals was the way in which women participated. Lady Sheil's account, which was quoted in the previous chapter, serves as a rare example of how Iranian women participated in public life. She describes how women attended these events in large numbers. Many similar accounts claim that women were often in the majority. For example, Samuel Benjamin reported in 1887 that "[Kalians were] smoked by women as well as men. The masculine sex was in but a small minority in the arena; what few men were there stood behind the compact army of women."[12] Furthermore, in the police reports compiled in 1885–87 under the supervision of Count De Mount Forte, who was in charge of public security in Tehran, are hundreds of reports of *Moharram* rituals in the homes, *takyeh*s, and mosques of Tehran in 1886. In most of these ritual events women are listed as participants.[13]

While there were numerous female characters in the scripts of these rituals, women's involvement did not usually include performing as actors. Female characters appear in many of the narratives, but one of the more elaborate ways in which female characters are included in the performances is the procession of prisoners. One such case is described by Samuel Nweeya:

> On two of them [Arabian horses] are seated two girls representing the daughters of the martyrs; the tops of their heads covered with mud and straw. The third horse is riderless, to remind one of the missing martyr. Following next is a large number of women, boys and girls and some men, all with yokes about their necks, their hands chained behind them, seated on horses and mules. . . . Near them are men in helmets to represent the soldiers of Yazid. They are armed

with whips and are driving these women and children of Moslems into captivity.[14]

However, female characters were almost always played by male actors, as documented in numerous written accounts. For example, Lady Sheil reported that "young lads represented the wives of Hoossein, in whose favour I can say nothing;"[15] And as Charles James Wills reported: "Small boys, chosen for their clear and sympathetic voices, from among the singers of the town, sustain the little parts of the granddaughters, and grandsons of the prophet. The wives are veiled, and these characters are played by bearded men, as are the angels and prophets, who are also veiled by glittering handkerchiefs."[16] Eustache De Lorey and Douglas Sladen reported a similar scene of boys representing female characters, although in this scene the common practice of wearing Western clothing is also described. "Then came his [Yazid's] wives, *with their faces uncovered,* represented by boys who had been dressed in costumes lent by European women, a device which without doubt was intended to make them more odious to the public."[17] This practice of wearing Western dress was not unheard of. Sometimes the soldiers of Yazid dressed in British or other Western military uniforms. Time and space were often stretched beyond logical temporal boundaries. However, on a deeper symbolic level, it is not surprising that Iranians made these sorts of connections between the evil troops of Yazid and the non-Muslim Western imperial troops.

Space was usually gender specific, with men and women being allowed to occupy designated areas during the ritual events. Women were sometimes restricted to the second floor, separate rooms, a curtained-off area, the roofs of nearby buildings, or the "pit" in the middle of the takyeh. The definitions of gendered space, along with the degrees of enforcement, varied considerably. For example, in an account by Sven Hedin, enforcement could be rather strict at times. He reported on one of the provinces in 1910: "Here [the governor's takyeh] a number of spectators, mostly women, had assembled, but the place was cleared at once by the switches of the ferrashes. They have not the slightest respect for ladies."[18] He also records examples of women sitting on rooftops: "On the flat roofs around the arena women sit wrapped up in their veils, and chattering like jackdaws. Those of higher rank have a white veil before their face with an opening for the eyes, just as in the larger towns, but the poorer women have blue veils or rather sack-like wraps which cover the whole head and body." "There are certainly as many as 3000 people in the court, and on the roofs around some 340 women have taken their seats."[19] Dorothy De Warzee, H. G. Winter, and other Western travelers to Iran give similar reports.[20] Some Iranians did not like the presence of women in the rituals. For example, following a noisy outbreak among the women participants in a ritual sermon given in the Sepahsalar mosque, Mirza Lotfollah claimed he would not give any more sermons if women were going to be present in the audience.[21]

Wealthy women were kept separate and out of sight, while poorer women sat in the "common" area. For women, seclusion has generally been one of the primary signs of wealth in most Muslim societies, and *ta'ziyeh* performances were no exception to the rule. Charles James Wills, a Westerner attending a *majles,* wrote in 1883 that, "the women having been crowding in from an early hour, the wives of the grandees and officials are accommodated with seats with the princess and her ladies, while the less favoured have the places retained for them in good situations by their servants, and according to rank."[22]

Wealthy women also reinforced their social standing in a more direct way by being generous supporters themselves of such rituals, including women's *majales* and *sofrehs* (ritual dinners), as well as *rowzeh khanis* and *ta'ziyehs*. Women-only rituals were regularly held in private homes and even in the *Takyeh Dowlat*.[23] A typical example was a women's *rowzeh khani* that was held in Reza Qoli Khan's house in Tehran on the fifth of *Moharram* of 1886. In *Safar* of the same year, the wife of Mohammad Hoseyn Javaheri sponsored a *ta'ziyeh* in the *takyeh* of Melkabad.[24] Other examples of women patrons include Qamar al-Saltaneh, the wife of Mirza Mohammad Khan Sepahsalar, the notable Aziz al-Saltaneh, and at least one of the daughters of Fath Ali Shah.[25]

One of the better-known female patrons of such performances was Naser al-Din Shah's sister Ezzat al-Dowleh, who regularly sponsored elaborate *ta'ziyeh*s in her home in Sarcheshmeh.[26] Abdollah Mostowfi gives in his memoirs the following brief account of one of the rituals she sponsored:

Ezzat od-Dowleh, the sister of Naser ed-Din Shah, provided one such program in her neighborhood. At this time the Princess was on her fourth husband, Mirza Yahya Khan Mo'tamed ol-Molk, the minister of foreign affairs, and the brother of Mirza Hoseyn Khan Sepahsalar. This was a very elaborate and beautiful event. The main courtyard of the reception quarters was covered with a three-steeple tent. The large center pool, covered with planks of wood, was converted to a platform and serves as the center stage. Three side walls of the courtyard were covered with black cloth. The fourth opened to a large garden. A temporary wooden building with an awning was erected for the season, providing six additional areas to serve as boxes. The interiors of the boxes were elegantly decorated with candelabra and hurricane lamps. Exquisite Persian rugs hung from the walls. The curtains were made of gold and silver brocade. The lower level of this building was designated for the young people, and the upper level for the older guests. . . . Other members of the royal family and aristocracy attended these shows, and were received in the large reception hall by Moshir od-Dowleh himself. The rooms opposite the temporary boxes were for the Princess Ezzat od-Dowleh and her guests. A transparent curtain provided privacy for the ladies. There were three other rooms on the south side of the courtyard, for the male public, and the courtyard level was for the women. The steel band occupied the porch of the temporary building, or sometimes the roof of the house. The military band, with band director Shokrollah Khan, sat on the front porch. The street served as back stage for the performance, where the animals and crew awaited their turn.

These passion play performances were very elegant and fully equipped. Mo'in ol-Boka and the government cast performed here also. It was a smaller version of the [*Takyeh Dowlat*] productions, but not inferior in any way. The introductory parade of mourners and wailers was limited to a few groups, and they were usually neighborhood organizations of Sartakht and Sarcheshmeh. Lady Ezzat od-Dowleh rewarded the participating groups with a gift of an Amiri shawl tied to the banner on the last day of the performance. Other well-known mourners, such as the Borujerdi group, came to this location during the sermon and preaching sessions only. These functions lasted well into the night, and the public was served tea and water pipes. During the day performances, refreshments and water pipes were limited to the guests who were received inside the quarters.[27]

Women were active participants in *Moharram* rituals, which is one of the factors that prompted Ayatollah Khansari (a prominent religious scholar and jurist of the late nineteenth century) to write the following humorous comment:

> It is the consensus of the ulama and is obligatory that women should go anywhere in the streets and markets where there is a *ta'ziyeh;* and it is said, "Woe to any woman, near whom there is a *ta'ziyeh* taking place (within one *farsakh*), but who does not attend it." Furthermore, if a pregnant woman goes into labor and gives birth while attending a *ta'ziyeh* or *rowzeh khani* her child will be considered blessed and should be named Ramadan.[28]

Another interesting dimension of women's involvement in *Moharram* rituals were the numerous accounts of fights breaking out among the female participants. Numerous reports by Western travelers and by law enforcement officials in Tehran describe female participants being involved in either arguments or actual fights.[29] These fights were usually broken up by servants in charge of the event in question.

More interesting were police reports regarding women involved in arguments and physical fights with their husbands over the issue of attending religious rituals. It was not uncommon during the Qajar period, much like today, for some women to attend these religious rituals either without the husband's permission or in defiance of his instructions that she should not attend.[30] For example, according to one of the more interesting police reports from 1887: "Last night the wife of Karim Nam got into a fight with her husband because he would not give her permission to leave the house in order to attend a *ta'ziyeh*, it led to physical fighting between them. Residents in the house calmed them down. Afterwards, this woman ate some opium (i.e., to commit suicide) in order to threaten and punish her husband. She was diagnosed, given help, and recovered . . . in the end her husband was forced to give her permission to go to the *takyehs*."[31]

Law enforcement reports document many such incidents where women called on officers to resolve conflicts with their husbands over *Moharram* rituals. The use of opium as a threat of suicide was also not uncommon. Another interesting example of a woman ignoring male authority involved a female servant: "Hajji Mohammad Bazzaz reported to the head of the *mahalleh* that one female slave left the house to attend a *rowzeh khani*. She has not returned for two days and is missing . . . as a result of [our] investigation, she was located in the *Emamzadeh* of *Sayyed*

Esma'il . . . [and was returned to him]."[32] Stories like these give brief glimpses into the everyday experiences of women in Qajar Iran, whose lives would otherwise be little understood by modern scholars.

Accounts of *Moharram* rituals also give glimpses of social, cultural, and political discourse during this period. These rituals served as one of the more important means for expressing political, religious, or social ideals. Ulama routinely preached about social ills, political problems, and cultural habits, a practice that continued throughout the twentieth century. For example, on the fourth of *Moharram* during a *rowzeh khani* in the home of a wealthy patron, one of the speakers, by the name of Sayyed Mazandarani, complained of how the people were suffering because of price gouging of bread.[33] In *Ramazan* of 1887 in the *Chaleh Hesar* mosque, the giver of the sermon complained about how too many Iranians eat, drink tea, and smoke opium rather than fast for this holy month.[34] A few nights earlier in another local mosque, women were criticized for not obeying their husbands sufficiently.[35] In the month of *Safar* of the previous year in the *Dangi* mosque the speaker criticized *ta'ziyeh* and expressed the desire that it would be outlawed by royal decree.[36] A few days earlier Westernization was also criticized in a sermon: "Mirza Mohammad Reza Va'ez said on the pulpit, 'I don't know why people are so unaware of God, and have given up their religion to such an extent. Most servants of the Westernized wear Western cloths in accordance with recent trends. They have the right to do this. However, why do most other people wear Western cloths, and make themselves appear Westernized?' He went on to criticize ideals of imitating Westerners."[37]

Another, similar incident occurred the previous year in the month of *Ramazan* during a *majles* in the home of Sadeq al-Molk that was attended by several people from the foreign ministry. "Two or three people were smoking cigarettes during the sermon of Naqeb al-Sadat. He criticized Westernized Iranians severely from the pulpit. He said 'People aren't you ashamed? Have all of you become Christians? Have you forgotten your religion? The only thing that remained of Islam was these four days or so of mourning, and now you want to even lose that?'"[38]

In another sermon delivered in *Ramazan* of 1886 in the mosque of *Chaleh Hesar*, the same Agha Sayyed Mohammad Reza denounced elites for shirking their financial responsibilities to the public. "He criticized and complained about the notables, nobility, and aristocrats saying that they are hoarding wealth and do not pay their *zakat* and *khoms*, and are usurers. If they pay their alms taxes why are the needy so poor and unfortunate. . . . [He then criticized women for gossiping and being worldly]."[39]

The following week in the same mosque he again raised similar issues. "He criticized the notables and government officials. He said that they ride their metal carriages throwing their silver staves in front of them and when a poor person begs for a *shahi* from them they refuse to give it to him/her. [He then went on to criticize one of the chief scholars among the ulama for shirking his duties as an educator, scholar, and religious leader]."[40]

The topic of oppression was always fair game in sermons. Usually, these monologues on royal corruption were abstract and were not necessarily intended to be a criticism of the current ruler. The symbolism or narratives could be understood in different ways by different listeners. However, they did serve as means to promote popular ideals on how a ruler should behave. One story regarding the corruption of a ruler was told in a *majles* in a private residence. One of the speakers told of a ruler who was oppressive. According to the story, the tyrant had developed a headache as a result of his evil conduct, and God had told him as a test that if he sacrificed a baby in front of the baby's parents, his headache would be better. The king tries but cannot go through with it. In the end he changes his ways and repents, which causes his headache to go away. The story wraps up with this warning: "Therefore, no sultan should ever abandon justice."[41]

Of course, the notables and the shah had their defenders as well.[42] In one exchange between religious sermonizers, Va'ez Kashani endorsed the Shah: "Giving prayers to his highness [the shah] is a religious obligation for all Muslims, because unless the ruler takes care of the people they will not be able to worship God. In Isfahan I said that saying the prayer for the ruler is a religious obligation, and they labeled me a heretic [*kafar*]."[43] The following week participants in the Marvi mosque refused to allow Kashani to go up onto the pulpit to give a sermon. They threatened to drag him down forcibly, and it became necessary to bring in another person to give the sermon. Several days later, in another sermon in the mosque of *Amin al-Dowleh,* Kashani tried to defend himself: "I am a Muslim [i.e., not a heretic or *Kafar*], and I had no intention [other than adherence] to the holy Islamic law when I said that the shah is the representative of the imam." He expressed deep sorrow at having been labeled a heretic, or *kafar.*[44]

The accounts of debates surrounding the perceived heresy of Kashani provide a good indication of the potential debates and conflicts that could result from political views being expressed within ritual sermons. Throughout the nineteenth and twentieth centuries it was common for social and political debates to take this form. In another account of 1886 in the mosque of *Chaleh Hesar*, Agha Sayyed Mohammad Reza complained: "Whenever one of our respected ulama have labeled someone as a *kafar* or heretic, the notables still consider him to be the 'king of sermonizers' [*Soltan al-Zakerin*] and then allow him to give a sermon in a major mosque like the mosque of *Marhum Amin al-Dowleh*."[45]

In a sermon given on the following night in the above-mentioned mosque of *Amin al-Dowleh*, Sayyed Hasan Kashani criticized the hypocrisy of the Sadr al-Olama's labeling anyone a *kafar*.[46] Rivalries and political infighting between sermonizers or ulama was a relatively common feature in the ritual sermons. This practice is significant because it illustrates how religious rituals were used by most factions in the society, including those associated with the state, as a vehicle to promote certain ideals or to attack political rivals. This practice is strikingly different from that of the Pahlavi period, where it is limited almost exclusively to groups and factions not associated with the state.

The above analysis demonstrates how the Qajar rulers and elites were able to promote their religious and political legitimacy through patronage of both public and private Shi'i rituals, thus maintaining and strengthening their relationships with their subjects at various levels in society. They were not exactly maintaining "public" support in the same sense that modern nationalist governments try to construct a national citizenry, while at the same time promoting nationalistic loyalty to the state. It can be reasonably concluded that these rituals served as a means for legitimizing various power relationships within Qajar society, including, but not limited to, the ruling elite.

While the Qajar elites were at the top of the hierarchy of patrons, they were not the only beneficiaries of this system of patronage. The Qajar state was built on relationships of mediation. Taxation and the enforcement of commercial regulations, for example, were greatly facilitated by the state's reliance on such associations as guilds. Various community relationships were strengthened within a broader system that allowed for relatively diverse identities and loyalties. These were not absolute categories of identity, but rather they were fluid and overlapping identities based largely on existing social, political, and economic relationships, which manifested themselves in ritual form. The religious culture prevalent during the Qajar period was aggressively challenged with the rise to power of the Pahlavi dynasty. Economic and political changes in Iran, along with new identities like nationalism, helped to transform these social relationships. As these relationships evolved over time so did the patterns of ritual patronage, performance, and participation.

4 ᴣ

The Pahlavi Regime and the Emergence of Secular Modernism (1925–1979)

*A*s this study turns its focus from the Qajar period to the Pahlavi era, it becomes evident that there was a great deal of both continuity and change in relation to *Moharram* symbols and rituals. Whereas the relationship between the Qajars and their subjects was characterized by mediation, the Pahlavis slowly moved in a new direction. During the Pahlavi era the government became much larger and more bureaucratic, the country's dependence on Western powers increased, and the sale of oil eventually added a new source of revenue that allowed the state to be relatively more independent of society. A new class of middle-strata bureaucrats emerged, and the social status of some traditional elites was challenged by the state. Nationalism was proposed as the primary identity for Iranians, and cultural ideals were much more influenced by the West.

As new cultural paradigms from the West became more influential, Iranians were forced to rethink some cultural values and identities. At one end of a fluid spectrum were the cultural values imported from the West. At the other end of the spectrum were preexisting cultural models. However, very few Iranians subscribed completely to either of these two simplistic models. Instead, Western cultural values were modified and adapted, often in rather awkward and inconsistent ways, to Iranian values and social realities. Preexisting cultural attitudes also evolved in accordance with modern forces of social, economic, and political change. Many new identities and cultural ideals also came into being.

It would be problematic to describe Iranian society as having exactly two cultures, a "modern," Western one and a "traditional," Iranian one. However, it can be said that there were two general cultural ideals, one associated with Western ideals, the other with Islamic ideals. There are two reasons why the term "Islamic" is used here rather than "Iranian." First, the conceptualization of Iranian culture and identity was shared by both these cultural ideals. Second, by the 1960s and 1970s, two separate discourses had developed, one associated with Western-oriented ideals and the other with Islam. The former was promoted by the state and by some elites and middle-strata Iranians. The latter continued to be dominant in most of Iranian society. This cultural divide was also associated with class divisions. There was a pronounced tendency for educated elites associated with the state to disassociate themselves from Shi'i rituals. These groups were often associated with new economic activities like large-scale industrial production and some middle-income technical professions. Meanwhile, the vast majority of Iranians continued to participate in these rituals for a variety of social, political, and cultural reasons. This tendency toward polarization was not universal, but it is a useful frame of reference for analyzing this period.

The analysis below begins with the state and its policies regarding *Moharram* rituals. A discussion of attitudes of modernizing elites associated with the state and new economic sectors follows. Concluding this chapter is an examination of the role of religious rituals as a means for expressing alternative social and political ideals, finally culminating in a crisis of legitimacy of the Pahlavi state.

With regard to state patronage specifically, Reza Shah Pahlavi (r. 1925–41) was fairly consistent in his hostility toward Shi'i rituals, although his actual policies were tempered by political pragmatism. Because of his friendly relations with Germany during World War II, Reza Shah was forced by the British and the Russians to abdicate his throne in 1941. His son, Mohammad Reza Shah (r. 1941–79), who was then placed on the throne, was less consistent in his attitude toward these symbols and rituals. Unlike his father, he was not hostile to all forms of *Moharram* rituals. He objected only to representations that he viewed as promoting hostility to his regime. This position helped to undermine his religious credibility when religious opposition groups challenged his right to rule in the 1960s and 1970s. Meanwhile, many of the popular trends in ritual performance and symbolic discourse evolved relatively independently of the actions and policies of the state and the ruling elites. The argument presented here is not intended to underestimate the influence of the government's policies. It is merely meant to acknowledge the relative gap between the government's modernization program and the broader processes of transformation underway in Iranian society.

Poster of Abu al-Fazl al-Abbas, the young standard-bearer at Karbala. This poster was hung in a store in Qom. Abbas is famous for being killed by Yazid's troops while trying to obtain water for the women and children.

A "coffeehouse" painting, depicting the Battle of Karbala in its entirety. These types of paintings were used as visual aids by professional storytellers, who recounted the Karbala story in tragic detail. (Tehran)

A "coffeehouse" painting, depicting single combat between Abbas and one of the Yazid's henchmen.

A "coffeehouse" painting, depicting the return of Hoseyn's heavily wounded horse, Zu al-Jenah, from the battlefield without his master. Zu al-Jenah, with his wounds and blood-soaked empty saddle, has served as a symbolic reminder of Hoseyn's tragic and bloody martyrdom. In this image, the women and children, who remained in the camp during the battle, mourn the tragic death of Hoseyn, while in the background Yazid's troops begin their assault on the camp.

In this *taʿziyeh* performance, the young bridegroom Qasem recites poetic refrains expressing support of Hoseyn's cause. His youth, along with the fact that he was about to start a new, married life, heightens the sense of tragedy in the Karbala story. (Tehran)

In this *taʿziyeh* performance, Hoseyn recites poetry in which he articulates his religious message, while at the same time expressing his sadness and sense of loss as his family members are killed one by one. (Tehran)

This truck had been converted for the purpose of reciting *taʿziyeh* elegiac poetry on a loudspeaker, thus functioning like a "mobile *taʿziyeh*" of sorts. (Mashhad)

A rider, in full military costume, wearing red to symbolize that he is one of the villainous troops of Yazid. (Tehran)

A typical banner for a *heyʿat*. Such banners usually have religious slogans praising the family of the Prophet and extolling their nobility. They usually have the name of the *heyʿat* woven into the design as well. (Mashhad)

A procession carrying a model replica of a tomb/shrine of Hoseyn in front of the entrance to the *Masjed-e Karbala'i-ha* in front of the Tehran Bazaar. (Tehran)

Inside the *Masjed-e Karbala'i-ha* was an elaborately decorated replica of a ship, which symbolizes the household of the Prophet. This association is based on the hadith in which the Prophet is believed to have compared his family to Noah's Ark (i.e., whoever gets on board the ark is saved, and whoever stays away from it will drown). The replica was decorated with fake white pigeons, which symbolize peace as well as Imam Reza, who loved and raised pigeons. The white carnations symbolize peace and purity, and the red carnations represent martyrdom. Candles and lamps are lit in honor of the dead. Lamps also represent the light of Mohammad, which is a divine light that Shi'is believe shines through his progeny. This boat is pushed along in the public procession in front of the Tehran Bazaar.

A procession of mourners beating their chests and crying after having
rubbed mud on themselves as a symbol of mourning the death of a loved
one. (Tehran)

A drummer in a ritual procession in front of the Tehran Bazaar. The drums provide a steady rhythm so that the ritual participants can chant and perform flagellations in unison.

A man spraying rosewater on the ritual participants, as a symbol of purity. The Prophet is believed to have loved the smell of perfumes, and roses in particular. Rosewater is sprinkled on the believers at a wide variety of ritual events, including regular communal prayer. (Tehran)

A drummer leading the group of mourners during *Arbaʿin* in a *hoseyniyeh* in Mashhad. The drum provides a steady rhythm, allowing participants to chant and perform flagellations in unison.

Above: Mourners wearing burial shrouds (*kafan push*), in front of the Tehran Bazaar, as a symbol of their willingness to be martyred.

Right: A proud father holding up his infant son, who has been dressed up in miniature Arab costume for the day. Dressing up children as the children of Hoseyn and his family is a favorite activity for parents, who are happy to take any opportunity to share their excitement about their children. (Tehran Bazaar)

Below: Women do not normally participate in the self-flagellation with chains ritual, although in extremely rare cases girls participate. This small girl is simply having fun playing with her father's ritual chains. (Tehran)

Above: Two elderly mourners, who have fallen behind the main procession. Even though the older man is no longer able to chant or swing the chains, he is determined to participate in the ritual with the help of the other man, who is keeping him from toppling over. (Tehran Bazaar)

A standard, or *alamat*, being carried in front of a typical procession. (Tehran)

A standard-bearer carrying a very large ritual standard, or *alamat*, which weighs several hundred pounds, as part of the ritual procession. These standards symbolize the military standard of the Prophet's family at Karbala. The ability to carry the standard is not only a pious honor, it is also quite a feat of strength and power for the men. (Mashhad)

A close-up shot of a ritual standard, or *alamat*, which is carried in front of most large processions and is displayed in *takyehs*. In Islam, lions are symbolic of manly heroism and loyalty. Beginning in pre-Islamic Iran, the lion and sun have served as a symbol of royalty, as have peacock feathers. Beginning in the modern period, the lion with a sword has been used in Iran to represent Ali. The peacocks are symbolic of paradise, because they are considered to be one of the "birds of paradise." (Tehran)

A standard-bearer spinning in circles while carrying a different type of ritual standard, called a togh, as part of a ritual greeting of another *hey'at*. The *togh* is different from the military standard in that it is symbolic of a death, a funeral, and martyrdom. This one had a picture of Hoseyn with a replica of *Zu al-Feqar*, which is believed to be the double-bladed sword of the Prophet that was passed down through Ali to his descendants. (Tehran)

A "parade" of more than two hundred ritual standards (*alamat*), in front of the Tehran Bazaar. Since these *alamat* often weigh several hundred pounds, it is no small feat to carry them in processions. Even though the standard-bearers are extremely strong, they have to switch places constantly with each other after traveling short distances. Normally, each standard represents a specific *hey'at*. (Tehran)

Women carrying the cradle of Ali Asghar, on which is placed the poster of *The Night of Ashura*, along with a painting of the severed head of Abu al-Fazl al-Abbas. That the women are carrying the cradle/funeral bier is significant in that the women are associated with the children at Karbala. The cradle serves simultaneously as a funeral bier, in that the infant Ali Asghar went directly from cradle to grave. The replicas of tents represent the camp, where the women stayed during the battle itself. The tents are usually ritually burned at the end of the ritual day, symbolizing how the troops of Yazid attacked and burned the camp at Karbala, after which they took the women as captives to Damascus. (Tehran)

A man in full costume riding on a camel, representing Zayn al-Abedin, as he was taken to Damascus in chains. He was Hoseyn's only son to survive Karbala. Shiʿis believe that he was unable to participate in the fighting because he had fallen ill. (Tehran)

A procession of women, including the cradle of Ali Asghar, with the tents. However, now they have been joined by women on camels who represent the *osara*, or women captives, who were taken to Damascus in chains.

A miniature military standard has been placed, interestingly, on top of the cradle, which the women are carrying. This act is unusual, because usually only men carry the ritual military standards. (Tehran Bazaar)

A close-up of the cradle of Hoseyn's martyred infant son, Ali Asghar, on which is placed the poster of *The Night of Ashura*, along with a painting of the severed head of Abu al-Fazl al-Abbas. The cradle serves simultaneously as a funeral bier, in that the infant Ali Asghar went directly from cradle to grave. (Tehran)

Women participating in the central procession holding banners with political and religious slogans. They also carry jars of water, to quench symbolically the thirst of Hoseyn and his followers, and shovels to bury symbolically the martyrs.

Osara, or prisoners, being taken in chains on camels to Damascus. (Tehran)

Osara, or prisoners being taken in chains on camels to Damascus. Children are often brought along in these rituals, partly for practical reasons, partly to show them off and have fun, and partly to allow them to share in the pious merit of the rituals. (Tehran)

Mural in which Fatemeh, the mother of the martyrs, is in the background holding red tulips (symbols of martyrdom) in her hands. She is symbolically holding the martyrs and the blood of the martyrs on her hands. In the foreground, a young girl is planting tulips, which symbolizes that she is continuing the legacy of Fatemeh, by rearing a new generation of martyrs. This mural is painted on the wall of an enclosed martyrs' cemetery called *Bagh Behesht-e Ali*, located in Qom.

A large billboard located at the entrance of the martyrs' cemetery, named *Behesht-e Zaynab*, in Isfahan. A young girl is portrayed sitting on the post-revolutionary Iranian flag, while the image of Khomeini looks on from above. She is surrounded by the religious symbols of the revolution. The tulips symbolize the fallen martyrs of Karbala as well as the revolution; the goblet conveys the act of drinking the martyrdom; and the dove represents peace and the imams. The image says, "Peace unto you, O Ruh Allah [Khomeini]." It also states, "Dedicated to the memory of the martyrs of the Islamic Revolution." The banner that has been hung under the billboard declares, interestingly, "Peace unto you, O Fatemeh Zahra: We give our condolences for the martyrdom of Fatemeh Zahra, to the Imam of the Age [the twelfth imam, al-Mahti], to Khomeini, the great leader of the revolution, and to the respected families of the martyrs."

Opposite page, bottom: A large billboard with a picture of Khomeini and his son Ahmad Khomeini. The banner that was hung underneath the billboard says, "We give our condolences for the innocent daughter of the Prophet, her holiness Zahra-e Marziyyeh, to the lovers of Velayat [al-Faqih]."

Behesht-e Zahra, the martyrs' cemetery, located just south of Tehran.

Behesht-e Zahra, the martyrs' cemetery, located just south of Tehran.
The graves are small memorials to the fallen martyrs.

Another martyrs' cemetery, named *Behesht-e Zeynab*, located in Isfahan.

A memorial at one of the tombs of the martyrs' cemetery in a small town outside of Isfahan, named Shahreza.

The tomb of the martyred soldier Reza Qane'a in the martyrs' cemetery in a small town outside of Isfahan, named Shahreza. These memorials typically have a picture of the martyr, often in uniform and in civilian clothes. In this picture, the young soldier stands in uniform at the front lines, with a Qur'an his right hand and a standard-issue rifle in his left hand. This picture clearly symbolizes his willingness to fight to defend his country and his religion, under the guidance of Imam Khomeini. Next to the picture are his dog tags, prayer beads, and a prayer stone. Pictures of Khomeini are common, as are flowers, letters, prayers, and poems. The memorials are also adorned with religious, personal, or decorative items.

The discussion turns first to the early reign of the first Pahlavi ruler, Reza Shah (originally called Reza Khan). He was from a Mazandarani family with a modest military heritage and rose through the ranks to become head of the Cossack Brigade in Qazvin. His career began during the reign of the Qajars as the officer in charge of the Cossack Brigade, which had been formed in 1879 and fashioned after the Russian military. This elite military force, which was initially used primarily for the personal protection of the shah, was the only significant modernized military force in Iran during the later decades of Qajar rule. As commander of this force, Reza Khan was in a strong political position once he decided to take over the government because the Qajars did not have any military force that could effectively defeat the Cossack Brigade.

In 1920–21, there was a political crisis in Tehran caused by the government's inability to deal effectively with military and political pressures from Russia and Great Britain. Popular political pressure from various segments of Iranian society, including the ulama, modern educated elites, and merchants in the bazaar, contributed to this crisis. In February 1921, the forty-two-year-old officer Reza Khan marched into Tehran, arrested dozens of potential political opponents, and made a political deal with the shah. According to the terms of this arrangement, Reza Khan was to be appointed commander of the military (sardar-e sepah). Some of his political allies were to be given prominent posts (notably a reform-minded journalist named Sayyed Ziya Tabataba'i, who was appointed prime minister), and Ahmad Shah Qajar would remain in power, at least for the time being.

Reza Khan's rise to absolute power, which began with his military takeover, continued over the next few years until he declared himself shah in 1925. During this five-year period, Reza Khan gained political advantage within the government by using the military to eliminate political rivals, while at the same time putting down rebellions and mutinies around the empire. He enforced a new sense of order and absolute governmental authority. After becoming shah, Reza implemented a modernization program with the state and the military at the center. He set out to eliminate all forms of political opposition associated with traditional elites such as rural warlords and tribal leaders, landowners and village leaders, ulama, bazaar merchants, and the old ruling elites allied with the Qajar dynasty. His primary base of power was the military, supported by a new and highly dependent elite. As part of this program, Reza Shah developed a model for modernization that excluded traditional Shiʿi ideals. His actions and policies evolved over time in accordance with his objectives and his relative political strength. He was a participant in *Moharram* rituals in the early years of his career, but became more and more hostile to these rituals as his position became stronger until he finally banned most of the public rituals entirely.

While during the Qajar period court officials and military personnel participated in public rituals along with the rest of the population, this practice was slowly abandoned under the rule of Reza Shah. This shift is indicative of the divide between the state and some sectors of Iranian society characteristic of much of the Pahlavi era. During the last few decades of Qajar rule, it was customary for the governor or shah to put some of his troops at the disposal of ritual organizers to construct necessary structures and to participate in the actual performances. The Cossack Brigade was no exception to this rule, and Reza Khan as its leading officer had regularly participated in such rituals. According to the account of the famous Iranian poet and writer Mohammad Taqi Bahar (Malek al-Shoʿara, 1886–1951):

> It was the day of *Ashura* a band of Cossacks under the command of Reza Khan (he had not yet become Shah) moved down into the bazaar in special formation, order and pomp. Several music detachments playing mourning marches were with them together with spare horses. Reza Khan led the procession bareheaded pouring straw on his head [a symbolic act of self-mortification]. . . . Also, on the night [before] the 11th of *Moharram* the Cossack band came to the bazaar and performed the *sham-e ghariban* ritual (literally the night of the strangers; in this ritual mourners symbolically search, candle in hand, for the corpses of the fallen martyrs). The *sardar-e sepah* himself (Reza Khan's title at that time, meaning commander of the army) was also with them bareheaded and barefooted with a candle in his hand. He accompanied his group into the *Jameʿ* Mosque of Tehran and the Sheykh Abd al-Hoseyn Mosque in which some of the *rowzeh khani* gatherings were held. The troops circled around the gathering place once. Such demonstrations showed that the *sardar-e sepah* [Reza Khan] regarded religious services and sanctities as important. He continued these performances for two or three more years until he became Prime Minister.[1]

Ja'far Shahri, in his account of his childhood days in Tehran, gives another eyewitness account of the Cossack *dasteh* (ritual procession) led by Reza Khan:

The Cossack *dasteh* led by their division leader Reza Khan, followed by brigadier generals, colonels, and majors, chanting . . . wearing typical military uniforms, but with bare heads and feet, went from *Mashq* square to *Tupkhaneh* square, then to *Naseriyeh*, and *Sabzemeydan* and then to the [shoemakers] bazaar, and the mosque of the Turks, where they circled around, performed *sineh zani* [ritual beating of the chest], sat down and had tea and sweet cold drinks, after which they rose and returned to the Cossack barracks by way of the *Pachenar* bazaar and *Khalilabad* street.[2]

The two accounts given above provide clues to the ways in which the Qajar military under Reza Khan were integrated into public religious rituals. They also illustrate the slow shift in policy undertaken by Reza Shah upon assuming the throne. Additionally, the Cossacks are described above as forming one of the most prominent *dasteh*s (processions), which implies that they had a distinct identity, or, at least, that the Cossack Brigade was viewed by others as a distinct group of ritual performers. This identity was expressed in a similar fashion to that of the goldsmiths *dasteh* or the Arab *dasteh*. It is also a typical example of how a *dasteh* or *hey'at* (a social unit around which rituals are usually organized) traveled around the neighborhood and visited other *hey'at*s or *dasteh*s before returning to their own *takyeh*. This military identity was integrated into the social fabric of early twentieth-century Tehran, but this practice would not continue for long.

Reza Khan's participation in *Moharram* rituals was restricted mostly to the early years of his rise to power (prior to 1926) before he had the independence and strength to oppose such ritual performances. It was also during this period that he pursued alliances with the ulama.[3] It is not clear what his attitude toward *Moharram* rituals was in his early years, but as his power increased his opposition to such practices also increased and became more uncompromising. It is clear, however, that he did not attempt to co-opt these rituals. The cornerstone of Reza Shah's policies was the elimination of all potential political opponents. Because popular religious rituals were one source of popularity and legitimacy for elites outside his direct control, he viewed these rituals as a potential threat to his authority. This is one of the main reasons he opposed such ritual performances, eventually banning them in the 1930s.

Another prominent reason he was hostile toward these rituals was that he wanted to portray a different image of Iran to Westerners. Reza Shah's ban of *Moharram* rituals, like his banning of certain traditional clothes, notably, the hijab and traditional Iranian hats worn by men, required firm and sometimes violent enforcement. Rosalie Slaughter Morton, a doctor visiting Iran in the late 1930s, commented on this general pattern: "The quiet opposition [toward Reza Shah] of many of these mullahs is the strongest conservative force in the land. But the shah will brook no opposition. And as their power wanes, they see their aristocratic position vanishing. They have not taken it lightly, and have tried to rouse the people against the new customs, but they have been chastised and given to understand that their business is entirely within their mosques."[4]

Negative reactions to Reza Shah's new policies are confirmed in other accounts as well. There also seem to have been difficulties in administering these new laws, indicated by the uneven levels of enforcement across the country. It would seem that "the long arm of the law" was not so "long" in this case, because the laws were much harder to put into effect in areas outside of the government's direct sphere of authority. Hence, cities like Tabriz and Tehran experienced a higher degree of enforcement, while smaller cities and villages experienced a lower degree. There are also accounts discussing how, in response to the government ban on rituals, many professional *ta'ziyeh* performers relocated to rural areas. Still others formed small troops of three to four professionals and performed on a very small scale in back alleys and neighborhoods.[5] Performances of this sort were observed by this author in Isfahan in the 1970s.

The process of progressively restricting the performances of *Moharram* rituals culminated in the banning of such rituals in the 1930s.[6] While this ban was not the first example of a state official's restricting ritual performances, it was the first outright ban of such activities. The few earlier examples in sources that are available were usually of temporary restrictions, often having to do with security concerns.[7] Reza Shah's policies were therefore a departure from previous patterns of rule. *Moharram* rituals ceased to be a primary means for maintaining the position of the ruling elites within Iranian society. Still, it took time for him to implement his policies. Before 1925 he participated in rituals himself, and until the early 1930s *Moharram* rituals were merely discouraged in some areas or were diverted to certain neighborhoods.[8] Furthermore, only extreme rituals such as *qameh zani* (striking the shaved head with a sword in order to shed blood for Hoseyn) were banned at this time. These ritual practices were specifically targeted by Reza Shah and some others because they believed that if Westerners saw what they considered to be barbaric and backward rituals, they would develop a negative impression of Iran as a modern nation. This concern over Iran's image and place in the international community continued to be of central concern throughout the Pahlavi era and resurfaced after the Islamic Revolution of 1978–79.

On June 1, 1931, an article appearing in the *Ettela'at* (the national newspaper, controlled and heavily censured by the state) harshly criticized *qameh zani* and praised the shah's ban of such practices. It goes on to condemn such violence on both rational and religious grounds, although, as a matter of interest, it does not refer to any specific condemnation of this practice by the ulama. This position is significant when one considers that the ulama have historically criticized this particular practice in rather strong terms. Later, Ayatollah Khamenei, the successor to Ayatollah Khomeini as spiritual leader of the Islamic Republic of Iran, in a speech to an audience of religious scholars said that "this practice [*qameh zani*] is wrong. . . . This is ignorance. These things are contrary to religion."[9] *Qameh zani* was again banned by the government of the Islamic Republic in 1994. The concern for Iran's international image was not restricted to secular nationalists or the Pahlavi regime, but eventually became a common sentiment among many Iranians.

Ettela'at articles condemning *Moharram* rituals indicate changing attitudes among some Iranians concerning potential Western perceptions of Iranian culture and civilization, particularly the embarrassment these rituals could cause to Iranians. This attitude gained more and more currency beginning in the late nineteenth century and continuing throughout much of the twentieth century, especially among the new, modern-educated elites. One concerned citizen wrote in another article:

Is it possible to imagine that the Prophet (S.A.S.) who is even recognized by the Europeans themselves as a great man of wisdom and a philosopher of high standing, and from whose great and noble ideas they learn, could be content with [such behavior] on the day of *Ashura*. . . . Are there still films which the Westerners have taken of these strange spectacles and of [the processions mutilating themselves with swords on the day of *Ashura*], which they have shown to millions of civilized people from around the world at public shows as an example of Iranian civilization? . . . [if one of these Iranian youth were to see such a film] how embarrassed and ashamed he would be. What would he say in answer to the questions of these foreigners who say in a ridiculing manner "Is this mourning ceremony an example of your civilization?"[10]

The banning of extreme ritual practices by the Pahlavis and the leaders of the Islamic Republic is indicative of an important shift that took place in the twentieth century. The ambivalence of the ulama and some elites toward the more extreme ritual practices goes back for centuries, but the state rarely made any effort to ban such activities. The Qajars and early rulers had not been centralized enough to be able to control significantly public forms of religious expression. As the state expanded during the twentieth century the realm of state control dramatically expanded. In other words, this was the first time that such a ban on public rituals was realistically possible. During the Qajar period, concerns were raised about Iran's negative international image, but it would not have been practical to try to end all such public displays. Therefore, the only action leaders took was to ban Westerners from attending the rituals organized by the rulers themselves. This shift in policy also points to a rising consciousness, at least in the circles of government and some nationalist elites, of Iran's place in the international order.

The banning of extreme ritual practices also indicates a shift in attitudes concerning the role of government in society and the relationship of ideals like nationalism to actual popular practice. Throughout the twentieth century, the state and some elites promoted a particular vision of what they believed Iran should look like. Meanwhile, the state increasingly tried to control public space and public activities in order to promote its particular program of social transformation. In other words, it was assumed at least by some nationalist elites that the ideals propagated by the Pahlavi state should be implemented in the public sphere. This pattern continued under the religious leadership of the

Islamic Republic. Under the Pahlavis, the state was used to implement a particular set of secular nationalist ideals. Following the Islamic Revolution of 1978–79, the revolutionary elites similarly believed that the official Islamic interpretation of the revolutionary ulama should be implemented by the state. In both cases, Iran's international image was important, but there was also another important issue. In modern Iran, the expanded state bureaucracy has been used to implement a series of national ideals for social practice and identity. This shift reflects a new role for the state in trying to shape and control Iranian society in the modern period. These trends also parallel efforts by Reza Shah to co-opt the religious establishment, by taking over pious endowments and increasing the government's role in religious education and curriculum.[11]

The relative success of Reza Shah's efforts to restrict ritual performances is illustrated by changing patterns of advertising for such rituals in major newspapers. During the later years of Qajar rule, government officials and wealthy patrons often advertised *ta'ziyeh*s and *rowzeh khani*s in major newspapers. As late as 1928, an advertisement appeared inviting all of the residents of Tehran to attend a *ta'ziyeh* performance in the famous *Takyeh Dowlat*.[12] And on July 2, 1927, Sayyed al-Mohaqqeqin Diba of the national assembly advertised his annual *rowzeh khani* in his home.[13] Other organizations, such as the *Givehforushan* and *Jurabchiyan* guilds (sellers of shoes and socks), as well as respected notables (such as Ayatollah Zadeh Esfahani or Haji Molla Abbas Ali Qazvini), also advertised such events.[14]

Advertisements for rituals continued until 1933, after which they ceased until 1941 when Reza Shah had abdicated his throne and was no longer the ruler of Iran. The discontinuity in advertising is a good indicator not only of the efforts by Reza Shah at restricting the performance of such rituals but, more important, of his efforts to control access to the "public sphere" through censorship of the popular press. However, many of the rituals continued to be performed to varying degrees by different individuals and organizations, especially in private residences, long after they were condemned by the shah. The large public events, however, were officially banned and became much less common in the larger cities. The public promotion of these events in newspapers was discontinued.

The state, under the guidance of Reza Shah, tried to dominate the public sphere, allowing only discourses that conformed to the state's

program. Reza Shah both tolerated and promoted a secular nationalist discourse, sometimes originating from the state and more often proposed by the modernizing elite. This discourse was allowed in the
public press. As a result, Islam was mentioned less often in the press,
and national symbols and ceremonies usually excluded Islamic referents. Such activities were more and more considered to be outside the
realm of nationalist discourse and appropriate nationalist behavior and,
therefore, were not to be publicized in the public press.

Many Iranian nationalists during this period disassociated Islam
from Iranian identity, often rewriting Iran's history to stress its pre-
Islamic heritage at the expense of its Islamic heritage. Such intellectuals often did not explicitly reject religion itself, but rather they criticized
what they characterized as being examples of "backward" or "barbaric"
practices of Shi'is. Some scholars, such as Abd al-Hoseyn Zarrinkub,
an influential nationalist historian and ideologue, went even further
by claiming that Islam and Shi'ism were distinctly "un-Iranian." His
1957 publication *Do qarn-e sokut* (*Two Centuries of Silence*) represents
this secular nationalist depiction of Iran's history. Zarrinkub's account
describes a typical primordialist construction of Iran as an organic
nation in which citizenship is based on ethnicity, shared language,
shared history, or membership in a unified culture or civilization. While
the Islamic identity is assumed to begin with the establishment of the
Islamic community in 622 CE, the Iranian community is described as
going back to pre-Islamic times. This national identity served to portray Iran as a nation like European nations, while at the same time dis-
tancing Iranian patriots from other Muslim nations and from religious
leaders.[15]

Zarrinkub's work begins with the seventh century Arab invasion
of Iran, which he portrays as a tragedy for the Iranian nation.[16] He represents the first two centuries of Iranian history following the invasion as a period of darkness characterized by constant struggle between
two peoples, the Iranians and the Muslim Arabs. Iranian national
heroes such as Afshin and Maziyar, rebelled against Arab rule and
struggled against Arab and Islamic oppression.[17] The Muslim Arab
conquerors are presented in this book as abusive, racist barbarians who
are intent upon suppressing Iran's national spirit by systematically
destroying everything Iranian.[18] However, he claims that Iranians soon
proved their superiority in matters of state, culture, warfare, and knowledge and eventually took over the ruling institutions.[19]

Zarrinkub argues that during this period the most that Iranians could do was to participate in failed rebellions and preserve what they could of Iran's culture, until after two centuries of oppressive Arab/Islamic rule the Iranian consciousness could again emerge victorious. Likewise, in 1943 an amusing attack on Shi'ism was published in the *Parcham* newspaper, which was edited by Ahmad Kasravi (1890–1946). While this newspaper was not directly produced by the Pahlavi regime, it espoused views that were more or less in line with those of the shah. Shi'is are sharply satirized in a short piece titled "The Invisible Imam; or [Merely] an Excuse for Lazy People?" in which believing Shi'is are characterized as being unwilling to do anything about social and political corruption, claiming that nothing of value can be done until the vanished imam returns.[20] Ahmad Kasravi is more specific in his critique of *Moharram* symbols and rituals:

The issue of weeping and religious mourning [celebrations] must be dealt with separately. This, too, has harmful results . . . which I will only list briefly.

1) Recounting a story that occurred thirteen hundred years ago and weeping and mourning because of it is to turn one's back on and to trample wisdom. The belief that God will be pleased with such weeping and moaning and will reward them is another manifestation of their ignorance. God is pleased with action that is rational and beneficial. What would be the benefit of crying and weeping about an old story of a thousand years ago? Why should God reward it? . . .

2) Chest beating, beating oneself with chains, rubbing mud on one's face, pouring dirt on one's head, cracking one's skull, jumping and falling, yelling, and other such actions are merely signs of a violent nature and savagery. Shi'is consider this to be a gift, and if there are one or more Europeans among the audience, they [the Shi'is] show off by beating themselves even more and crying even louder. But the truth is that such ignorant behavior has given an excuse to the Europeans to call Iranians and other Easterners "semi-savages" and to consider them undeserving to live free. . . .

3) Besides the fact that weeping and mourning suppress emotions and extinguish the sense of honor, all those religious mourning ceremonies and processions became a preoccupation for the people preventing them from attending to the affairs of life. . . . Rather than

becoming aware of world events and the advancement in science and other areas, or contemplating the condition of the country and the masses, they engage in such futile exhibitions. What we see is the result of such preoccupation. They are the victims of the greed of the Europeans, but complain of the injustice of Yazid.

Iranian women are oblivious to everything and do not have the slightest interest in the country and the nation. The educated, as well, do not display any intelligence or understanding in this regard. As a result, they spend most of their time in religious mourning ceremonies and using their intellect and abilities for such purposes.

4) The practice of weeping and pilgrimage, with all the rewards promised, results in another great harm, which is that Shi'is unabashedly engage in evil deeds . . . [Ordinary people] do not understand that evil deeds harm life and cause disorder in life. Hence, when they hear that a person who weeps for Hoseyn or makes a pilgrimage to his shrine will be absolved of all sins and is bound to go to heaven, they no longer fear, and they engage in evil.[21]

It should be pointed out here that there were exceptions to this general trend. These exceptions tended to attempt a compromise of sorts between religious and secular nationalist ideals and practices. The new nationalist discourse, which is exemplified by such ideologues as Ahmad Kasravi, usually rejected *Moharram* symbols and rituals outright, but exceptions were made to this pattern as well. For example, in an *Ettela'at* article published in 1938, the *'Eyd-e Ghadir* holiday was discussed along with the mutual responsibilities and rights men and women have toward each other according to Islam. In this article it is argued that "there is no difference between religious celebrations [such as *'Eyd-e Ghadir*] and national celebrations," because they both strengthen the sense of brotherhood and of national unity among the population.[22] In any case, such efforts at bridging the ever-increasing gap between Islamic ideals and nationalist identity were the exception to the general rule.

The second Pahlavi ruler, Mohammad Reza Shah, continued many of his father's policies. For example, he continued the ban on the more extreme rituals such as *qameh zani*. However, he followed a less consistent path than his father had done. He allowed most rituals to be performed publicly and even allowed articles and editorials about Hoseyn and Karbala to appear in the national newspapers during the ritual season. He also portrayed himself as a good Muslim leader and sponsored *Moharram* rituals in the tradition of previous Iranian dynastic rulers. He incorporated a diverse set of strategies to legitimize his rule. He claimed that his government was a democratic, Islamic monarchy in the tradition of the ancient Persian kings. At the same time, he tried to encourage only the politically pacifist interpretation of the symbols and rituals of Karbala.

One of the reasons Mohammad Reza Shah followed a less decisive path was that he started off in a much weaker position compared to his father. Unlike his father, he was placed in power following Reza Shah's forced abdication at the hands of Britain and Russia. From 1941 through 1953 his authority was limited by several factors including the eventual rise to prominence of the Mosaddeq-led parliament, which maintained some degree of popularity and legitimacy. In 1953, he was placed in power following a Western-supported overthrow of the Mosaddeq government. The ulama reasserted themselves beginning in 1941, when they called for an end to the restrictions on *ta'ziyehs* and *rowzeh khanis*, and the previously banned Islamic veil reappeared in the streets.[23]

Another major difference between Mohammad Reza Shah and his father was that he could not claim to be a military leader with any real credibility. Like his father, Mohammad Reza Shah started out by tolerating *Moharram* rituals. As time passed, his position grew stronger and oil revenues provided him with greater independence from economic interest groups. By the 1960s and 1970s, he relied far less upon strategies for religious legitimacy. He put less and less time and money into religious rituals and activities and promoted secular nationalist ideals more aggressively. Eventually a crisis of legitimacy resulted. One of the factors contributing to this crisis of legitimacy was his failure to make effective use of *Moharram* symbols and rituals.

As stated above, many of Mohammad Reza Shah's policies regarding religious symbols and rituals differed significantly from those of his father. One of the policies Mohammad Reza Shah continued was the banning of the more extreme *Moharram* rituals. An article appeared in 1950, long after the abdication of Reza Shah, that credits Mohammad Reza Shah with the banning of rituals in which swords were struck against the head, as well as certain forms of theatrical representations of Karbala.[24] However, Mohammad Reza Shah departed from the example of his father in other ways. Until 1955 he gave financial support to groups that held processions in Qom.[25] He also sponsored a *majles* (i.e., a *rowzeh khani*) every year in the Golestan palace (by 1969 the location had been switched to the *Sepahsalar Madreseh*). His ministers and other top government officials attended this *majles,* which was publicized in the national newspapers.[26] It was reported that in addition to his ministers and other top officials, military officers, a variety of guilds, merchants, and "notable men" attended the *majles.* The comment of the famous orator Falsafi, who was one of the three speakers giving sermons at this event, is paraphrased in this article: "Agha-ye Falsafi stressed that [promoting] such commemorations [*majales*] which will bring the shah and the nation [i.e., the people] closer together is the greatest service his Majesty the Shah can perform."[27] The article goes on to dismiss the allegations that the shah was disassociated with his people, labeling such accusations as anti-shah propaganda.

Mohammad Reza Shah's strategy of demonstrating piety through attending or even sponsoring religious rituals was not restricted to the central government. Many government officials in the capital and the provinces followed suit. There were also reports of provincial appointees of the shah attending similar *majales* in the provinces. In the same year Brigadier General Shahbakhti (governor-general of Azerbaijan and the commander of the Azerbaijani armed forces) attended *majales* in Tabriz, and his troops held similar sessions in their barracks where they said prayers for the shah.[28] This practice of saying prayers for the shah, dating back to the earliest ritual performances under such dynasties as the Buyids, the Safavids, and the Qajars, was also followed elsewhere.[29]

Another way Mohammad Reza Shah tried to promote his own religious legitimacy was by visiting holy places like Qom, Mashhad, Mecca, and Karbala. This practice has a long heritage in Iranian history. Traditionally, rulers were expected to make such pilgrimages in order to demonstrate their piety. One of the earliest examples of Mohammad Reza Shah's efforts to perform Shi'i pilgrimage was his visit to the holy shrine in Qom on the eleventh of *Moharram* in 1950, at which time he also met with the highly respected religious leader Ayatollah Borujerdi.[30] He often visited Borujerdi and other prominent ulama, particularly in the earlier decades of his rule. He made another heavily publicized pilgrimage to Mashhad in *Moharram* of 1953, during which it was claimed that the populace lined up along roadsides holding up flowers and reportedly shouting praises to him as he passed by.[31] It is further claimed that when the people saw the shah arriving by car at the *majles* in the Golestan palace they spontaneously shouted out *salavat* (a religious formula wishing peace upon the Prophet and his family, traditionally said on special religious occasions). The shah is even reported to have claimed that the eighth imam, Reza, visited him in a vision. This vision was widely criticized by many religious leaders.

Mohammad Reza Shah seems to have wanted to make use of Shiʿi symbols and rituals on a more selective basis than his father had done. While he was hostile to the politically radical potential of these rituals, he attempted to avoid direct conflict with religious ideals. This stance is consistent with his general pattern of claiming to represent Islam, while at the same time trying to minimize the importance of Islam as a legitimizing factor. He also at times tried to co-opt religious institutions such as pious endowments and religious seminaries, while still stressing the importance of religion in Iranian society. For example, Shahrough Akhavi quotes him as saying in a 1971 press conference: "It is not improbable that we may create a religion corps in the future so that if some of the students of the religious sciences have to perform their service, they can do it [within the framework of this corps]. Just as we say religion must be separated from politics (and a few years ago we saw the results of mixing the two), and just as we are insistent in that respect . . . so, too, we encourage the people to piety and religion. No society is truly stable without religion."[32]

His somewhat indecisive strategy may reflect the fact that he felt fundamentally less secure about his political authority than his father had. After all, his father could make at least some claims to being a strong and heroic military leader, while he had come into power as a result of a Western-led coup, which overthrew the nationalist government of Mosaddeq.

The inconsistency of Mohammad Reza Shah's use of Shiʿi symbols and rituals to legitimize his rule undermined his credibility as a ruler. It is true that he participated in and even sponsored *Moharram* rituals; that he did make highly publicized pilgrimages to holy cities such as Qom, Mashhad, Mecca, and Karbala; and that he claimed to be representing Islam and to be a believing Muslim. However, his aggressive promotion of a social order that ran contrary to more commonly held religious ideals made it difficult for him to claim any real religious legitimacy.

There were many contradictions inherent in Mohammad Reza Shah's rhetoric and actions. An excellent example of this inconsistency was the 2,500-year anniversary celebration of the Iranian monarchy that Mohammad Reza Shah sponsored in 1971. This ceremony, which was largely held to boost Iran's international image, stirred up a great deal of controversy in Iran, particularly among religious leaders. It was a celebration of twenty-five centuries of monarchy at a time when a variety of opposition groups were questioning the very institution of monarchy. This ceremony was severely criticized as an outlandish waste of government revenues and for many was the ultimate symbol of the disparity between the extremely wealthy ruling elites and the impoverished masses. This criticism may have been a fair assessment considering that the celebration was postponed for over a decade largely because of financial problems.

What is more important for the purpose of this study is the fact that the symbolism of this event was perceived as contradicting the symbolism of the *Moharram* rituals that the shah was also sponsoring. He stated the purpose of the celebration in this way: "This glorification [the 2,500-year celebration] is actually the glorification of the foundations of our national identity, civilization and glorious [achievements] and it is done in an effort to awaken a sense of Iran's honor and glory."[33] In order to bring to life Iran's pre-Islamic heritage, he had a coronation ceremony in 1968, and later in 1971, a major national celebration of Iran's heritage, featuring grand parades with all the participants in full costume in the style of the ancient Persian empires. To maximize the effect further, the ceremony was held on the site of the ancient capital of the Persian empire, Persepolis. This major event was accompanied by a variety of other cultural and academic promotional efforts, such as a film dealing with the ancient Iranian shah, Cyrus the Great.

In planning this event, the shah went far beyond merely presenting Iran's pre-Islamic heritage. With a few exceptions, such as the inclusion of Safavid troops from the sixteenth through eighteenth centuries, he excluded any significant representations of Iran's Islamic heritage from the celebration. Discontent over this issue was further compounded by the arrangements for mixed seating of men and women (unveiled) and the drinking of alcoholic beverages. These allowances, along with the Western-oriented lifestyle of his wife, Farah, undermined his religious credibility in many circles in Iran. Opposition to the celebration did not take long to surface. According to the SAVAK's (the shah's secret police) report to the shah:

> From the moment the subject of holding the 2500-year anniversary of Iranian monarchy became known, the religiously extremist clerics and preachers, and opponents of the state started speaking [publicly] about opposing this celebration. As the date of the event approached their efforts and actions became sharper, such that when Khomeini's speech condemning this event was broadcast on Baghdad radio some of the religious extremists started reproducing this speech in the form of announcements and propaganda and have distributed them. Some of the religious extremist clerics and preachers and opponents of the state have spoken against the celebration in their speeches, some of them even from the pulpit. As the date of the celebration approaches, they will likely mobilize people from the religious classes to oppose the 2500-year anniversary of Iranian monarchy.

The report goes on to discuss how these "enemies of the state" should be identified and arrested. Another SAVAK document reported:

> The aforementioned demonstrations, each in its own way and under the influence of certain conditions, expressed their uneasiness and sometimes overt opposition to this celebration; and [as for] one of these processions of opponents, which was large enough in number to be significant, the primary basis of their criticism was the harshness of living conditions [in Iran].[34]

The contradictory nature of the shah's actions did not escape the notice of others present at the time of the ceremony. This situation is perhaps best illustrated by an assessment attributed to the British ambassador at the time, Sir Anthony Parsons:

> Should he [the shah] have allowed the Queen to call together a council of Zoroastrian clerics? And afterwards to entertain the participants in a celebration in the royal palace, serving them champagne? And right in the middle of the month of Ramadan?!! . . . These sorts of actions, much more so than various economic issues . . . left a deep

and negative impression upon Muslim masses and religious leaders; perhaps for him and the Queen, this was a sort of emergency medical procedure intended to separate [surgically] the people of Iran from Islam.[35]

In addition to Mohammad Reza Shah's contradictory uses of symbols and rituals, there was another highly problematic issue. His personal lifestyle was considered by many to be far removed from Islamic ideals. The reference to "the Queen" is significant because she came to represent the female ideal articulated by the shah's Westernization program. She never appeared in public wearing hijab, was well educated, symbolized a career woman, and mingled freely with men. She, therefore, was eventually viewed by conservative Shi'is as a symbol of the moral corruption of the shah.

The behavior of the shah, according to many Iranians of that period, contradicted the image he sometimes projected of himself as a very pious Muslim. Sayyed Mohammad Baqer Najafi, in a speech broadcast on the radio in 1976, quoted Mohammad Reza Shah as having said the following in a speech given in Qom in 1967:

"Today I assure you that nobody, either by trying or by actively [succeeding] can claim to have done nearly as much for God or for the infallible *imams* as I have done. In fact, I have done everything that I could possibly have done in the path of God. I have repaired every holy shrine that could be repaired. Every night before going to bed I have said my prayers [*raz va niyaz*] to my God, and I have said my prayers [*do'a*]."

[Ministry of Information:] The shah thought he was a good and pious Christian; as if repairing holy places and saying prayers [*do'a*] before going to sleep (according to his honest claim) [are] an indication of closeness to God and to the infallible *imams*. In reality he did not understand, nor did he live according to, religion and Shi'ism. On the contrary, his actions and behavior and opposition to Islam and Shi'ism [were] a sign of his deeply [ingrained] hostility toward religion. One of the other important actions of the shah in opposing Islam was his changing of the calendar of the country, which had formerly been calculated beginning with the Hejrat of the Holy Prophet (S.A.S.), and which he personally decreed should be calculated starting from the establishment of the monarchy.[36]

The moral corruption (from a religious Shiʻi perspective) of the shahs of Iran has been a recurring trope through the centuries. Qajar rulers often drank wine, watched dancing girls, and lived a lifestyle in sharp contrast to the prescriptions of the ulama. However, it was usually done behind closed doors, and the wives of the shah did not violate Muslim sensibilities regarding female seclusion. So, the earlier shahs were often able to avoid direct and harsh criticism from religious leaders.

An important change was the spread of the modern media in Iran. The behavior of the Qajars could not have been as objectionable to the populace because very few people observed them directly. The Pahlavis, like other modern rulers, had to deal with the fact that their lifestyle was far more visible because of mass media coverage. However, there is another way in which Pahlavi rule was different from that of the Qajars. While the Qajar shahs were sometimes faulted for not living up to Islamic ideals, they were not often criticized for overtly challenging Islamic ideals. Thus, they were not perceived as being a threat to the overall social order. Unlike the Qajars, the Pahlavis deliberately violated Iranian standards of Islamic conduct, and in a very public way.

In the last century and a half a new discourse slowly emerged in which moral and political legitimacy has been more closely associated with issues of modernization, Westernization, and patriotism in the face of a perceived threat from the imperialist West. During the early nineteenth century, the Qajars were criticized for not looking after Iran's interests vis-à-vis European encroachment. However, the nature of their failings was often restricted to specific policy decisions. In the late Qajar period a new trend developed according to which the position of Iran within the international imperialist order became a central concern. This tendency became more pronounced during the Pahlavi period, leading to periodic open challenges to the shah's authority by the ulama and other social elites, such as the bazaar merchants and the modern Western-educated elites.

As modern educated elites emerged, some of them proposed new social ideals that challenged both the state and various social conventions. These elites questioned not only the policies of the state but also its fundamental nature. This was the political climate when the constitutional revolution took shape during 1905–11. The Pahlavis adopted some of the social ideals of these Western-educated intellectuals, such as aspects of secularism, enlightenment ideals, and nationalism. However, they essentially had an authoritarian political vision and force-fully transformed Iranian society. The government also ignored alternative visions of Iran's future that had gained popular currency. As a series of opposition views progressively gained acceptance, they eventually influenced the ways in which the authority of the shah was challenged. Karbala symbols and rituals were among the more important manifestations, or vehicles for expression, of these alternative social and political visions.

5 ✍

Religious Rituals, Society,
and Politics during the Pahlavi Period

*W*hile the state tried with futility to control *Moharram* rituals, these same rituals continued to evolve independently of the state's direct control. During the Qajar era, *Moharram* rituals (such as the *ta'ziyeh,* the *rowzeh khani,* and the *Moharram* procession) were among the most important means of promoting religious and political legitimacy. These rituals were also important in strengthening patron-client relationships and a variety of social identities, including ethnicity, profession, regional affiliation, and quarter/neighborhood alliances. Compared to the Qajars, the Pahlavis were aggressive about supplanting these identities with a "national" identity that would supersede this multiplicity of identities.

Moharram rituals had previously served as a means of mediation between the state and society, thus allowing for a plurality of identities. Reza Shah viewed *Moharram* rituals as a threat to this program and therefore set out to eliminate them. Mohammad Reza Shah followed a similar yet less consistent path. The fundamental similarity in their policies was the trend toward using a model of national identity, which either was overtly hostile toward *Moharram* rituals or, at the very least, would allow only a subordinate and more limited sphere of influence for such rituals. It is interesting that the government of the Islamic Republic, which came into power in 1979, has followed yet another path, involving the transformation of these rituals into a vehicle for a single identity accompanied by a "revolutionary" movement led by the state.

While the overall patterns of patronage and organization of ritual performances were influenced and informed by the actions and policies of the state, they also evolved independently of the Pahlavi agenda. During the Qajar period, merchants, ulama, ministers, government officials, military officers, landowners, and heads of guilds were patrons of *Moharram* rituals.[1] This pattern was interrupted beginning with the early reign of Reza Shah. At this time, ritual ceremonies sponsored by ministers and wealthy elites associated with the state became noticeably less prevalent. Elites no longer considered ritual patronage to be a desirable means of promoting social status. In addition, there was a complete break in such elite patronage when Reza Shah outlawed many of these activities in the 1930s.

Things changed with Reza Shah's abdication, which was followed by a period of liberal national government led primarily by secularists surrounding Mosaddeq. During these years of decentralization of government authority, and relative tolerance of political diversity, there was a shift on the part of the state toward a tolerance of *Moharram* rituals. For example, some members of the legislature, notably Ayatollah Kashani, publicized their participation in such rituals.[2] While such trends do not indicate a complete turnaround on the part of Iranian elites associated with the government, they are symbolic of a relative shift toward participation in these rituals. The modernizing nationalists did not adopt such rituals en masse, but, rather, segments of society, which had enthusiastically supported such rituals previously, now did so in the open. Old organizations such as guilds and ethnic associations reemerged in the public sphere as sponsors of *Moharram* rituals. It is also at this time that there was a flourishing of new *hey'ats*, some associated with the state and some developing independently.[3]

Some *majales* sponsored by elites praised the shah and his program. Some of these patrons praised the shah in the traditional way by praying for him, while others praised him in their public pronouncements. For example, below an advertisement for a *majles* in 1956, the organizer Abbas Namavar said: "Especially because of the attention paid by the agents of his Majesty the Shah, new buildings and decorations have been built in this holy shrine which are worthy of being seen and which warrant saying prayers to his Majesty the 'promoter of religion.'"[4] Another example of sponsors supporting the shah is a *majles* in the bazaar (*Takyeh-e Dabbaghkhaneh*) that was attended by government ministers, members of the national legislature, various bureaucrats, diplomats from Islamic countries, and military officers and that ended with prayers for the shah.[5] One of the most striking trends during this period was the persistence of various preexisting identities in ritual performances and patronage. Ethnic groups, regional alliances, guilds, and neighborhoods all began publicly advertising such ritual events as they had done before the ban.[6] These identities certainly still existed, and they were quick to take advantage of the change in government policy to begin publicly promoting themselves through patronage of *Moharram* rituals. In a similar way, individuals such as the ayatollahs Borujerdi, Behbahani, and Nuri, all of whom were among the highest and most respected ulama, began to sponsor and publicly promote such rituals.[7]

Many prominent ulama sponsored *Moharram* rituals in their homes and in mosques and *madresehs*. For example, Ayatollah Sayyed Ahmad Khansari (d. 1963), who was the prayer leader in Tehran and rose to the stature of the leading religious scholar of Tehran, sponsored *Moharram* rituals in his home every year.[8] These rituals were attended by participants from diverse social and economic backgrounds. Some prominent ayatollahs, such as Mirza Khalil Kamarch'i (d. 1962) and Sayyed Ahmad Shahrestani (d. 1963), even gave the ritual sermons and occasionally even participated in the more popular rituals that involved physical self-mortification.[9] Rituals were also sponsored in major mosques, *madresehs*, and *hoseyniyehs*. For example, rituals were held every year in the *Madreseh-e Marvi*. These rituals were often attended by the elite members of the ulama as well as wealthy bazaris and political leaders.[10]

Rituals and ritual sites continued to be associated with specific social groups. For example, *Masjed-e Shah* was associated with the silversmiths, jewelers, and goldsmiths; *Masjed-e Mirza Musa* with cloth merchants; and *Masjed-e Hajj Sa'id Azizolluh* with the spice, sugar, and tea guild, as well as the haberdashers guild.[11] There were also new identities. As more and more people migrated from rural areas (or from other countries) to big cities like Tehran, they maintained their regional identities. Many mosques and *hey'ats* were associated with ethnic groups or groups with strong regional affiliations, such as the Azerbaijanis and Arabs, who continued to be associated with specific mosques and *hey'ats* in the bazaar and elsewhere. Also, as cities transformed, new urban identities based on neighborhood or cohort also formed (e.g., the South Tehran Association, new "youth groups," etc.).[12] As new occupations became common, new associations were created, including associations of mechanics, electricians, truckers/transporters, drivers, newspaper and journal distributors, and cigarette sellers.[13] Some of these consisted of government employees, such as the Railway Workers Association or the Retired Officers Association (for military personnel), and others of modern educated elites, such as the Islamic Association of Engineers.[14] Following the abdication of Reza Shah, *Moharram* rituals reflected new versions of preexisting social identities, along with new associations and their corresponding identities. Communities and neighborhoods also continued to work together as groups to sponsor rituals and to deal with neighborhood problems. Of course, individuals and families continued to maintain their social networks by means of these rituals.

Patterns of ritual patronage also changed as Tehran grew from a population of fewer than 150,000 in the mid-nineteenth century and 200,000 in the early 1920s to an estimated three million in 1970.[15] A comparison of the census data from 1852 and 1973–74 shows that one of the most noticeable changes was that while the number of mosques increased from 47 to 752, the number of *takyeh*s or *hoseyniyeh*s only increased from 54 to 86.[16] This dramatic difference points to a relative decline in the prevalence of these ritual sites as compared to both the growth in population and the expansion of the number of other religious buildings like mosques. For example, in 1852 there was roughly one *takyeh* for every two mosques and every 1,500 people. In 1973–74, there was an average of one *takyeh* for every nine mosques and every 35,000 people. The data are approximately the same for the years 1974–75, and 1975–76. These figures indicate that the *takyeh* became less prevalent than mosques during the Pahlavi period. However, the patterns on a national level are quite different. While there is insufficient data for a comparison with the nineteenth century, in 1973–74 there were 1,235 *takyeh*s or *hoseyniyeh*s and 5,166 mosques in the rest of Iran.[17] These numbers mean that there was roughly an average of one *takyeh* for every four mosques in other regions of Iran that were outside Tehran. The leading regions for *takyeh*s in 1974–76 were the provinces of Khurasan, Mazandaran, Yazd, Semnan, and the Central Province (i.e., Markazi).[18]

There is also a noticeable correlation between both income and location in relation to religious buildings, as pointed out by H. Bahrambaygui in 1971. In short, the older neighborhoods, which were consequently the closest to the center of the city and contained the lower-income communities, had the largest number of mosques. The newer parts of the city, which were located mostly on the outskirts of Tehran, had far fewer mosques. The northern districts in particular contained the wealthiest populations and the lowest number of mosques.[19] Comparing the data for *takyeh*s in this period reveals a similar pattern. In 1971, for example, 70 out of 93 registered *hoseyniyeh*s or *takyeh*s (i.e., 75 percent of Tehran's total) were located in the southern districts of the city (districts four, five, seven, and ten). Twenty-five percent were in the bazaar district alone.[20] The outlying districts and the wealthy northern districts contained far fewer ritual buildings. The correlation between wealth and ritual sites emerged during the twentieth century. As was discussed in a previous chapter, during the Qajar period there was no significant relationship between the wealth of a neighborhood and the number of *takyeh*s located within that neighborhood.

These changes were brought about by several factors. One important factor was the decline in patronage of such rituals and ritual sites on the part of elites and the state. In fact, Sadeq Homayuni argues that while the *ta'ziyeh* had strong roots in popular culture, they became increasingly dominated or even co-opted by elites. Later, when they withdrew most of their support for the *ta'ziyeh*s, they contributed significantly to its decline.[21] Their eventual withdrawal from the role of patrons of these rituals, then contributed significantly to the decline of the tradition. *Takyeh*s were expensive to create and maintain, which means that elites often played a prominent role in creating and running these pious endowments. As elites increasingly abandoned this practice, fewer ritual sites were built. Also, as the Pahlavi shahs stopped using *Moharram* rituals as a primary means of promoting their religious legitimacy and maintaining bonds with their subjects, they virtually abandoned support for *hoseyniyeh*s. The state also restricted ritual performances and, by extension, ritual sites, especially during the reign of Reza Shah. Shahrough Akhavi discusses this trend during the Pahlavi period in relation to *madreseh*s, or seminaries, which were increasingly controlled by the state and were reduced in number.[22] The same pattern can be seen in relation to *hoseyniyeh*s during this period. As the patronage of these sites by elites and the state was reduced, it was more practical for neighborhood organizations to sponsor rituals on a smaller scale or to use temporary ritual sites that were located on private property or even in large professional or commercial buildings. Temporary ritual sites were common during the Qajar period as well, but during the Pahlavi period there was an increase in the percentage of ritual sites that were temporary. This trend is also related to the proliferation during the early Pahlavi period of religious associations called *hey'at*s, which often had no specific ritual site at all aside from someone's house or some other form of private property. There were also fewer rituals in some neighborhoods, especially newer and wealthier neighborhoods, such as in northern Tehran. The reduction in ritual participation and patronage was restricted mainly to the wealthier urban classes.

The rituals themselves also evolved. For example, the pool of speakers changed over time. Initially, speakers were primarily lower-ranking ulama and professional *rowzeh* preachers, usually referred to as the *sheykh* or the *va'ez*. In the nineteenth and early twentieth centuries, they were often famous orators, which was sometimes reflected in such names as *Soltan al-Va'ezin* (the king of orators). This sort of speaker continued to be dominant throughout the Pahlavi era, but as each decade passed, the number of speakers with different backgrounds slowly increased. For example, more and more doctors or researchers (*mohaqqeqin*), such as Dr. 'Ali Shari'ati, spoke at these events. Eventually, especially following the Islamic Revolution in 1978–79, it became common to advertise lectures by women speakers.

The emphasis in rituals shifted from sermons to lectures. Sermons, as the primary vehicle of expression, however, were not displaced by lectures. Rather, in the 1960s and 1970s, there is a noticeable increase in the number of these events in which the lecture is emphasized. During this period, advertisements for some of the *majales* refer to the content of these ritual events as being lectures (*sokhanrani*) as opposed to mentioning only sermons, mourning sessions, and public performances (*rowzeh, ta'ziyeh, sugvari,* and *'azadari*). In such cases, the method for targeting an audience also shifted. Previously, the targeted audience had usually been guild members, ulama, notables, neighborhood residents, fellow members of an ethnic or regional group, or all classes of society. During this later period, some advertisements used the speaker and the topics of the lectures as the hook that would draw in interested individuals. Thus, the audience was self-selecting based partly on the political orientation of the speakers. Such lectures placed stress more on national or international issues than upon fragmentary identities and thus contributed significantly to national discourse. This is not to say that such components were completely absent before, but rather there is a relative shift in emphasis during this period.

The Islamic Association of Engineers sponsored an event in which Morteza Motahhari and Salehi Najafabadi spoke about the ideas presented in Najafabadi's controversial book *Shahid-e javid* (*The Immortal Martyr*). And a more famous example would be the *Hoseyniyeh-e*

Ershad, where both Motahhari and Shari'ati gave lectures on Hoseyn in the late 1960s and early 1970s. In 1968, Mohammad Taqi Shari'ati ('Ali Shari'ati's father) spoke on "Role Models for Islamic Society," Fakhr al-Din Hejazi spoke on *"Shahid-e javid"* (Najafabadi's book), and Motahhari gave his famous lectures titled *"Hamaseh-e Hoseyni"* ("The Epic of Hoseyn").[23] The contents of these lectures, along with other ritual sermons and publications, are analyzed in detail in the next chapter.

Moharram rituals, much like during the period of the Constitutional Revolution, were sites for political expression. *Moharram* rituals were among the most effective means by which religious opposition groups mobilized the masses against the state. This result was due partly to the inability of the state to control these rituals effectively, but it was also due to the deep societal roots of these rituals, along with the important role the ulama played in the rituals themselves.

Much like in the period of the Constitutional Revolution, political sermons were not uncommon during *Moharram* rituals. While the main topic of sermons was religious piety or personal or community issues, political themes were sometimes woven into the sermons. Gustav Thaiss, in an unpublished dissertation, points to the "multi-vocality" of the symbolism of Karbala.[24] Thus, the symbolism can simultaneously convey multiple meanings. For example, any statement about the "tyrant Yazid" could also be understood to refer to all tyrants, generally, and to the shah, specifically. Political sermons could challenge the state, the shah's legitimacy, Israel, the Baha'is, or the role of colonialist powers in Iran. For example, Thaiss quotes a sermon in which the British are criticized for having a Christian missionary agenda in Iran and for leading Iranians into immoral conduct.[25]

There are numerous other instances of orators at *rowzeh khanis* directly opposing the state. An example is provided by a mourning session that was held in June 1962 at the house of Mr. Navid, located in *kucheh-e Qa'in* in Tehran. This event was held in cooperation with *Maktab-e Towhid* and *Anjoman-e Eslami-e Mohandesin* (the Engineers' Islamic Association) and was attended by an audience estimated as high as 1,500 that included people from a wide variety of social groups, but especially the youth of the universities, the bazaar, and the ranks of the bureaucrats. The yard and residence were filled to capacity. This was not the only time Mr. Navid held such rituals in his home. Of the many sermons and lectures given during the *majles,* two stand out as examples of opposition sermons, those by Morteza Motahhari (on the tenth and eleventh of *Moharram*) and Sayyed Mahmud Tale-qani (on the twelfth of *Moharram*). Both of these two religious leaders became active in the oppositional movement that eventually led to the Islamic Revolution of 1978–79.

In his sermon, Motahhari stressed the importance of using religious sermons and lectures as a vehicle to inform the public about political issues. He said that religious lectures and sermons, which have roots in the tragedy of Karbala, constitute one of the most important pillars of society and religion. He argued that Hoseyn's movement was a model that should be kept alive in these sermons and then should be used as a model for action by believing Muslims, who are obliged to "promote good and prevent evil." This aspect of his argument is discussed in greater detail in the following chapter. For the purposes here, it is sufficient to consider his appeal to use these sermons as a vehicle for political discourse. Motahhari said the following:

Some people who were rational, wise, and pious suggested that since these rituals [*Moharram* rituals] are always being held in the name of the Prince of Martyrs, and since people already gather in the name of Imam Hoseyn, why not use them for another purpose? Why not promote another principle at the same time? And this principle is "promoting Good, and preventing Evil." . . . And what a wonderful thing to do, and what a wonderful tradition that has been brought into action. They put the feelings of the people toward Hoseyn Ebn-e Ali, which are sincere feelings, to a wonderful use. . . . Why should we not follow the principles of our own religion?! They are very good principles, and should be used. . . . Just as Mr. Beheshti said, the struggle between truth and falsehood has always existed in the world and still exists. There is always a Moses and a Pharaoh, an Abraham and a Nimrod, a Mohammad and an Abu Jahl, an Ali and a Mo'aviyeh, a Hoseyn and a Yazid.[26]

Motahhari then went on to "practice what he preached" by using his sermon as a vehicle to critique the government and a host of international political problems, including what he called "the threat of Communism and Zionism." He gave this appeal:

Today we face two great threats. . . . Of these two dangers, the first is Communism, and the other is Zionism, in other words the threat of the Jews. I can plainly state that the threat of Zionism is greater and more pressing than the threat of communism, even though the foundation of communism is materialism, . . . Zionists have spread their networks of espionage in all the Muslim countries. . . . We must understand what Materialists and Zionists are doing. We must be more aware of these issues than the government is. Even if the Government neglects this duty, we must make the government aware of such things. Telling, informing, and recounting these things is a religious obligation. . . . This is the philosophy of mourning for Hoseyn Ebn-e Ali. Otherwise, what good does it do to cry for Hoseyn? What need does he have for someone to cry for him. Hoseyn wants his name and ideology to remain alive; for us to fight against all evil in accordance with his belief system. He wants us to fight against Communism, tyranny, injustice, corruption, immorality, gambling, and intoxicants.[27]

On the following night (the twelfth of *Moharram*), Taleqani continued with anti-Communist and anti-Zionist rhetoric, but was even more direct in attacking the Pahlavi regime. His speech focused upon the theme of jihad. He argued that jihad is obligatory under certain circumstances. After discussing the complex moral and legal restrictions placed on warfare, he argued that in Iran at that time the conditions existed to warrant such a struggle. He went on to make the following comments, which are worth quoting here at length:

Who in this country is working hand-in-hand with the enemies of the Muslims? . . . I want you to confess. Who steals the wealth of the Muslims and gives it to assist the international Zionists and Israelis? Who forces Muslim women outside the bounds of chastity? . . . If a government or state has ties with them, what will the duty of Muslims be toward such a government? . . . On one hand they make the Muslims homeless in the desert, and violate the boundaries of Islam; on the other hand they take the wealth of Muslims for different purposes, without putting it to proper or productive use; they encourage moral corruption; if a government opened an embassy for them, and the leaders and diplomats of a Muslim nation go there and "eat, drink, and be merry," what would the duty of the people be toward such a government? You tell me what their duty would be? Should a government that is not governed by Islamic law rule over Muslims? Please tell me. If it is a lie, call me a liar; if this is true then it does not conform to the boundaries set by Islam.

Today Zionism is the second [or new] form of colonialism. Colonialism, in its first form [or stage,] was defeated, and has now taken the form of Zionism, and Zionism has taken the form of Israel, and Israel itself has taken on another form in our country, and that is Baha'ism. And they have influence over all the embassies and the pillars of this Shi'i government, to which prayers of peace should rightfully be sent, and which all of Islam should [be able to] take refuge. O you agents of the government who are present here today, both undercover and not undercover, this is the issue raised by Islam, the issue raised by religion, whether it be the ruler, above the ruler, or beneath the ruler. You ask why do I say these things, which upset you? Then don't allow me to say them. Stop me. Then it will no longer be my responsibility. However, once I have come here I am obligated to tell the laws and bounds of Islam. I am not working on behalf of anybody. I do not want anyone to put me in charge of the government. Like it or not, I am simply what I am. . . . I am responsible for what I say. Don't take the owner of this house tomorrow and interrogate him and ruin his life. It is not his affair. Tell me that I am a liar, that I have spoken against religion, that I am a troublemaker, or that I have colluded with [foreign] embassies; well say whatever you like; you can even start a file on me. . . . O Minister of Agriculture, is there no Muslim Advisor in this country? Do we not have engineers? If we do not, then bring one from Switzerland; if we don't, bring one from India; if we don't, bring one from Germany; Does the advisor of redistribution of property [i.e., land reform] have to be a person who is Jewish and Zionist?[28]

Taleqani then went on to accuse the government of tyrannical and dictatorial rule. He was arrested the following day and sentenced to a ten-year prison term.

Khomeini repeatedly spoke out against the government during *Moharram* in 1963. His criticisms of the government focused mainly upon several issues, including land reform laws, generally referred to as the White Revolution, and women's enfranchisement. The Local Council Laws of 1962, which allowed for non-Muslims' participation in the vote, were also targeted, as was the shah's dependence on the West (in particular the United States). He also expressed concern over the perceived threats of Communism, Zionism, and Baha'ism. Another unpopular action of the regime was a loan from the United States, which also provided for extraterritoriality for some American servicemen and government officials stationed in Iran. This association, of course, opened an old wound going back to the Qajar era. The timing of this opposition activity was also related to the confusion that followed the death in 1961 of the great Shiʿi scholar and sole *Marjaʿ al-Taqlid* (the highest rank of the ulama), Borujerdi. He had maintained a cordial relationship with the Pahlavis and had avoided any involvement in government politics or oppositional protest. He was upholding one of the traditional ideological strains within Shiʿism according to which it is argued that associating with governments or most forms of politics has the potential to lead one to corruption and injustice. Therefore, the most prudent thing for the ulama to do is to avoid such worldly concerns. Khomeini broke with this tradition by openly participating in oppositional politics and eventually establishing a theocratic state.

Khomeini gave one of the most well-known opposition sermons at the Feyziyeh seminary on April 22, 1963, which was the symbolically important fortieth-day anniversary of the government's attack on protesters at the famous Qom seminary in the Feyziyeh. In it, he declared the following:

> Forty days have passed since the beating, wounding and killing of our dear ones; those the victims of the slaughter at Feyziya Madrasa left behind have now been plunged into mourning for forty days. Yesterday the father of Sayyid Yunus Rudbari (may God have mercy upon him) came to see me, with his back bent and his face deeply marked by the great tragedy he has suffered. What words are there to console those mothers who have lost their children, those bereaved fathers?
>
> Indeed, we must offer our condolences to the Prophet of Islam (peace and blessing be upon him and his family) and the Imam of the Age (May God hasten his renewed manifestation), for it is for the sake of those great ones that we have endured these blows and lost our young men. Our crime was defending the laws of Islam and the independence of Iran. It is because of our defense of Islam that we have been humiliated and brought to expect imprisonment, torture, and execution. Let this tyrannical regime perform whatever inhuman deed it wishes—let it break the arms and legs of our young

men, let it chase our wounded from the hospitals, let it threaten us with death and violation of our honor, let it destroy the institutions of religious learning, let it expel the doves of this Islamic sanctuary from their nests!

... I have repeatedly pointed out that the government has evil intentions and is opposed to the ordinances of Islam. One by one, the proofs of its enmity are becoming clear.[29]

He gave a similar speech on the tenth of *Moharram* (June 3, 1963) in the Feyziyeh:

If the tyrannical regime of Iran simply wished to wage war on the *maraji'*, to oppose the *'ulama*, what business did it have tearing the Qur'an to shreds on the day it attacked Fayziya madrasa?

... Let me give you some advice, Mr. Shah! Dear Mr. Shah, I advise you to desist in this policy and acts like this. I don't want the people to offer up thanks if your masters should decide one day that you must leave. I don't want you to become like your father.[30]

Khomeini was particularly active in using *Moharram* rituals as a vehicle to promote opposition to the shah. Like Motahhari, he stressed the importance of using these religious rituals in the opposition movement against the Pahlavi regime:

Do not take for granted that [the uprising of] 15 of Khordad would have occurred even if there were no mourning rituals, or mourning processions in which they beat their chests and chanted slogans. No force could have caused the 15th of Khordad to take the form it did, except for the power of the blood of the Prince of Martyrs; and no force could have [preserved] this nation, which has been subjected to attack from all sides, and against which the great powers have conspired; [no other force could have] countered these plots, except for these mourning rituals.[31]

In 1963, Khomeini encouraged a wide variety of oppositional activities to be carried out during the ritual season. More specifically, he worked very hard to coordinate a multi-city opposition movement centered on *Moharram* rituals. He gave antigovernment speeches himself while encouraging others to do the same. He also exerted his influence to encourage ritual organizers to compose and use protest slogans and chants in their rituals. During the ritual season, Khomeini attended *rowzeh* sermons on most nights, traveling from one religious gathering to another. As was customary, he did not give *rowzeh* sermons, which were usually given by specialists and lower-ranking ulama. Rather, he gave sermons that would more properly be called lectures. However, Khomeini was unusual in that he was very active in giving such sermons, from which higher-ranking ulama like him tended to refrain. He also held frequent mourning rituals in his own home. Even when he did not give a sermon himself, his presence, and sometimes his active encouragement, prompted those who were giving the sermon to shift the topic to criticism of the government, the United States, or Israel. While many protest activities were clearly spontaneous and uncoordinated, Khomeini and other opposition leaders actively tried to coordinate protests. For example, as an act of protest Khomeini cancelled celebrations of the Iranian New Year holiday. He also called for people to boycott any celebrations related to the shah, such as those accompanying his visits to various cities. Khomeini even called for a three-day interruption of Shi'i rituals. The shah, however, did not cancel his mourning rituals held in the Golestan palace on those three nights and reportedly was himself in attendance on at least one of those nights.

There are also numerous accounts of how Khomeini encouraged orators to include protest themes in their sermons.[32] In fact, in *Moharram* 1963, he gave specific instructions that orators should give nonpolitical sermons for the early part of *Moharram,* and then after the seventh of *Moharram,* as the climax of the ritual season approached, they were to change their sermons to include antigovernment themes.[33] He sent messages throughout Qom, Tehran, and other cities with instructions on how to organize religious rituals that also served as political protests. He relayed both verbal and written messages to other cities by means of his students, the ulama, and other activists.[34] There are numerous accounts of his sending instructions, or protest materials, for ritual organizers and other activists. For example, Sayyed Esma'il Zarribaf, an opposition activist, described how Khomeini estimated that there were at least five hundred *hey'at*s in Tehran and that there had to be at least one hundred participants in each of these. He then gave Zarribaf materials for dissemination at these rituals.[35] Tape recordings of Khomeini's speech on the twelfth of *Moharram* were also disseminated nationwide.[36] Because of these networks, the sermons made it possible for all timely news to spread quickly from city to city, often within hours. Dedicated to helping him in these protest efforts were members of a wide variety of community and activist organizations, professional associations, political parties, community and occupational guilds, and religious/political networks, such as the *Hey'atha-e Mo'talefeh*. Khomeini and his followers also encouraged the composition of *Moharram* chants and slogans that had political content. For example, Abbas Zarribaf, a composer of elegiac chants and poems for *Moharram* rituals, provides an account of how he was encouraged by representatives of Khomeini to compose political chants and poems. One such chant was "The Feyziyeh University; Like the desert of Mariyeh; The students of religion; O despair! O despair! The body of each of them has fallen from the roof; Khomeini, Khomeini; You are the descendant of Hoseyn; You are the protector of religion."[37] He also quotes another chant, which he attributes to the clothiers, but that spread throughout the bazaar: "Qom is the desert of Karbala; Its every day is Ashura; Feyziyeh is a place of slaughter; The life-blood of the Ulama; O despair! O despair! The time has come to join with our [religious] leader Khomeini."[38] Many of the chants treated the government's attack on the Feyziyeh as a *Moharram* tragedy (like Karbala) to such an extent that it almost took on the status of a new *rowzeh*.[39]

The rituals of *Moharram* constituted one of the most important vehicles for protesting against the Pahlavi regime. Sometimes these protests were coordinated by opposition organizations, while at other times they were spontaneous expressions of popular discontent. Religious treatises about Karbala were, of course, among the most important vehicles for protest and are analyzed in detail in the following chapter. It can be said here briefly, however, that protest themes were often woven into the narratives of the ritual sermons by equating the shah with Yazid and the revolutionaries with followers of Hoseyn. At other times, sermons were much more direct, as the speakers commented explicitly on political issues, but, even in these cases, the speakers usually began and/or ended with appropriate selections from *rowzeh* sermons. Chants, like those quoted above, were also important. Some common themes of sermons, speeches, and chants/slogans were criticisms of imperialism, the United States, or Israel, along with condemnations of the shah and his policies. The most common policies that were attacked were dependence upon the West; alliance with Israel;

land reform; changes in laws governing gender roles, such as giving women the vote; the ever-increasing gap between rich and poor; and government corruption, tyranny, and incompetence. The discussion returns to these themes shortly.

When rituals turned into political protest, the basic structure of the rituals usually was not fundamentally altered. The rituals still consisted of ritual mourning, self-mortification, self-flagellation, or public processions. Protesters still traveled in processions in the bazaar or attended mourning rituals in homes, mosques, *madreseh*s, or *takyeh*s. For example, in numerous accounts of protests mourners wore shrouds in preparation for the *qameh zani* ritual, in which they strike their heads with swords, producing blood. As the clashes and violence escalated, especially in the late 1970s, the protesters who wrapped themselves in shrouds confronted armed soldiers, symbolically expressing their readiness to become martyrs. In some protests, they carried pictures of Khomeini or other political leaders, sometimes attaching these pictures to the standards that they carried in front of the mourning processions. As the numbers of martyrs increased in the 1970s, protesters increasingly carried pictures of fallen martyrs. In many cases, protesters carried banners with political slogans. Protest chants were generally intermingled with more abstract mourning chants, creating a symbolic connection between the Battle of Karbala and the protest movements underway in the 1960s and 1970s.

Many advantages to this particular method of protest existed. One of the most important was that most Iranian Shi'is had spent much of their lives participating in these rituals. Therefore, it was extremely easy to coordinate mass marches and protests without having to worry about chaos or confusion on the part of participants. The form or structure of the protests was usually familiar to the participants. It was also helpful that these rituals were already being organized by individuals, guilds, corporatist associations, and community and professional *hey'at*s. These efforts provided the necessary infrastructure, manpower, and financial resources for carrying out protests. In short, these rituals were taking place anyway, so it was a simple matter to influence them to be more protest oriented.

Another advantage was that these gatherings could simultaneously serve as religious rituals and political protests. Because these gatherings were ostensibly for the purposes of performing the Shi'i religious obligation of mourning for Hoseyn, it was difficult for the shah to prevent them. However, following the 1963 uprising, he tried to ban any rituals that he viewed as a politically dangerous. These rituals also allowed protesters to decide selectively how explicit they wanted to be with their protests. It was easy to speak either in abstract terms about Karbala or in specific terms about the shah's regime. In most cases of political protest, it was somewhere in between, combining both of these elements. Another important factor in these rituals-turned-protests was that the networks of ulama and ritual organizers made it possible to have at least some level of coordination of protest activities in numerous cities simultaneously.

One other major advantage was that most of these religious organizations were self-sufficient and had deep roots in the community. Some were founded during the Qajar period, while many others were established in the 1940s, in part to fill the gap left by the changes in patronage patterns of the state and the elites associated with the state. These organizations, usually called *hey'at*s, were involved in all sorts of activities. Many restricted their efforts to religious function, for example, organizing ritual events or funding and maintaining religious sites, such as mosques and *madreseh*s. Many were involved in charitable works such as running orphanages and religious schools for children or taking care of the poor. In addition to strengthening patron-client relationships, most served the further function of preserving a variety of identities, including ethnic, community, or corporatist identities. In the 1960s and 1970s, many of these *hey'at*s became increasingly politicized. This long-term trend helped the opposition leaders tremendously, because these organizations became political organizations, committed to protest and to serving as informal networks for spreading ideas, pamphlets, and protest materials. Khomeini actively encouraged this trend, and even worked to build coalitions between these groups, such as the famous *Hey'atha-e Mo'talefeh,* which consisted of a diverse grouping of *hey'at*s that worked together to promote protest against the regime. They printed and duplicated protest materials and helped to disseminate pamphlets, letters, telephone messages, tape recordings, and other protest materials broadly. This coalition increasingly grew to resemble an underground political organization with secret cells and clandestine networks and with Khomeini as its religious and political model. Because their functions were technically religious in nature, it was difficult for the shah's agents to shut them down. These groups were instrumental in the 1963 uprising.[40]

Throughout the 1960s and 1970s, *Moharram* rituals frequently became sites for conflict as opposition groups and government forces clashed during these rituals-turned-protest. The SAVAK (the shah's secret police) and other government agents regularly attended these rituals to collect information, monitor dissidents, and disrupt political sermons. Many accounts exist of government officials intimidating speakers, surrounding or even closing down rituals, or picking up ritual participants for questioning. On occasion they attended rituals undercover and tried to disrupt rituals either by shouting or, in extreme cases such as the attack on the Feyziyeh in Qom, through violence. From his previously quoted statements, it is clear that Taleqani believed that members of the government's secret service were present "undercover" at the ritual in which he spoke, which is likely to have been true, since he was arrested the next day.

It was fairly common for men who gave religious sermons to be arrested or "picked up for questioning." Michael Fischer comments that "in early 1975 Falsafi was not being allowed to speak, S. Abdul Reza Hejazi was in prison, Khasali was banished to Baluchistan, Shariati was in prison, Bazargan and Hasheminezhad were not being allowed to speak. But Bahlul, after his forty-year exile, was back and speaking. Shari'ati was released from jail later that year, so seriously ill that he died within two years. Another akhund—Ghaffary—allegedly died in jail under gruesome conditions."[41] Naser Makarem Shirazi gave an account of being arrested on his way to give a *rowzeh* sermon in Shemiran, in which he was planning on "mentioning the name of Khomeini."[42] Another eyewitness named Vaseqi Bakhshayeshi similarly described how the government agents surrounded a mosque in Tabriz, in which an orator by the name of Naserzadeh was giving a sermon containing the "*rowzeh* of Feyziyeh-e Qom." Armed government representatives ordered him to shorten his sermon and to stop talking about revolution and protest.[43] Similar incidents occurred to speakers such as Khomeini, who was arrested during the height of the ritual season, and Falsafi, who was eventually arrested because he protested openly in his sermons given at the *Masjed-e Azarbaijaniha* in Tehran.[44] In another account, a witness describes how the *hey'at* of Tayyeb Reza'i, a neighborhood leader who took part in protests and was later tortured and executed by the government, placed a picture of Khomeini on one of the standards that they were carrying in front of their procession. The police stopped them and tried without success to intimidate them into removing the picture.[45] In fact, many of these confrontations ended in a standoff or a stalemate of sorts. According to one account from Tabriz, tens of thousands of mourners were gathered in the bazaar to participate in mourning rituals and to take part in political protests; when the government troops correctly realized that the people were there to take part in protests, they tried to disperse the crowd without much success.[46]

These confrontations often erupted into violent clashes between protesters and government officials. Even *taʿziyeh*s had the potential to lead to violence. For example, in the Tehran bazaar, violent clashes erupted between government forces and protesters who started off as participants in a *taʿziyeh* performance.[47] Of course, the clash at the Feyziyeh seminary in Qom is one of the best examples of the type of clashes that took place in ritual events. In March 1963 in the Feyziyeh, the prominent theologian Golpaygani organized a ritual to commemorate the death of the sixth imam, Jaʿfar al-Sadeq. Among the speakers were the well-known Hajj Ansari Qomi and political activist Al-e Tahah. According to numerous accounts of ritual participants, government agents followed a plan they had used in many other rituals, including ones in which Khomeini was giving the lecture. They attended wearing normal dress (i.e., not wearing official uniforms) and initially tried to disrupt the ritual by shouting out prayers to the royal family (*salavat*), as was a common practice for rituals sponsored by supporters of the regime. When this was met with hostility on the part of other participants, they pulled out sticks and other crude weapons that they had hidden in their clothing, and a violent conflict ensued. Many students were injured or killed, some of them being thrown from the rooftop.[48] Khomeini was quite vocal in condemning and publicizing this tragedy.

Khomeini now openly criticized the shah. When he was arrested on the twelfth of *Moharram* (June 5) violent protests broke out for several days in most major cities throughout the country. In Tehran, for example, violent clashes broke out in front of the bazaar and the military opened fire. Many of the protesters were killed or injured. Estimates for the death toll for the 1963 uprising vary, ranging from the hundreds to the thousands. In 1975, the violent confrontation in the Feyziyeh was destined to repeat itself, both there and elsewhere, as students and scholars in this famous seminary took part in protests against the shah. This second clash, which was strikingly similar to the first confrontation, was also accompanied by arrest and imprisonment of participants, who were mostly seminary students.[49]

There are also many reports of the government using mobs to control protesters. This is an old tactic that had been used by the Qajars and other regimes. When mobs were used, a common practice was to arrange for soldiers, policemen, or hired men to attend these rituals in normal dress. Another common method was to convince local community leaders "to round up" a number of men, often manual laborers, unemployed youth, or just thugs, to show up with sticks, shovels, or other crude weapons to disperse the protesters by force. In pursuing this latter strategy, it was important to win over the neighborhood leaders, or strongmen, such as Sha'ban Ja'fari, Hajji Nuri, Tayyeb Hajji Reza'i, and Esma'il Reza'i. It stands to reason that protest organizers would in turn try to counter this force by bringing similar support of their own. There are numerous accounts of both the government and the opposition leaders desperately trying to win over the support of Tayyeb Hajji Reza'i.[50] In the end, Tayyeb, Esma'il, and Hajji Nuri sided with the revolutionaries, whereas Sha'ban Ja'fari sided with the shah. Tayyeb was able to bring large numbers of men to counter the government's plans to disperse the crowds by using violent mobs, which included the men that Sha'ban Ja'fari provided, along with support from government agents. Tayyeb's support was instrumental in several protests, which is why the government eventually arrested him and Esma'il and Hajji Nuri, after which they were tortured and Tayyeb and Esma'il were executed. According to reports, they were tortured and told to admit that Khomeini had given them money (i.e., a bribe) to participate. They reportedly said that they had not received any money from Khomeini. Quite the opposite was true, for they had given him money and would continue to do so.[51] In fact, the logistical and financial support they provided for the protesters was indeed important in making the protests possible. The government hoped that their fate would serve as a deterrent to others who might follow their example. It was also much easier to punish these men than it would have been to try to punish prominent religious leaders, such as Khomeini or Motahhari.

As the government promoted a particular variant of nationalism, other alternative identities and ideologies were also being articulated and debated in Iranian society. Iranian ethnicity (e.g., Persian, Turk, Arab, and Armenian), race, cultural heritage, and shared national culture were all included in discourses on religious identity. The vast majority of Iranian citizens accepted variants of ethnic and civic nationalism that stressed Iran's shared history, culture, language, and, in some cases, race. What they disagreed about was the place of that nation in the modern world. How were they going to modernize or Westernize? Is there a difference between these two? What would the role of religion generally, and of Islam and Shi'ism specifically, be within this national identity? Perhaps most important of all, what would be Iran's political position vis-à-vis the West? As the government promoted its programs for dealing with these questions, alternative views contested these ideals that inspired these government programs. As a broadly based discourse evolved surrounding these issues, *Moharram* symbols and rituals constituted a particularly prominent vehicle for expressing diverse views within this discourse. The following chapter analyzes in greater detail this discourse as it relates specifically to the "Karbala Paradigm."

6 ᧒

Hoseyn, "The Prince of Martyrs"

$\mathcal{B}$y the 1960s and 1970s, *Moharram* rituals had become effective means for critiquing the shah's regime and for expressing alternative social and political views. Lectures, often the centerpieces of these rituals, became increasingly politicized. Their use for this purpose was an important development within the oppositional discourse under Pahlavi rule. As many historians of the Iranian Revolution of 1978–79 have pointed out, the religious leadership surrounding Khomeini used religious symbols effectively to motivate the Iranian masses to rebel against the shah's regime.[1] One of the most important sets of symbols used in the oppositional political discourse was the Karbala Paradigm. In the 1960s and 1970s this narrative was cast in a new light. The shah and his followers were labeled as followers of Mo'aviyeh and Yazid, and the Iranian masses were equated with the martyrs who died with Hoseyn in 680 in the deserts of Karbala. This recasting can be seen in mass media, political pamphlets, books, political slogans, posters, and stamps, as well as in Khomeini's speeches and the political literature of various revolutionary groups in Iran.

It is not surprising that the Karbala narrative was used in this way, because it is based on a historic rebellion against what was perceived to be corrupt leadership. In addition, since it has traditionally been the symbolic event most central to Shi'i rituals and beliefs, it was easily comprehensible to most Iranians. However, Hoseyn's martyrdom has not always been interpreted in such an overtly revolutionary way. This symbolism, depending on the context, has been used both to defend and to fight the political status quo. As the different ideologues set about reinterpreting the Karbala Paradigm in more revolutionary terms, some of them encountered a great deal of resistance or even hostility from other religious scholars, who attacked them on grounds of heresy and who set out to systematically refute their arguments. This change is best understood as a complex process of revision of the narrative, followed by critiques of these revisions, and ending with a synthesis of a new "Karbala narrative." These competing narratives were accepted, rejected, or modified based on a series of factors related to contemporary political and social discourse.

Several issues were contested in this discourse on the "appropriate" understanding of the Battle of Karbala: the relative importance of the soteriological dimension of the Karbala Paradigm, the issue of whether or not to rebel actively against unjust rulers like the Pahlavi regime and what is characterized as the oppressive international imperialist order, the nature of jihad and martyrdom, the nature of the "self" and the "other," and, finally, the construction and propagation of different conceptions of gender roles in society. Prior to the mid-twentieth century, Karbala narratives tended to stress the soteriological dimension of the symbolism. This view did not, however, preclude the use of these narratives as a means for challenging or promoting the legitimacy of the state, as was frequently the case. During times of political crisis or upheaval, such as the period of the tobacco protests, the anti-Baha'i campaigns in the nineteenth century, the period of the Constitutional Revolution, and the revolutionary activities of the 1960s and 1970s, these narratives were used for more explicitly political purposes. However the narrative was not fundamentally reformulated until the 1960s and 1970s.

Two basic terms are used below to illustrate how the Karbala narratives were debated. The "core-narrative" is defined as the basic narrative of Hoseyn and his movement, including such things as the moral qualities and infallibility of the imam, loyalty to the imam, courage, honor, and a willingness to be martyred, with the battle dominating the drama. The term "meta-narrative" is used to refer to the broader narrative context in which the core-narrative is situated and from which it gains relevance to social and political discourse.[2] The core-narrative, which is relatively universalistic and static in meaning, includes the ideals of justice and piety that are embodied in the person of the imam. An example of the meta-narrative in the Karbala narrative is the representation of the "self" and the "other," which was transformed during this period. In earlier narratives the just and righteous self tended to be defined as consisting of the pious and loyal followers of Hoseyn (i.e., the Shi'is), whereas the corrupt and oppressive other was defined as consisting of the Sunnis and the hypocritical followers of Hoseyn, who had abandoned him at the crucial moment. However, in the revised narratives, the self was usually defined as the universal brother-hood of Muslims who have been subjugated by the oppressive other, most often represented as including the imperialist powers and the shah's regime. In some narratives, the class struggle between the pro-letarian masses and the oppressive bourgeoisie became central to the meta-narrative. In others, Muslim solidarity, Iranian solidarity, or even third world solidarity in the face of imperialism figured prominently.

This discussion should begin with the earliest and most influential Karbala narrative, Hoseyn Va'ez Kashefi's 1502 composition titled *Rowzat al-shohada* (The Garden of the Others), which has been consid-ered by many to be the canonical text within this tradition. It was based on earlier sources by prominent ulama like Sa'id al-Din's *Rowzat al-Eslam* (The Garden of Islam) or al-Khwarazmi's *Muqtal nur al-'a'em-meh* (The Site of the Murder of the Light of the Imams). However, Kashefi's book became the standard text for a new set of Karbala nar-ratives. It was also one of the most often quoted sources in later nar-ratives and histories retelling the story of Karbala.[3] What is most important for the purposes here is that Kashefi's text is sufficiently rep-resentative of the more commonly accepted narratives of the later part of the Qajar period and the early reign of Reza Shah. It was one of the primary scripts used in *rowzeh khani* sermons that bear the same name as his text (*Rowzat al-shohada*). This type of narrative is critically impor-tant to the study of Karbala symbols and rituals because it served as the "text" in sermons and was performed in ritual form.

This text serves as a good reference point for discussing the narra-tives that were later produced, because its basic approach was not fun-damentally challenged until the mid-twentieth century. There were, of course, numerous similar narratives produced by prominent schol-ars during the Qajar era. For example, Mirza Mohammad Taqi Sepehr, in his 1879 book *Nasekh al-tavarikh* (*Abrogator of Histories*), developed similar themes, although he partially restructured the narrative. He spent more time outlining the proper ritual practices that are to be observed when making a pilgrimage to any of the tombs of the imams. His narrative, which was significantly longer and more detailed than Kashefi's text, also included a series of theological interpretations, such as the creation of the imams before the creation of the world, that were not developed in Kashefi's version. Another interesting narrative from that period was Vaqqar Shirazi's 1880 book *Ashareh-e kameleh* (*The Com-plete Ten*), in which he made more liberal use of poetry and less consistent use of the narrative format, but his basic themes were not fundamentally different.

The relative continuity of this narrative tradition can be seen in the twentieth century as well. For example, the only significant variations in Abbas Qomi's 1941 *Romuz al-shahada* (*The Mysteries of Martyrdom*) and Sayyed Ebrahim Miyanji's widely circulated Arabic text *al-Uyun al-ibra fi maqtal sayyed al-shohada* (published in 1959), were their exclusion of the experiences of the prophets and their reduced focus on the lives of Fatemeh and Ali. The same can be said of Mohammad Yazdi's 1967 text *Biyayid Hoseyn Ebn-e Ali ra behtar beshnasim* (*Come, Let Us Better Understand Hoseyn*), which appeared only one year before the first "revisionist narrative" appeared. These stories also focused more explicitly upon Hoseyn as the central character in the narrative. Hence, these narratives followed fairly closely the core themes that Kashefi develops in his narrative *Rowzat al-shohada*.

Va'ez Kashefi was born in the fifteenth century in Sabzivar, in northeastern Iran, and died in 1504. His father was probably one of the elite ulama of the period. He spent much of his life in Sabzivar. He lived in Mashhad for a short time, visited Neyshapur, and later on traveled to Herat in search of the famous mystical teacher Sa'd al-Din Kashghari, who had already died. He stayed in Herat and came to know another famous Naqshbandi master, Mowlana Jami, before joining the Naqshbandi Sufi order. He began writing his famous book *Rowzat al-shohada* by the order of Sayyed Mirza, a local notable, and finished it in 1502. *Rowzat al-shohada* is the first book of its kind to be written in Persian and was so widely accepted that it was regularly recited from the *menbar* (the pulpit in a mosque). Reciters of Kashefi's text were called *rowzeh khans*, or *rowzeh* preachers. The basic structure of the narrative consisted of reciting in a chain the names of prophets and imams (beginning with Adam and ending with the vanished twelfth imam), all of whom suffered as a result of injustice and oppression. Kashefi used a series of Shi'i hadith collections and other classical works to construct the story.[4] The basic style of the text was narrative Persian prose with many Qur'anic verses in Arabic, as well as poetry and Arabic phrases interspersed throughout.

The main theme of Kashefi's narrative was commemoration of the tragedy of Karbala through acts of ritual mourning and crying. Unlike some of the later narratives, Kashefi's did not use the symbolism primarily as a symbolic set of political role models to be emulated literally. Instead, these symbols were represented as an ideal to be remembered and commemorated by the true believers (the Shi'is). There were several accounts according to which Mohammad and Hoseyn both promised spiritual and earthly rewards (*savab*) to anyone who sheds tears for his suffering. This narrative reinforced the soteriological aspect of mourning, which also became a contested issue in later narratives. This idea of receiving blessings (*shafaʿ*) has always been central to the ritual practices of Shi'is. According to Kashefi, mourning can preserve the message of Hoseyn, which is the message of true Islam. According to this view the unjust "other" consisted of the *monafequn* (Muslims labeled as hypocrites), among whom the Sunnis were the most prominent, while the true believers were portrayed as those who were loyal to Hoseyn. The key issue being reinforced by Kashefi was that mourning for the imam leads to rewards in this world and the next. The idea of Shi'is literally following Hoseyn's example by rebelling against corrupt and oppressive rulers was notably absent in his work. He also argued that taking revenge for the tragedy of Karbala was the exclusive right and responsibility of the Mahdi (the last imam).[5]

Kashefi created a definite dichotomy between the evil material world and the purity of the esoteric dimension of human existence, a dichotomy that remained characteristic of Iranian Shi'i culture. Kashefi stated that the basis of mourning and crying for the tragedy of Karbala is Hoseyn's suffering. He portrayed Karbala as the central axis around which all human history revolves. Moreover, the repeated pattern of suffering of earlier prophets was presented by him as the prelude to Hoseyn's movement. Hence, both Hoseyn's suffering and the cause his movement represented were connected to the broader prophetic mission that began with Adam and culminated with Mohammad (and the imams).

Kashefi's narrative began with the story of the creation of the first human being and prophet of Islam, Adam, and his wife, Eve. He recounted their fall in detail, stressing the inherently corrupt nature of humanity. This ended with a detailed account of the treachery and murder of Abel at the hands of Cain, for which Adam suffered.[6] This was followed by a telling of how Noah suffered as a result of oppression by his society. The story ended with an account of the seven-year-old daughter of Hoseyn. She was in Medina when he was martyred, and she noticed a crow sitting on the wall, whose wings had been soaked in the blood of Hoseyn. She likened the bird to the dove that was sent from Noah's ship and said, "My family is like Noah's ship."[7] The most obvious way in which Hoseyn and his follows suffered was through martyrdom. Furthermore, martyrdom as a symbolic act was central to all references to Karbala in political discourse. In Kashefi's account of the Battle of Karbala itself, a series of martyrdom stories were told in graphic detail.

The climax of the sequence of martyrdom stories was the martyrdom of Hoseyn himself. While he was central to almost all the other martyrdom stories, it was only at this point in the narrative that he took center stage as "the Prince of Martyrs" (*Sayyed al-shohada*). He wore the turban of Mohammad, the shield of the early Islamic hero Hamzeh, and the sword of Ali (*Zu al-Feqar*). He rode his famous white horse, *Zu al-Jenah*. This description is another example of the connection between Hoseyn and earlier prophets, imams, and Islamic heroes, which was constantly reinforced in this narrative. Hoseyn addressed the enemy troops with a series of speeches dealing with God, death, good versus evil, oppression versus justice, and honor versus shame, stressing the nobility of the family of the Prophet Mohammad throughout. Kashefi's account of Hoseyn's martyrdom is summarized below:

> In the first wave of attacks, fifteen thousand troops shoot at Hoseyn with arrows but fail to hit him. At this point he returns to the tents and a supernatural creature comes to him offering to help with an army of similar supernatural beings, but Hoseyn rejects this offer on the grounds that it would be unjust for such powerful creatures to be unleashed upon mere humans. In the second wave of fighting he reportedly kills 400 soldiers and is only taken down when Yazid's troops abandon the traditional (and honorable) system of single combat, rushing him from all sides instead. However, none of the troops has the courage to kill Hoseyn at first, until their leader Shemr comes in for the kill. Right before being beheaded, Hoseyn sees that Shemr has the teeth of a pig and remembers a dream he once had in which the Prophet Mohammad foretold of the tragic events of this day.[8]

One of the most important themes developed in Kashefi's narrative was the idea that Hoseyn had foreknowledge of his impending martyrdom. Hoseyn and all the other imams and prophets were portrayed as having known in advance of the suffering they would have to endure in the future. The fact that the prophets both foretold and mourned Hoseyn's loss set the example of mourning Hoseyn's death, which was to be followed by later Shi'i Muslims everywhere. Moham-mad's knowledge of the events at Karbala established the fact that Hoseyn's movement was preordained by God (an issue that eventu-ally became a major source of contention in the later narratives).

The treatment of women in this narrative is also important. The role of Fatemeh was quite central to the Karbala narrative even though she was not actually present at the Battle of Karbala itself. She was one of the most developed characters in the story and was held up as the most perfect of women. She was also the only female character in the story who shared in the infallibility (*esmat*) of the imams and prophets. In later texts, Fatemeh sometimes became the central character and was more explicitly used as a vehicle for debating gender issues within a broader discourse on gender roles in society. Kashefi stressed Fatemeh's moral character throughout his text, including her suffering in the face of oppression and her loyalty to the family of the Prophet.

The themes developed in Kashefi's text were consistent with the political environment in which it became so popular. During the Qajar era, the religious symbolism of Karbala was used to legitimize the rulers, while at the same time supporting the social status of other elites and sub-elites in society. Kashefi's narrative similarly stressed the inap-propriateness of active political mobilization in the face of political injustice. It is the role of the Mahdi and not of the average believers to avenge Hoseyn's unjust death. Narratives like Kashefi's were not explicit efforts at contesting the legitimacy of the ruling elites; rather, they stressed patience and perseverance instead of action.

Salehi Najafabadi, a religious scholar who studied with Khomeini in the 1960s, was the first person to attempt a revision of the Karbala narrative. His unorthodox views regarding the Karbala Paradigm were the subject of many lectures and sermons that he presented in public gatherings and public religious rituals in the 1960s and 1970s, espe-cially during the ritual season of *Moharram.* These lectures provoked debate and criticism from other speakers at such gatherings. In 1968, he wrote *Shahid-e javid,* in which he demystified the Karbala Paradigm as part of the process of reinterpreting it in a more politically activist light. Najafabadi's revision focused on two key points. First, he argued that Hoseyn intended to overthrow Yazid, who had transgressed to the point where it was imperative for someone to remove him from power. Second, he proposed that Hoseyn did not know in advance that he would be martyred at Karbala. According to Najafabadi, Hoseyn's movement was an utter failure.

Najafabadi argued that Muslims should follow Hoseyn's example by actively rebelling against corrupt rulers. His methodology was rather extreme and radical, breaking with previous trends of interpretation of Hoseyn's movement. He even rejected fundamental tenets of Shi'ism concerning the powers and abilities of the imam. It is not surprising that he received a great deal of criticism following his public lectures and speeches. Many of his views are still not fully accepted by most Iranian religious scholars, even if they accept the politicization of the paradigm. However, the majority of the critics of his views did not condemn him for encouraging Muslims to emulate actively Hoseyn. Rather, the primary reason for this criticism was that he fundamentally revised the core-narrative of Karbala to the point where his views were regarded by many as heresy. In the political climate of the 1960s and subsequent decades, there were limits to how much flexibility was allowed to ideologues in interpreting the Karbala Paradigm.

In his public lectures and sermons and in his book *Shahid-e javid*, Najafabadi dealt with the issue of what caused Hoseyn to lead the rebellion against the Umayyad rulers of his day. He spoke primarily about the need to defend Islam from corruption and heretical innovation, accusing Yazid and his family of religious corruption and of incompetence. This idea was not in itself unusual. However, he argued that the only way Hoseyn could have achieved this objective was to take over the government and reform it from within. Hoseyn, he argued, was intent upon seizing power from the Umayyads and taking over the government itself.[9] He went so far as to criticize the long-accepted view that Hoseyn's movement and sacrifice had the important benefit of preserving true Islam for future generations. He even denied that the long-term effects of the massacre were positive. He said that the Umayyads were not really weakened by the event. Nor did Hoseyn accomplish anything in the way of exposing the corruption of the Umayyads because it was already well known to everyone (e.g., territorial gains at the expense of foreign powers).[10] Muslims did not suddenly become better Muslims (not even the Shi'is), and his sacrifice did not even inspire others to rebel to any large extent. Finally, Najafabadi referred to a hadith attributed to Hoseyn, which states that "in me you can see what is incumbent upon you to do" (*lakum fiya uswa*). He said that if Hoseyn's intention was to commit suicide, then we should all commit suicide. Najafabadi also naively stated that if Hoseyn truly wanted to be killed, then the Umayyads did him a favor and should not be blamed for what they did. According to the traditional view, Yazid, the true loser in the massacre, fell right into Hoseyn's trap. This was necessary in maintaining Hoseyn's greatness. Najafabadi violated this basic belief, for which he was viewed as compromising Hoseyn's status as a holy figure in Shi'ism.

Najafabadi's views inevitably led to another highly controversial claim, that Hoseyn did not have prior knowledge of his impending martyrdom. This is where one of his classical sources, Tusi, became important. Tusi, a highly respected eleventh-century Shi'i scholar, gave a ruling that Hoseyn could not have had prior knowledge of his death, nor could he have consciously committed suicide. Unlike recent centuries, among early Shi'is there was greater diversity of opinion regarding Hoseyn's movement. This was part of Najafabadi's strategy for revision. He did not refer to more commonly accepted Shi'i sources, but instead he consulted early Shi'i works. He also made use of Sunni sources like the great medieval Arab historian al-Tabari's account of the events at Karbala.

Najafabadi further argued that Hoseyn could not have planned on bringing along his family and friends (including women and children) only for the purpose of having a tragic massacre, because that would be absolutely unethical from an Islamic perspective. Nor would such a strategy make any logical sense. According to Najafabadi, nobody commanded the respect and honor that Hoseyn did, nor did anybody possess his character and qualities. Thus, it would make no sense for him to sacrifice himself in order that those less qualified could take power at some later date. Nor does it stand to reason that he should plan the death of his closest companions, who were also among the greatest Muslims. Perhaps the boldest statement of Najafabadi, and the summation of his position, was that Hoseyn did not intend to create anything resembling the Karbala Paradigm. Najafabadi seems to have been interested in ridding the symbols of symbolically static interpretations in order to reinterpret them in a more politically radical light, which would allow for active political opposition to the shah's regime.

Opposition to Najafabadi's revisionist interpretations did not take long to surface. The popular and highly respected Ayatollah Hoseyn Montazeri wrote the introduction to Najafabadi's book as a show of support, but many ulama reacted quickly and with much hostility. For example, the conservative Hojjat al-Eslam Shamsabadi condemned both Najafabadi and Montazeri from the pulpit in Isfahan. This conflict escalated to the point where some of Montazeri's followers murdered Shamsabadi.[11] However, other critics followed Shamsabadi's example. Three typical responses to Najafabadi's book were Lotfollah Safi Golpaygani's *Shahid-e agah*, Nuriyan's *Pasokh beh ketab-e shahid-e javid,* and Sayyed Ali Akbar Hojjat's *Pasokh beh ketab-e shahid-e javid.* All three works criticized Najafabadi's claim that Hoseyn was not aware of the fact that he was going to become a martyr. They further claimed that Hoseyn's motive was not to take power but rather was to instill in Muslims the true spirit of Islam. These works were overtly hostile to Najafabadi himself. At times they attacked, wished bodily harm upon, insulted, and even cursed him repeatedly for heresy, spreading falsehood, confusion, and generally weakening the faith of the true believers. They also accused him of promoting the views of Orientalists and non-Muslims. They even accused him of not being a Muslim at all, or at least a Muslim without any real faith.

Contemporary accounts of SAVAK agents described Najafabadi's book as containing views that violated the basic tenets of Shi'ism.[12] One SAVAK report discussed the hostile response to his book on the part of religious students and religious scholars (*rowhaniyun va tollab*), and another stated that the position of the followers of Khomeini (namely, Najafabadi and Montazeri) would be severely weakened by the negative responses to this book.[13] According to these accounts, the main criticism directed at Najafabadi was the idea that the imam had no prior knowledge of his martyrdom at Karbala, which violated the Shi'i view that he was aware of the past, present, and future generally and of the events at Karbala specifically.

While there were many attacks leveled against Najafabadi's construction of a new Karbala narrative, few were as comprehensive as Lotfollah Safi Golpaygani's critique, which he presented in public speeches, in sermons, and in his book titled *Shahid-e agah* (*The Martyr [Who Was] Aware*). This critique was unique in that it was more than just a competing narrative. It was a direct assault on Najafabadi's narrative. The title *The Martyr [Who Was] Aware* was a direct contradiction of Najafabadi's claim that Hoseyn did not have knowledge of his martyrdom beforehand. Golpaygani's text was organized according to the structure of Najafabadi's narrative. He referred to Najafabadi's ideas point by point and then presented a counterargument for each of them, thus abandoning the earlier narrative structure to take part in a direct debate with his opponent. This was somewhat of a departure from earlier conventions and marks the beginning of a general trend. During this period, most of these writers began referring to each other's arguments directly, either affirming or rejecting them. They also spent a great deal of time presenting general analytical discussions as counter arguments to ideas presented in earlier speeches or publications. Debate took the form of competing narratives.

Golpaygani began his critique with a discussion of the current state of the Muslim world, which he characterized as being in a state of war with the evil imperialist West. In this period of crisis, the most important factor in the struggle was the need to preserve Islamic unity through Islamic national sentiment or pan-Islamic feeling, because the "imperialists" have tried to create disunity by diverting Muslims from the true message of Islam.[14] Najafabadi's book was then characterized as a study filled with errors and false conclusions that would aid the enemies of Islam by creating disunity and dissension within the Muslim community.[15]

Golpaygani was particularly disturbed by the fact that, while he had previously critiqued the book before its publication and believed that he had convinced Najafabadi not to publish it, the book resurfaced despite his instructions. In sharp contrast to Najafabadi's probable intention, Golpaygani believed that this book would weaken the potential influence of the Karbala Paradigm as a mobilizing force in the struggle against oppression and imperialism. He criticized several of Najafabadi's ideas.[16] He rejected the idea that the imam was rebelling with the intention of establishing an Islamic state by saying that the imam would only have pursued that goal under favorable circumstances, which were not prevailing at the time.[17] He also rejected the assertion that Hoseyn did not know he was going to be martyred, claiming that Hoseyn's martyrdom not only was God's will but was predicted by angels, the Prophet Mohammad, other prophets and imams, and Hoseyn himself. Golpaygani also summarily dismissed Najafabadi's idea that Hoseyn's battle was fought in defense of his life and for survival in the face of an Umayyad plan to eliminate him. He argued instead that the imam would not have surrendered and reached terms of peace with Yazid in an effort to prevent his impending military defeat, as Najafabadi claimed. Golpaygani was particularly outraged by Najafabadi's view that Hoseyn's movement was a failure, with more negative than positive results.

A particularly telling statement Golpaygani made is that Najafabadi's ideas were eventually going to help the oppressive imperialists by weakening the faith of Muslims. In this argument, he accused Najafabadi of following in the footsteps of previous generations of both Sunni and Western scholars who failed to study properly the movement of Hoseyn. He also took an interesting turn in his argument by saying that this particular interpretation of the Karbala narrative would not be acceptable to his Muslim brothers elsewhere in the Muslim world. He made specific reference to Sunnis as well as Shi'is and quoted a Sunni scholar from al-Azhar University in Egypt, Mohammad Abd al-Baqi, from his book *al-Tha'ir al-awwal fi al-Islam, al-Husayn, Sayyid al-Shuhada*. Abd al-Baqi was quoted as saying that "Husayn's rebellion was for the preservation of Islam's nobility, which Yazid had tried to destroy . . . he rebelled to label as an 'oppressor' anyone who is oppressive toward others, to become a martyr, and to make 'right' victorious over 'wrong.'"[18]

Golpaygani's general discussion of Islamic brotherhood was indicative of another trend that can be identified in this process of revision, namely, the relative shift away from the earlier construct of the "just, Shi'i self" versus the "unjust, Sunni other." This model shifted during this period more toward a model of the "just, Muslim self" (i.e., Sunnis and Shi'is) versus the "unjust, imperialist other." In many places, the oppressed masses of the world (i.e., the developing world) were spoken of as the "self." This change was part of a general political-cultural shift away from seeing Sunnis as the main enemies of Shi'i Iran to seeing Western imperialists as the main enemies and Sunnis as political allies against the greater enemies in the West. In some cases, Iranian Muslims went as far as to consider non-Muslims who have been subjected to imperialism as allies in this struggle.

Najafabadi's attempted demystification of the Karbala Paradigm, by provoking such intense hostility, sparked a debate on several important aspects of the Karbala narrative. This is not to say that debates would not have ensued without his attempt, but rather it is to acknowledge the significant effects his views had on the content and form of this discourse. Golpaygani's critique illustrates the commonality of certain key trends in this process of interpretation. The key issue was not whether to oppose actively the evil threat posed by the "oppressors." Rather, the debate centered on the core symbols of Hoseyn's movement, which were considered to be sacred and timeless. In other words, Najafabadi was criticized not for his more overtly activist interpretations of the Karbala symbolism but, rather, for violating the sanctity of the core symbols themselves (i.e., the core-narrative), which includes the moral and spiritual qualities of the imam and his followers.

Reactions to Najafabadi's narrative were not restricted to Iran, nor were they homogeneous. Opinions regarding Najafabadi's book have been mixed both in Iran and abroad.[19] Outside Iran, many scholars criticized some of the new narrative themes presented by Najafabadi in terms similar to those of Golpaygani. For example, Seyyed Hosayn Jafri, Sayyid Mahdi Shamsiddin, Muhammad Jawad Mughniyya, and Ali Naqi Naqvi, along with many others, resisted some of these new views. While many Shiʻi writers began to adopt some of the themes of the new narrative, most reacted with hostility, and still others continued to hold to earlier narrative traditions, refusing to take part in these political debates altogether. A contributing factor in this last trend has been the general distrust Shiʻi ulama have often shown toward government and politics. Thus, the most respected members of the ulama class have often stayed aloof from politics generally and government specifically.

While Najafabadi faced a great deal of opposition to his views, he also had some supporters. Ayatollah Montazeri, Abu al-Fazl Musavi, Mohammad Shariʻat Esfahani, Mohammad Taqi Jaʻfari, Ahmad Aram, and other members of the revolutionary leadership surrounding Khomeini himself praised some of his views both verbally and in writing. This debate raged until Morteza Motahhari, also a religious scholar associated with the Iranian revolutionaries of the 1970s, tackled the issue by attempting to find a compromise position that would require Muslims to follow the revolutionary model of Karbala without violating the fundamental tenets of Shiʻism. This method proved to be more palatable to other religious leaders as well as the popular masses. Still, many of the more conservative religious leaders like Allameh Mohammad Hoseyn Tabataba'i, Mohammad Reza Hakimi, and Seraj Ansari have only slightly modified their traditional views or have even remained silent in the debate. Furthermore, while Najafabadi initially provoked hostile responses from some of the ulama, his work did have an effect and was eventually followed by a series of competing narratives that presented the traditional Karbala narrative in a more activist mold.

Najafabadi's attempted revision of the Karbala narrative marks the beginning of a process of debate that began taking shape in the 1960s and carried on through the 1990s. While many later ideologues rejected most of Najafabadi's fundamental ideas, many of them were nevertheless greatly influenced by his views. For example, Morteza Motahhari drew upon some of Najafabadi's ideas in his construction of the Karbala narrative. His more moderate view gained general acceptance among the revolutionary opposition in the 1970s and later the revolutionary government (following the Islamic Revolution of 1978–79). The influence of Motahhari's narrative can be seen throughout the 1980s and 1990s. Opposition leaders with a less traditional education and orientation, such as 'Ali Shari'ati and Ahmad Reza'i, also made important contributions to this debate. Shari'ati was an influential Iranian intellectual influenced by leftist ideas; however, his ideas were formulated within a self-consciously Islamic framework. Ahmad Reza'i also actively opposed the shah in the 1960s and 1970s as a member of the *Mojahedin-e Khalq,* the Islamic-oriented socialist party whose members were also active in attending *Moharram* lectures and sermons.

Like Motahhari, Shari'ati actively motivated intellectuals and the masses of Iranian Shi'is to oppose the shah in the 1970s. He similarly joined in public lectures and debates sponsored by such organizations as the *Hoseyniyeh-e Ershad.* Like Najafabadi, Motahhari, and other religious oppositional leaders, he gave lectures at a variety of *Moharram* ritual events. Shari'ati argued a very unorthodox revolutionary interpretation of Shi'ism in his public lectures, some of which were eventually published. His efforts, while quite influential, failed to gain general acceptance within the ranks of the ulama. The reasons for this were fundamentally different from the reasons for the attacks directed at Najafabadi. They had to do with the general rejection of Shari'ati's meta-narrative by the ulama. The main value of his work, however, was that even though the ulama were critical of this meta-narrative, many leaders were profoundly affected by his views. Khomeini himself adopted Shari'ati's slogan, "Every place should be turned into Karbala, every month into *Moharram,* and every day into 'Ashura."[20]

Beginning in the late 1960s and early 1970s, a variety of revolutionary activists with liberal or even explicitly leftist interpretations of Islam emerged as active participants in the opposition movements against the shah. These activists are distinct from the communist Tudeh Party, which in most cases rejected Shi'i symbolism. However, many individuals who were influenced by Western liberal and socialist ideals, such as Shari'ati, were not formally affiliated with any political parties and, therefore, are best understood as Western-educated, liberal, middle-class activists who were much influenced by Western ethical and philosophical thought, including Marxism and Leninism. These intellectuals were committed to what they called the liberation of the masses of humanity (especially in the third world), whom they considered to be oppressed by the elites of their countries and the international imperialist order. They often referred to the ideals of Islam and sometimes used Islamic symbolism extensively in their political discourse. 'Ali Shari'ati is by far the most influential of these individuals. However, the views of Ahmad Reza'i are also briefly presented here in order to represent the more partisan perspective of the *Mojahedin-e Khalq*. The final narrative interpretation discussed below is that put forth by Morteza Motahhari.

'Ali Shari'ati was born in Khorasan in 1933. He was the son of Mohammad Taqi Shari'ati, who was a religious scholar in the traditional sense but was somewhat unorthodox in his views and lifestyle. For example, in the mid-1940s he formed a local branch of a short-lived organization known as the Movement of Socialist God-Worshippers. He was also an enthusiastic supporter of Mosaddeq in the early 1950s, and even held regular discussions at his home along with such ideologues as Ahmad Kasravi who had incurred the wrath of many clerics. Both father and son were active speakers on issues related to politics and the Karbala Paradigm in the *Moharram* ritual events in the 1960s and 1970s.

After receiving his master's degree in French and Arabic from the University of Mashhad, 'Ali Shari'ati went to France in 1959 on a government scholarship to pursue graduate training at the Sorbonne in philology. He had been an active supporter of Mosaddeq in Iran, and while in France he continued his active opposition to the shah's regime by helping to publish two anti-regime periodicals (*Nameh-e Pars* and *Iran-e azad*). He was particularly influenced by the writings and teachings of Louis Massignon and Henry Corbin, both French experts on Islamic mysticism. Having received his doctorate in 1965, Shari'ati returned to Iran only to be arrested for political activities upon entering the country; his prison term lasted six months.

In 1969, he began perhaps the most influential three years of his activism when he took on a permanent position at the *Hoseyniyeh-e Ershad* in Tehran, a religious institution of learning endowed by an anti-regime philanthropist. Like Motahhari and similar ideologues, his lectures given at the *hoseyniyeh* were usually taped and then distributed widely by his students and later, during and following the Islamic Revolution in 1978–79, were collected, transcribed, and published in book form. The *Hoseyniyeh-e Ershad* was closed in 1972, partly because of government concern over the anti-regime character of the teaching and partly because of internal differences between such individuals as Shari'ati and Motahhari. Shortly afterwards, Shari'ati was arrested on charges of propagating Marxism and was imprisoned again, this time for eighteen months. He then spent 1975–77 generally under house arrest in Tehran, where he continued to tape lectures, until he left in 1977 for England, where he died of a heart attack one month later.[21]

Ervand Abrahamian calls Shari'ati "the main ideologue of the Iranian Revolution." Hamid Dabbashi similarly calls him "the Islamic Ideologue Par Excellence."[22] Shari'ati used the symbolism of Karbala extensively in his public speeches condemning the shah's regime. Some of the best examples of these speeches were given at the *Hoseyniyeh-e Ershad*. Shari'ati's ideology was heavily informed by Western ideas derived from Orientalism, sociology, and Marxist political philosophy, as well as traditional Islamic doctrines and Shi'ism. He sought egalitarian justice and equality through a revitalization of a more revolutionary interpretation of Islam generally and of Shi'ism specifically. To this end, he was very critical of both the shah's regime and most of the ulama. Shari'ati made many enemies among the more conservative ulama who were uncomfortable with his views. He developed a relatively large following among the educated, young, urban middle classes who were familiar with Western ideologies and were looking for an ideologue who could successfully engage the West in dialogue. His ideas had a great deal of influence both during and well after the Islamic Revolution. His lectures were distributed widely on tape and in pamphlet form before and during the Islamic Revolution and were published in multivolume books that sold tens of thousands of copies afterwards.

In his numerous public speeches and writings, Shari'ati presented the Karbala Paradigm in rather unorthodox terms. He was much less concerned than more traditionally oriented scholars about ruffling the feathers of the conservative ulama. Shari'ati divided Shi'ism into two types, the first being the Shi'ism of Imam Ali, which was pure, just, and populist. The second type was the corrupt and worldly Shi'ism of the Safavids, which he characterized as the Shi'ism professed by most of the ulama.[23]

The shah and the conservative ulama criticized Shari'ati for his unorthodox views. While the ideological framework of his interpretation was entirely unorthodox, many of his arguments were less radical than Najafabadi's views. Whereas Najafabadi's interpretations led to a hostile critique of his work, Shari'ati's use of this same set of symbols became very influential after his death. One of the most important differences between the approaches taken by Shari'ati and Najafabadi is that Shari'ati did not fundamentally violate the core-narrative. Rather, he kept this narrative intact while introducing a radically new meta-narrative that was derived largely from Marxist conceptions of universal class struggle and anti-imperialist rhetoric. Shari'ati's version of the Karbala narrative began with a worldview that has direct bearing upon the events at Karbala. Using the metaphor of competing "tribes," he articulated a vision of the world order characterized by two opposing groups in a constant struggle with each other. He then described the events of Karbala according to this framework.

Shari'ati described Hoseyn's movement using three core concepts: revolution (sar), struggle in the path of God (jihad), and martyrdom (shahadat). He traced the concept of revolution back to the founding of Islam by the Prophet Mohammad and even farther back to the beginning of human history with the Prophet Adam. Like Kashefi, who also began his story with Adam, Shari'ati argued that Islam came as a revolution against a conservative tribal social order.[24] This corrupt system was the antithesis of the system established by the original Islamic revolution (of the Prophet).

According to Shari'ati, there was originally only one order, the divine order that existed during the lifetime of the Prophet Adam. During this time, society was characterized by adherence to the divinely sanctioned social order. The division of humanity into the two groups was the result of Cain shedding the blood of Abel. This story was also central to Kashefi's narrative, although it was radically restructured here. According to Shari'ati, the first order was a type of egalitarian, primitive, just, pure, and God-conscious order, whereas the second was a hierarchical, civilized, unjust, corrupted, antihuman, and atheistic order. Likewise, the first was the true Islamic order, and the second was the un-Islamic order. The reestablishment of this order was the basic goal of the Prophet's original Islamic revolution (*sowreh-e Eslami* or *enqelab-e Eslami*). According to Shari'ati's account, Cain murdered Abel, just as a corrupt social order supplanted the pristine social order set in place by God. This resulted in an inherited conflict between the two groups that will continue until the end of time. Thus, it was a type of blood feud that was instigated by Cain's shedding Abel's blood. This inheritance was the essence of the conflict between Hoseyn and Yazid. They were merely adhering to their responsibilities inherited because of the feud. This is why Shari'ati called Hoseyn the heir of Adam/ Humanity (*vares-e Adam*).

Shari'ati associated Hoseyn's movement with the two traditional concepts of jihad and martyrdom. Hence, Hoseyn's action had to take the form of jihad, but he did not have the means to carry out such a jihad.[25] Therefore, the only option left open to him was martyrdom. However, if a person is not able to fulfill an obligation to undertake jihad, then he or she must choose martyrdom.[26] He defined *shahadat* as what occurs when a person sacrifices his entire being or character for a cause or concept. If the cause is holy, then the martyr's entire essence becomes holy. The concept of martyrdom in Shari'ati's narrative was essentially the same as in other narratives, with the notable exception of Najafabadi's version. Shari'ati argued that Hoseyn's movement was for the purposes of promoting good and discouraging evil.[27]

Shari'ati's central themes were similar to those developed in the narratives of Kashefi and others, and his views confirmed earlier interpretations of Karbala in many ways. He argued that Hoseyn knew that he would be killed in the process of rebelling but still insisted on proceeding with his plan. This response is because, in accordance with the responsibilities he inherited from the previous imams, it was incumbent upon him to act against Yazid and his men. In discussing the circumstances surrounding Hoseyn's uprising, Shari'ati said that the Prophet's Islamic revolution was in danger of extinction, and Hoseyn was the one responsible for its preservation.[28] Therefore, Hoseyn led the rebellion, along with his followers, in response to the cries of Muslims who were looking for a leader. Muslims who failed to support Hoseyn were, in Shari'ati's estimation, just as guilty as the followers of Yazid, because they were passive participants in the tragedy through their inaction.[29] Thus, Shari'ati fundamentally disagreed with Najafabadi on the issue of Hoseyn's foreknowledge of his own martyrdom.

One area where Shari'ati fundamentally disagreed with most ulama was his view that the ulama and the Muslim governments of the past had collaborated in misinterpreting the Karbala Paradigm. The Umayyad rulers co-opted the religious scholars of their period and used them as an army of intellectuals against the cause of truth. He said that scholars were pressured directly by the government; even more chose to remain acquiescent on their own. As a result, scholars ignored political issues and isolated themselves in a corner of the mosque and became lost in the complexities of ritual worship. This route was taken by many scholars, including Shi'i ulama. They exerted incredible amounts of energy studying and giving rulings on insignificant details of worship that need not have led to controversy in the first place. Shari'ati argued that many scholars also propagated false doctrines to support their positions as well as that of the government. For example, many promoted passivity and acceptance of corruption and instructed the believers to undertake the greater struggle (*jahad-e akbar*), which is against the self.[30] At the same time, fatalists propagated the doctrine of predestination, which condemns action as being useless and pointless. All these scholars ended up giving rulers like the Umayyads a type of divinely ordained legitimacy.

Shari'ati argued that the political motivations attributed to Hoseyn by Salehi Najafabadi did the movement more justice than other so-called traditional narratives because Najafabadi's understanding of Hoseyn's movement is the only "false interpretation" that called for action and did not ignore the historical function of the movement.[31] Thus, it is clear that, as with Najafabadi and others, revolutionary activism was Shari'ati's central concern. What was unique about his interpretation was the overarching narrative, which was rejected by the revolutionary ulama, who claimed that these ideas were un-Islamic.

The next ideologue under discussion is Ahmad Reza'i, who was an active member of the controversial political party called the *Mojahedin-e Khalq*. While Ahmad Reza'i was not as influential as Shari'ati, especially regarding mainstream revolutionaries such as Khomeini's followers, his use of the Karbala narrative is interesting, if nothing else, as "an exception to the rule." His interpretation may be best understood as an "experiment" that did not fully take root in the society, culture, and political discourses of the time. While the *Mojahedin* were heavily involved in the opposition movements against the shah in the 1970s, they became less influential after the revolution in 1978–79. After 1981, they actively opposed the Islamic regime and were banned from political participation in the new political system. Their popularity was particularly compromised when they sided with Iraq in the Iran-Iraq war in the hopes of achieving regime change in Iran. Most Iranians viewed this as an act of treason.

A very rare example of the *Mojahedin*'s use of Karbala symbolism is Ahmad Reza'i's Karbala narrative, which was published in 1972 as a book titled *Rah-e Hoseyn*.[32] This narrative was written with the help of Mas'ud Rajavi, another prominent *mojahed* who became the head of the *Mojahedin* after the 1978–79 revolution. This Karbala narrative was distributed by the *Mojahedin* in the late 1960s in pamphlet form and later in book form throughout the 1970s. It eventually served as one of the sources for Karbala symbolism among those opposed to the shah during the 1970s.

Reza'i was born in Tehran in 1946 and became a secondary school humanities teacher. He participated in the 1963 uprising against the shah and was active in such political groups as the National Front and the Liberation Movement before becoming one of the core *Mojahedin* theorists. He was one of approximately twenty young intellectuals who beginning in 1965, met regularly to discuss texts like the Qur'an and the *Nahj al-balagheh* (a classical Shi'i text attributed to Imam Ali), Marxist works like Lenin's *State and Revolution* and *What Is to Be Done?*, and Franz Fanon's *Wretched of the Earth*. By 1968, they had established a Central Committee of twelve people, including Reza'i. Reza'i became the first martyr for the *Mojahedin* when he was finally cornered by government forces in 1972 and reportedly killed himself with a hand grenade rather than be captured. His death was characterized by the *Mojahedin* in terms that are strikingly similar to his description of Hoseyn's martyrdom.[33]

Like Shari'ati, he stressed the importance of class struggle in human history. He divided humanity into two groups of people, the devourers of the world (*jahan kharan*) and the oppressed of the world (*setamdidehha*).[34] He developed the narrative around the Prophet Mohammad's elimination of wealth and privilege as a social reality and the resurgence of that elitism upon his death. He glorified the Prophet's companion Abu Bakr in a way that was strikingly similar to Shari'ati's narrative, in which Abu Bakr was presented as being staunchly opposed to the elitism of the early Arab Muslims.[35]

Reza'i's and Shari'ati's narratives demonstrate how easily the symbolism of Karbala could be adapted to liberal, leftist, third world, and anti-imperialist rhetoric. Reza'i and Shari'ati were intensely disliked by many ulama, who criticized them actively. However, there was no counter-narrative presented in response to their narratives. This is largely because it was not the narrative that the ulama took issue with, but rather the meta-narrative that they rejected. What the ulama rejected was the broader ideological construct in which Reza'i and Shari'ati situated the narrative. The ulama considered these two narratives to be too derivative of Western liberal and leftist ideas. Their criticisms of these two less orthodox intellectuals were based on fundamentally different concerns than were their criticisms of Najafabadi. This is significant and helps to illustrate several points. Because neither Reza'i nor Shari'ati violated the core symbols of the Karbala narrative, their interpretations were not viewed as heretical in the same way as was Najafabadi's. While it is true that Motahhari criticized Shari'ati's interpretations of the story of Cain and Abel, most of the criticisms were aimed at Shari'ati's Marxist ideas and not specifically at his interpretations of the Karbala narrative. The criticisms of the ulama were not based on the violation of the core-narrative, as was the case with Najafabadi. Reza'i and Shari'ati did not question the infallibility of the imam; his knowledge of the past, present, and future; his ultimate invincibility; or his active decision to martyr himself. Nor did they fundamentally challenge the basic ideals of Shi'ism. Their ideas were also consistent with the revolutionary feeling that was spreading during the 1970s. In other words, the symbolism of Karbala was integrated into new revolutionary dogma heavily influenced by Western political philosophies without violating the core-narrative. The versions of the Karbala narrative put forth by Shari'ati and Reza'i did not, however, put an end to the debate on the Karbala narrative. Many mainstream ulama who eventually opposed the shah were not willing to accept the new symbolism as it was initially articulated in the 1960s and 1970s. It was not until Morteza Motahhari tackled the issue that a revisionist narrative was able to gain sufficient acceptance among these religious leaders, allowing for the use of Karbala symbols on a mass scale in revolutionary political discourse.

Motahhari, whom Hamid Dabbashi dubbed "the Ideologue of the Revolution," was born in Mashhad in 1919. He received a traditional education in Mashhad and Qom and also studied at Tehran University, where he later took a position teaching theology. He was a prolific writer and participated in a variety of demonstrations and uprisings against the shah. He was imprisoned in 1964, following the 1963 uprising against the shah, and again in 1975. He was also an active teacher at the *Hoseyniyeh-e Ershad,* where he had extensive contact with ʿAli Shariʿati and various members of the *Mojahedin-e Khalq* who regularly attended lectures there. During this period, he was highly critical of the *Mojahedin.* He also criticized Shariʿati for being too confrontational and critical of the ulama, as well as being overly influenced by Western ideologies like Marxism, of which Motahhari was a well-known critic. He accused Shariʿati of bending Islam to fit Marxism and of misinterpreting the story of Cain and Abel, which was so central to Shariʿati's Karbala narrative. Motahhari was very close to Khomeini, and after the 1978–79 revolution he chaired the Revolutionary Council until May 1979, when he was assassinated by a terrorist bomb.

Motahhari's public lectures on the topic of Karbala, which were given as early as 1968, were later published and distributed widely under the title *Hamaseh-e Hoseyni* (*The Epic of Hoseyn*). In his numerous speeches and sermons, he presented a different view from those of Kashefi, Najafabadi, Shariʿati, and Rezaʾi. While he disagreed with more traditionally accepted interpretations of the Karbala narrative, he did not reject such accounts outright. Instead, he stressed the idea that scholars before him have placed too much emphasis upon the tragic side of the event (i.e., the traditional, politically nonactivist interpretation). This is one of the main reasons his views were much better received than Najafabadi's. In his lectures and speeches, Motahhari described the movement of Hoseyn as a holy epic or event (*hamaseh-e moqaddas*), as well as a movement for Islamic reform. He argued that it is more important to focus upon the heroic character of Hoseyn and compared Hoseyn to Alexander the Great and Iranian national heroes like Rostam. All were characterized by intensity of purpose, awe-inspiring dignity, bravery, zeal, and honor. However, Hoseyn's movement and character were unique because they were holy. That is, they were characterized by humanity, the love of truth, selflessness, and adherence to belief and to the holy burden or responsibility his great spirit inherited from the previous imams.[36]

Like Shari'ati, Motahhari defined the meaning of the symbols of Karbala as having two sides, a "dark side" and a "positive side." The dark side is the tragic side of the story and consists of the events at Karbala that led to the martyrdom of Hoseyn and his followers. It is an unparalleled tragedy in which Yazid and his followers are the central characters. This is the dimension of the story with which most people are familiar and is what stirs the passions of Shi'is everywhere. Crying is the proper response to this side of the symbol. Karbala is a tragedy, not only for Islam, but for all of humanity as well. It is a story of terrible injustice, of man's inhumanity to man, and of the brutal corruption of Islam by Yazid. Motahhari argued that if this were the entire story, then it would have had no lasting effects or significance. Therefore, the martyrdom of Hoseyn was not simply a case of senseless tragedy but, rather, a tragic event that resulted in a glorious outcome, which in turn has direct and immediate relevance to contemporary social and political issues.

Motahhari stressed active emulation of Hoseyn in the form of active rebellion against corrupt rulers. He explained that the movement and martyrdom of Hoseyn and his followers served four distinct functions. He said that the first two of these, which have to do with not legitimizing Yazid's rule (giving *beyʿat*) and responding to the call of the Kufans, have been the cause of much confusion. First, Karbala served as a tragic, but potent, example to the believers that the whole system of the caliphate is unjust and therefore un-Islamic and that the grandson of the Prophet would not condone a hereditary caliphate like that of the Umayyad dynasty. Furthermore, it exposed the moral and religious corruption of Yazid himself that reinforces the high standards of piety demanded by Islam. Second, it was an answer to the call of oppressed Muslims, which was not only a historic necessity of this specific period but also a moral obligation for all Muslims that cannot go unheeded at any time.[37]

The first two functions of Hoseyn's movement, according to Motahhari, were not the primary focus of his movement. Rather, it was the last two functions of the uprising that were the most important. The third function was to promote good and discourage evil, which is an obligation incumbent upon all Muslims. Acting against the religious corruption of the period was a religious obligation, and it was an example that had long-lasting effects upon the Muslims because it showed how this obligation should be carried out.

Hoseyn's movement also discredited the Umayyad government to such an extent that it hindered their efforts at expanding their influence over the Muslim community. The fourth and last, and one of the two most important functions mentioned by Motahhari, was that of *tabligh* (propagation of a concept).[38] By teaching the true meaning of Islam to the Muslims, it instilled them with the true spirit of Islam. The Prophet Mohammad instilled the true spirit of Islam in the hearts of Muslims.[39] However, this spirit was on the verge of being lost as a result of the corruption of the message by the usurpers of the rights of his household (in particular, Mo'aviyeh and Yazid). Hoseyn symbolically realized the true Islamic ideal that would otherwise be extinct. Hoseyn, therefore, sacrificed himself willingly in order to achieve these fundamental goals. Like the other revisionists, Motahhari placed the Karbala narrative within the context of imperialism and of Iranian nationalism. Hence, the primary role of Iran within the world political order was to struggle against oppression, corruption, and immorality, attributed to imperialism. Within this worldview, Hoseyn served as a model for rebellion against the shah and against foreign imperialist powers. This is a dominant trend across all these narratives.

Motahhari differed from the other ideologues in two basic ways. He did not violate fundamental Shi'i tenets that were usually preserved within the core-narrative. He also rejected the idea of contextualizing Shi'i symbolism within an explicitly socialist framework. He infused the narrative with immediate political relevance by positioning it within the framework of active political struggle against the shah's regime and the imperialist West. However, the struggle was to preserve justice and pure Islamic ideals.

When one analyzes these competing narratives, several trends become clear. As the political environment of the 1960s and 1970s resulted in an increase in open hostility toward the shah's regime, an oppositional discourse gained greater currency. Because the Pahlavi government was not able to make effective use of the religious symbolism of Karbala this symbolism became a discourse unto itself. The discourse did not focus upon the issue of whether the nationalist program of the Pahlavis could be effective. Instead, the discourse assumed that it was ineffective and provided alternatives to the government's program. Some leaders characterized this whole struggle as a class struggle in the Marxist sense. Others portrayed it as a struggle primarily between Muslims and non-Muslims, or of Iranians against corrupt Iranian rulers. Virtually all of the revisionists stressed active emulation of Hoseyn in a struggle against the tyrants and oppressors of their generation.

The oppositional discourse made justice versus injustice, a central theme in Shi'ism, its primary concern. It also made active, or even armed, struggle the primary method of emulating Hoseyn's movement. It identified the Pahlavi regime and the international imperialist powers with injustice and the suffering masses (i.e., the third world, Muslims, and Iranian Shi'is) with justice and righteousness. This in itself was a break from the earlier conceptions that placed Sunnis and hypocritical Shi'is at the top of the list of transgressors. Thus, a set of symbols that originally was used as a vindication of the Shi'i cause became a vindication of oppositional movements in Iran. In one way or another, the "imperialist order" was introduced into the narrative; the Sunnis were redefined as being included in the conception of the "just self," and the Pahlavi regime was cast in a mold similar to that of the imperialist powers.

The "multi-vocality" of these symbols was central to this process. Terms and concepts held dual meanings, such as the identification of the Pahlavis with Yazid or of the shah with Shemr (the murderer of Hoseyn at Karbala), and were a useful tactic to avoid government reprisals. In such cases, the shah would not be explicitly mentioned anywhere in the text, speech, or sermon, yet the audience would be aware that the government was being criticized. Furthermore, symbolic under standings of events in the basic narrative have always held multiple, and not necessarily mutually exclusive, understandings for Shi'is. The most explicit example of this is the conception of the so-called dual face of Karbala, according to which Karbala was tragic yet wondrous at the same time.

The Karbala narrative has undergone a process of reinterpretation that inspired critique at first. The symbols of Karbala both have served soteriological functions and been a source of active and literal emulation. While one or the other was generally stressed at any given time, these are not mutually exclusive concepts. The reinterpretation of the Karbala narrative is best understood as a process of both continuity and change. Hence, the more extreme break with traditionally accepted views, which Najafabadi's narrative represents, sparked harsh criticism based on its departure from the core-narrative and was seen as a violation of the sanctity of the narrative. The liberal or leftist constructions of the narrative were generally criticized for inserting un-Islamic ideas derived from Western ideologies like Marxism. However, more moderate attempts at revision encountered less criticism. Using Karbala symbolism as a form of political oppositional discourse became easier in the 1960s and 1970s. As long as core symbols, such as the nobility of the character of the imam, were not violated, the meta-narrative was not perceived as un-Islamic, and the general anti-shah and anti-Western sentiments were retained in one form or another. Thus, the Karbala narrative has proven to be a relatively (although not absolutely) flexible set of symbols, the interpretations of which have readily evolved in accordance with changing political trends.

7 ತಿ

Fatemeh, Zeynab, and Emerging Discourses on Gender

*L*ike most regions of the world, Iran witnessed the emergence of a new discourse on gender during the twentieth century. While some aspects of this discourse can be traced back to social and political trends in the late Qajar period, it did not achieve full force until the Pahlavi era. It is useful to think of the chronology of this period as consisting of four phases. The period 1925–41 marks the reign of Reza Shah Pahlavi, during which Iranian society underwent a modernist process of nation-building characterized by the development of a strong central government that promoted a comprehensive process of social, political, and economic transformation. This was followed by a period of weaker monarchy or political decentralization in 1941–53, accompanied by a short-lived flourishing of liberal nationalist sentiments in and around the circles of government power. The years 1960–78 mark the main period of social transformation under Mohammad Reza Shah Pahlavi. During this time there was a relative shift from a political context in which there was effectively one modernist political discourse dominated by the state to one in which this discourse was progressively supplanted by an opposition discourse dominated by diverse opposition groups. The decades following the 1978–79 revolution were characterized by a period of revolutionary consolidation, accompanied by a revolutionary religious discourse that was often dominated by the state. This chapter focuses on the years leading up to and following the Islamic Revolution of 1978–79.

Reza Shah Pahlavi, and later his son, Mohammad Reza Shah, introduced radical changes in the conceptualization of gender roles in society. For example, they encouraged women's education and employment as long as it was within the boundaries set by the state. Women similarly entered government service in all sorts of new capacities, including the police force and the Literacy Corps, and some schools became coeducational. The new Iranian woman was represented as being a mirror image of the "liberated" Western woman.

While the most dramatic changes can be seen in the roles of women, this analysis is not restricted to women exclusively. The concern here is with gender, which includes men as well as women. This distinction is important because throughout all of these phases the social transformation of male gender ideals has been somewhat different from that of female gender ideals. The dominant thread of discourse on the social ideals of male behavior (as opposed to political ideals) has consistently redefined male gender ideals (with some minor variations) along the Western "modernist" model. This is despite the changes in regimes and discourses that occurred from the 1920s through the 1990s.

With the rise in prominence of the religious oppositional discourse in the 1960s and 1970s, the political roles of men were redefined along more overtly activist or revolutionary political lines. Thus, in contradistinction to the Pahlavi model of Westernization, oppositional discourse argued that the proper social roles for men were not fundamentally different from those professed by most Western liberals and nationalists, except that Iranians need to follow Islamic laws and norms of behavior. At the same time, their political roles became more and more politically activist in nature.

The discourse on the female gender, however, was quite different: the social norms of female behavior proposed within this discourse distinctly contradicted most Western liberal conceptions of female social roles. The oppositional discourse stressed the idea that the only way for women to resist the Pahlavi program was to oppose transformations of female gender roles in society. This entailed the acceptance of restricted definitions of female gender roles, which, in turn, were reified as being "traditional" or "Islamic."

During the Pahlavi regime, the traditional feminine conception of womanhood managed to survive precariously in an environment in which there was an aggressive promotion by the state of a Western model of womanhood. A slow process of transformation of discourses on gender, which can be traced back to the Qajar era, took on a more pronounced character in the middle of the Pahlavi era and culminated in an oppositional discourse on gender. In its final stages, this discourse was characterized by the reification of a "traditionalized" conception of womanhood by religious opposition groups.

The Pahlavi model of womanhood was progressively associated

with the corrupting influence of the West. One of the best examples of the effective articulation of the concept of *Gharbzadegi* (or West-toxication) was in Jalal Al-e Ahmad's writings.[1] With the advent of the Islamic Republic, the traditionalist model of womanhood became the dominant state-supported model, while the Western "modernist" model continued to survive as an alternative model of womanhood. While the Islamist discourse on women predated Mohammad Reza Shah's reign, there was a reversal that slowly took place from the early Pahlavi period to the time of the Islamic Republic.

The approach used below was influenced in part by the analytical framework set up by Partha Chatterjee in his book *The Nation and Its Fragments*.[2] In this work, he identifies a dichotomy that is created by Indian nationalists between an esoteric, spiritual, inner cultural domain, which is perceived as being truly "Indian," and a material, external, outer cultural domain, which is perceived as having been subjugated by the colonialist powers. Thus, on the one hand, the battleground is the external world where the male is supposed to adapt to Western social and economic norms out of pure necessity, while at the same time preparing for the opportunity to fight for the honor and practical independence of the nation. The inner world, on the other hand, is the domain of women and the site of preservation of national identity rather than accommodation or battle. Therefore, the main emphasis in the gendered discourse is continuity within the female domain and discontinuity within the male domain. Perhaps the best summation of this process is this statement by Chatterjee: "In the world [i.e., the domain of men], imitation of and adaptation to Western norms was a necessity; at home [i.e., the domain of women] they were tantamount to annihilation of one's very identity."[3]

While the case of Iran does not conform exactly to Chatterjee's formulation, his insights are still instructive in analyzing the gender-coded symbolism of Karbala because the redefinition of gender roles followed a similar pattern. In other words, the ideal Iranian Muslim male was increasingly represented as needing to modernize economically, socially, and politically as a means to combat the dominance of the West, while at the same time fighting in the external world against oppression and corruption. The female-gendered symbols were used to promote what was articulated as being a preservationist model of womanhood, according to which the women of the nation are to preserve and pass on the "true" nature of the Iranian nation, or, more accurately, of the Shi'i cause. This phenomenon can also be characterized as a shift from "woman as symbol of modernity" to "woman as symbol of morality and resistance to foreign moral corruption." One of the main vehicles for expressing this new religious conception of gender was Karbala symbolism.

The process of construction of gendered ideals in Iranian society during this period was characterized by the use of a set of gender-coded symbols with an inherent multiplicity of interpretive possibilities. This discourse, which, in the case of Iran, was carried on almost exclusively by men, was characterized mostly by a process of restricting this range of possibilities of meaning to a small pool of traditionalist interpretations. In the twentieth century, as gender issues became more and more a source of contention within political discourse in Iran, many ideologues attempted to transform the potentially *dynamic* process of gender transformation in Iranian society into a *static* ideal or model that could then be legitimized using the Karbala narrative.

While certain aspects of the Karbala narrative were restructured and reinterpreted to allow for a new model of behavior for men, the female-gendered symbols underwent a different process of revision. Gender-coded symbols that dealt with male behavior were reworked to allow for a new ideal of political behavior, while gender-coded symbols promoting certain aspects of female behavior were used to reify traditionalist conceptions of women's roles in Islamic society. This is not unique to Iranian or even Islamic society, nor is it surprising to see this trend during a period of revolutionary transformation of the traditional interpretations of religious symbols.

Female characters have always served an important function in Karbala narratives. However, in narratives like *Rowzat al-shohada* the female characters have often been used as plot devices or as reflections of male characters rather than taking on the aspects of fully independent characters in their own right. As a discourse on gender developed during the 1950s and 1960s, Islamic ideals of womanhood were more explicitly articulated and placed in opposition to Western ideals. In more recent narratives, female characters have been presented as more self-aware than in earlier representations. Writers used these symbols to place gender issues at the center of political discourse. In the case of female characters, the modern era marks the first period in which female-gendered symbols were used as part of an anti-Western discourse focusing specifically upon gender roles. Thus, the transformation of the narrative form reflected a heightened consciousness of the issues of gender.

The shift that occurred in the focus of gender discourse in the late Pahlavi period defined gender roles in a context in which modernization policies were increasingly being viewed as detrimental to the nation. Preservation of social morality as conceptualized within gender categories was increasingly viewed as a fundamental goal of the opposition to the Pahlavi regime. The new female-gendered narratives were intended by virtue of their static representations of female-gendered symbols to subvert the transformations of conceptions of womanhood promoted by the Pahlavi regime. This shift was also not entirely unconscious, as Mehdi Moltaji, a religious scholar of modest reputation, pointed out in the introduction to his 1975 narrative on Zeynab. In it he stated that, unfortunately, "there are very few books on Zeynab in the Shi'i world." He then went on to name only eight books on Zeynab of which he was aware.[4] He consciously shifted the focus of the narratives in response to his concerns regarding social and moral corruption, which resulted from a lack of understanding and articulation of the role models of such characters as Zeynab and Fatemeh.

In addition to previously mentioned narratives of such ideologues as Shari'ati, Motahhari, and Kashefi, four examples of narratives that specifically focus on women are presented here. Moltaji's 1975 publication *Bozorg banu-e jahan, Zeynab* (*Zeynab: The Great Woman of the World*) is an excellent example of the discourse on gender in the mid-1970s. Moltaji, who usually confined most of his scholarly efforts to instruction manuals on ritual practices like the *hajj,* spiritual treatises, or moral critiques of social "ills" like listening to music, was not as politically active as the ideologues previously discussed above. Nevertheless, his contribution to the debate on gender was significant. Another important contribution was made by Bent al-Shate' (Bint al-Shati') with her book *Zeynab banu-e qahreman-e Karbala* (*Zeynab, the Heroine of Karbala*). This text was translated into Persian and widely circulated in Iran as early as 1953.[5] Bent al-Shate' (a pseudonym; her real name was A'esheh Abd al-Rahman) was an Egyptian Sunni Muslim woman who made a minor industry of writing about female members of the family of Prophet Mohammad. She wrote numerous books about many of these women. She also wrote books on hadith criticism and Qur'anic commentary.

Mohammad Eshtehardi's two books, *Sugnameh-e al-e Mohammad* (*Book of Sorrow of the Family of Mohammad*) and *Hazrat-e Zeynab, payam resan-e shahidan-e Karbala* (*Zeynab, the Deliverer of the Message of Karbala*), were also influential. The latter book provides an excellent example of the sort of female-gendered narrative that was produced after the establishment of the Islamic Republic in 1979 for use in educating young Iranian girls on their proper social roles. Eshtehardi was a self-styled "Islamic historian," researching and writing on such topics as the historical roles of Iranian Muslims in the early spread of Islam and the life stories of early companions of the Prophet Mohammad, like Belal and Habib Ebn-e Mazaher.[6]

Gender-neutral themes in these narratives included loyalty to Hoseyn, courage, self-sacrifice for Islam, and overall moral conduct. Leadership, fighting, and martyrdom are specifically male activities. Men were associated more closely with martyrdom, and women with the act of mourning. According to most narratives, women should be supporters of men and children and subservient to the authority of men. In general, men were actors in the story, while women were mostly acted upon. Throughout these narratives, both space and activities were characterized by gender difference or gender segregation.

One of the primary issues in most narratives was loyalty to Hoseyn and to the family of the Prophet Mohammad. For example, Fatemeh and Ali, who were Hoseyn's parents, have often been portrayed as defending both themselves and the Prophet Mohammad (Fatemeh's father) against persecution. Also portrayed as uncompromisingly loyal to Hoseyn has been Hoseyn's sister Zeynab, along with other female characters such as the old woman Tow'eh, who was said to have given shelter and a hiding place to Hoseyn's messenger, Moslim Ebn-e Aqil.[7] Zeynab was quoted as saying to her husband: "Oh Son of Abbas! Do you want to cause division or separation between my brother and I? I will never separate from my brother."[8] Zeynab's closeness and loyalty to her brother was a central theme throughout all of these narratives, as was Fatemeh's closeness to the Prophet and to her husband, Ali.

In the story of Moslem Ebn-e Aqil, the imam's messenger was hiding from the forces of Ebn-e Ziyad, who intended to kill him for treason, when Tow'eh risks her own life courageously in order to help him.[9] Thus, both Moslem Ebn-e Aqil and Tow'eh were portrayed as loyal, courageous, and self-sacrificing. Loyalty to Hoseyn and courage in defending him were presented as central themes in these narratives without being gendered in any significant way. Righteousness and piety have universally been praised as values appropriate for both men and women. There have been countless stories of pious behavior by male and female followers of Hoseyn. For example, in one account Zeynab's piety is praised by Hoseyn himself, as he says to her, "Do not forget me in your night-time prayers."[10]

Fighting and martyrdom have historically been portrayed as gendered themes, because men have been represented as being the ideal fighters and martyrs, while the ideal woman has been portrayed as sacrificing her loved ones rather than be a martyr herself. According to these narratives, women do not belong on the battlefield at all. Instead, they should lend support nearby. It has generally been argued in most sources that it was critically important for women to have accompanied Hoseyn to Iraq because their participation in the movement was significant to its successful completion. All the adult male followers of Hoseyn, except for Zeyn al-Abedin, were killed, and their martyrdom was recounted in great detail.[11] Examples include the heroic struggle of Abbas to obtain water for the followers, which eventually led to his death, as well as the struggle of the young and newly married Qasem, who killed many of his opponents in single combat before being killed himself.[12] The martyrdom of Hoseyn himself was the climax of the story.[13]

Even when a woman was martyred, her story is not recounted in the same degree of detail as that of the male martyrs. An example is the story of the newlywed Vahb and his wife, Haniyeh. In many of these accounts, she lost control out of love for her husband and ran out onto the battlefield to help him. She was called back to the tents by Imam Hoseyn, who reinforced the idea that she should not be on the battlefield at all.[14] It happened again and eventually she was martyred, but the story was passed over in only a few lines, as opposed to the story of her husband, which was given a much more elaborate treatment. Zeynab ran out onto the battlefield as well, which similarly resulted in Hoseyn's calling her back to the tent area with instructions to care for the women, the children, and the wounded.[15] It is clear that the ideal of the male martyr was well developed in the literature, while the female martyr not only was underdeveloped but was actually discouraged within the narratives. Furthermore, women on the battlefield were called back by Hoseyn himself, clearly defining this space as a male space and fighting as a male activity. According to these narratives, women were supposed to lend moral and logistical support to the martyrs from the sidelines during the battle. It should be noted here that under Islamic law fighting on the battlefield has usually been deemed unlawful for women.[16]

Women have generally been presented as being supporters of the martyrs and willing to sacrifice their loved ones. For example, the story of Vahb's mother's insistence (she is more enthusiastic than Vahb himself) on his going out and becoming martyred was a well-developed story, as were countless examples of other female characters who similarly supported the martyrdom of their loved ones. There were stories of young brides, such as Qasem's wife or Vahb's wife, who were willing to sacrifice their young husbands as martyrs.[17] Such stories were thoroughly developed, with the key theme being stressed throughout of women encouraging their loved ones to martyr themselves. For example, Zeynab willingly sacrificed not only her brother Hoseyn but also her two sons.[18] The primary ways in which women were expected to martyr their loved ones were either to encourage them to do so or to train and educate them during their childhood so that they would aspire to martyrdom later in life. Thus, they were the educators of the future generation of martyrs.

While female characters like Zeynab and Fatemeh have regularly been represented as having been active participants in Hoseyn's movement, their conduct on the battlefield was the subject of some debate. A particularly good example of the treatment of this theme is Bent al-Shate''s comparison of the role of A'esheh in the battle of the Camel and the role of Zeynab in the Battle of Karbala. She criticized A'esheh for contributing to factionalism and violent confrontation by provoking the Battle of the Camel. She was particularly harsh in her treatment of A'esheh's perceived disregard for accepted patterns of gender segregation. For example, she quoted a male soldier as having responded to A'esheh's call for vengeance for the murder of the third caliph, Othman: "Oh Mother of the Faithful, by God the importance of Othman's murder is less important than the fact that you have gone out in public and climbed onto this cursed camel, because God has commanded seclusion and *hijab* for you, yet you ignore this and discard your *hijab*."[19]

Bent al-Shate' went on to describe A'esheh as having committed a transgression by choosing to lead male troops personally in battle.[20] She compared this to Zeynab, who she represented as maintaining strict hijab during all her father's campaigns. Zeynab's abandonment of this strict hijab was ironically presented without comment during the Battle of Karbala. This seems to have been because her role at the Battle of Karbala was thrust upon her against her will, as well as the fact that the cause was considered to be worthy of merit, as compared to A'esheh's failed coup attempt. Bent al-Shate' quoted Zeynab as condemning Yazid for exposing the female members of the family of the Prophet Mohammad to the eyes of strange men and without their male family members there to protect them.[21] As a matter of interest, her role as spokesperson after the battle was not treated here or elsewhere as having been a violation of the basic parameters of hijab, even though it was not significantly different from A'esheh's public speeches condemning Ali. This was at least in part because of the fact that Zeynab never led male troops in battle but, rather, served in a capacity different than men that was not perceived as violating the accepted parameters of gender-segregated involvement on the battlefield.

Another important gendered theme developed in the Karbala narratives was women as victims of humiliation through captivity. While Zeyn al-Abedin was taken captive as well, the stories of women being mistreated and humiliated were much more dominant. These stories stressed disrespect of their status, their humiliation, and the general tragic nature of their being taken into captivity.

The theme of women as mourners of the dead has also been dominant in the Karbala stories. While men throughout history definitely have been presented as mourning this event, women have generally played a central, yet somewhat different, role in mourning rituals. Furthermore, there has historically been a hierarchy of involvement in rituals associated with Karbala. Crying has always been portrayed as being worthy of merit. However, it cannot provide exactly the same merit as that associated with martyrdom on the battlefield.

In *Moharram* paintings and other physical representations of the tragedy, women have often been used as graphic representations of the tragic loss of the martyrs of Karbala. In such representations, men have usually been the actual martyrs and warriors, while the women have generally been represented as mourning their loss. An excellent example is the popular postrevolutionary poster portraying the imam's martyrdom by showing his wounded horse with mourning women around it.[22] Thus, women become the embodiment of the tragedy by becoming mourners. This leads to a dichotomy between the ideal of "men as martyrs" versus "women as mourners." Following the massacre, when the female followers of Hoseyn went onto the battlefield, one of them "found the severed arm of her son, while another searched for the elbow of her husband, and yet another found the severed leg of her beloved brother."[23]

Women have also been portrayed as the conscience of the community. As the Kufans lined up beside the road to watch the women being taken as captives by Yazid's troops, they mourned the tragedy. This upset Zeynab to the point where she reprimanded them, saying that because of their hypocritical and cowardly abandonment of Hoseyn in his hour of need, they had no right to mourn for the martyrs. In this story, the Kufans were represented as being women. Another example of a woman in the role of mourner was given as one of Yazid's troops carried home Hoseyn's head, which caused the soldier's wife to run out of the house screaming and crying with grief.

This association of women with mourning and crying gains greater significance when contextualized within the broader discourse on Karbala. In the 1970s, political leaders such as Shari'ati, Motahhari, and Najafabadi stressed that mere mourning was to be abandoned. Instead, they advocated active rebellion. They often referred to the "wrong" practice as being what women commonly did, which was said to be pointless crying, rather than what men should be doing, which was active or even armed rebellion. This does not preclude men from also being mourners, but women as mourners were treated differently and were often given precedence. Furthermore, women as martyrs were not generally stressed to the same degree as male martyrs in this discourse.

The final gendered theme that was well developed was the ideal of women as spokespersons, preservers, and transmitters of Hoseyn's message. While men were the primary speakers before the battle, women served a critical function of becoming the spokespeople for the cause once they were taken into captivity and on to Syria. In particular, Zeynab was central to the preservation and spreading of the message at this point. This is significant because it clearly developed this role as a responsibility for women and assured the centrality of Zeynab to the story. The preservation and spreading of the message was related to the role of women as educators of men and boys. Zeynab coached the believers, and in particular her own sons, on the finer points of the ideology propagated by Hoseyn. The message of Hoseyn's move-

ment was similarly to be transmitted by women to the next generation of potential male warriors and martyrs.

Once themes are identified as gender coded in this basic narrative,
it becomes possible to see how men and women were encouraged to
take on the gender-neutral traits from role models of the opposite sex,
while adopting gender-specific traits only from role models of the same
sex. Hoseyn has been used as a role model for both men and women,
and in some cases female characters like Zeynab have served as role
models for both men and women. For example, Zeynab's loyalty can
serve as a model for men, and Qasem's piety as a model for women.
Martyrdom, however, is for men to adopt in most cases, and certain
gendered roles, such as sacrificing loved ones, are primarily associated
with women.

Most of the traits attributed to women in the narratives were presented as being acceptable for men as well, whereas the traits assigned
to men were not portrayed as being acceptable for women. Therefore,
these gendered traits were not rigidly exclusive categories but tendencies within a fluid dynamic of interpretation. A small digression
here is warranted, in that this phenomenon is similar to the general
Islamic practice of women taking the Prophet Mohammad as a role
model. Despite the spiritual equality of men and women articulated
in the Qur'an, the historical uses of Muslim role models have led to
much deeper ambiguities concerning the ability of women to be
equally pious believers. A male role model has generally been presented
as the ideal Muslim, yet women have usually been encouraged to adopt
only the gender-neutral traits of the male role model. The wives of the
Prophet have also been commonly portrayed as models to be emulated.
However, they have not been portrayed as spiritual equals of the
Prophet Mohammad himself, and traditional Islamic conceptions of
emulating the Prophet have been quite different from the idea of
women emulating his wives, Jesus' mother, Mary, or other female characters in the Qur'an and Islamic history.

In addition to the standard narratives that were being revised and
reinterpreted, a series of narratives that focused primarily on female
characters emerged beginning in the 1960s. These narratives were characterized by a focus on female characters, such as Zeynab and Fatemeh, within the standard narratives. While these two characters
figured prominently within Kashefi's narrative, there was a relative
increase in the focus on women in these newer narratives. This shift

is primarily a structural shift, but it reflects a more fundamental shift in the usage of symbols from the Karbala narratives, generally, and of gendered symbols, specifically. This shift is best characterized as a relative shift in the use of Karbala symbolism from "concept-elaborating" symbols to "action-elaborating" symbols. By creating a new style of narrative focusing on female characters, traditionalist ideologues presented men and women with gender-specific models of behavior.

One type of narrative focuses on Fatemeh, daughter of the Prophet, wife of Ali, and mother of Hasan and Hoseyn. The first example of a specifically female-gendered narrative, which is dealt with here, was the product of lectures on Fatemeh given at the *Hoseyniyeh-e Ershad* by 'Ali Shari'ati in 1971. This narrative is interesting in that it was both an explicit attempt to redefine Fatemeh as a model for women by rejecting what Shari'ati called "Western" conceptions of womanhood and a rejection of the traditional conception of womanhood. Most other narratives from the 1950s through the 1970s were primarily efforts at traditionalizing the conceptions of womanhood. It is also an excellent example of how the narrative form was transformed during this period into a discourse, with issues at times being raised explicitly within the narratives, along with a general theoretical discussion of these issues.

The starting point of Shari'ati's narrative was the question, "Who is Fatemeh?" followed by a long exploration of the character of Fatemeh. His basic concern was how to define womanhood in a society that is torn between two ideals. He said that there are three types of women: first are those who are traditional and who have no desire to meet the challenges of modernity; second are Westernized women who embrace everything Western without reservations; and third are the women in between the first and second types. The first two do not face any real identity crisis, whereas the third faces a fundamental one.[24]

As Shari'ati tried to create a new paradigm of womanhood in his narrative, he specifically stated that the women who face an identity crisis and who are neither traditional nor Western want to be the ones to define themselves. He said that these women want to be reborn and that they want to be their own midwives.[25] The irony of this is rather obvious, as almost the entire discourse, including his formulations, consisted of the constructions of various men. There were few women who took part in this particular aspect of the discourse on gender, namely, the uses of the Karbala narrative as a means for participating in gender discourse. After rejecting "tradition" and "revolution," Shari'ati pointed to what he called the prophetic model of reform, which was to preserve the external form of tradition while revolutionizing the internal components of society. Thus, superficial, external social institutions did not necessarily need to be destroyed to make room for the new, but rather there needed to be an internal reformulation of the very ideals of womanhood. This approach, he suggested, would allow for a reform in spirit of the conceptualization of women's social roles without requiring a fundamental reformulation of some social practices, such as clothing and hijab, which were among the most contentious issues in these gender debates.

The central obsession of most of these narratives was the promotion of what the authors considered to be the Islamic norm of female behavior, as opposed to what they defined as traditional and Western models of womanhood. Shari'ati, however, was just as concerned with criticizing both the model of womanhood that was promoted by the Pahlavi state and the model promoted by the traditionalizing discourse on gender. He rejected both in favor of a potential alternative. So what was this alternative conception of the ideal Muslim woman? She was to assume the role of Fatemeh, who in turn had a specific role in the broader scheme of history. Fatemeh was the link between the Prophet and Ali and the inheritor of the mission that is passed down from Adam through the imams: she was to take on the struggle of justice against the oppressive and corrupt elites of each era. This was presented in a leftist-style critique of corrupt Iranian elites, who fit more or less into the patterns of behavior of the bourgeoisie. Like Hoseyn, she was to struggle and sacrifice everything, including her life and property, in the path of social justice. While it is not clear how far his reformulation of women's models of behavior may ultimately have gone, it is clear that in Shari'ati's narrative everything was subordinate to the greater cause, which was class-based struggle against social corruption. He claimed to present an alternative to both the traditional model and the Westernized model.

The discussion now shifts to the other most commonly represented female character, Hoseyn's sister Zeynab. Eshtehardi's work *Hazrat-e Zeynab, payam resan-e shahidan-e Karbala* was one of the best examples of a text published after the Islamic Revolution as a means for educating young girls on the proper social roles of women in Islamic society. Unlike his much longer work, *Sugnameh-e al-e Mohammad*, this book was structured thematically, in an effort "to construct" the Zeynab role model. He was quite explicit about his purpose and clearly explained how girls and women should take Zeynab as a role model and should behave according to this gendered ideal: "We must learn these three lessons from Zeynab the Lioness of Karbala (especially the women). In all times and places we must protect our leader of the age, and drive home the message of our martyrs to the world. And we must care for the families of the martyrs, in order to have honored Zeynab's legacy."[26]

The themes presented in the text were the same as those analyzed here earlier; however, what was unique was the fact that the narrative form was in this case subsumed within the character construction project. He began with a discussion of how Zeynab was the perfect role model, demonstrating that she represented the (nongendered) qualities of her father, Ali, as well as all of the qualities of her mother, Fatemeh, and her grandmother, Khadijeh. From her mother, Zayneb learned chastity and hijab, courage and the desire for martyrdom (her courageous and dignified speeches criticized the enemies of Islam), simple living, and piety in faith. She learned courage, worship, generosity, and selflessness from her father, from his heroic actions and his passion for the cause of Islam. Eshtehardi described Zeynab in the following way: "Her personality was like Khadijeh, her modesty and chastity like her mother Fatemeh, and the sweetness of her speech was like her father Ali, her revolutionary dream and patience was like her brother Hasan, her courage and strength of heart was like her brother Hoseyn."[27]

This legitimization of Zeynab through association with other sacred personages was reinforced throughout Eshtehardi's text. This approach was a common feature of all the narratives. Eshtehardi then began a general construction of her character by discussing her most important qualities, which are presented here in two parts. The first set reflected her personal qualities as a Muslim, and the second dealt specifically with her involvement in Hoseyn's movement.

Eshtehardi began the first aspect of Zeynab's character development with her status as a scholar and an educator. He portrayed her as having been an educator of women during Ali's caliphate. He also said that she accompanied Ali and her husband to Kufa to teach some Kufan women moral conduct and Qur'anic interpretation, while at the same time giving aid to the poor and needy. She also served as Hoseyn's private secretary. Learning has generally been a gender-neutral trait in the symbolism of Karbala. However, the method of its application has not always been so. The fact that she did all of this under the direct supervision and with the support of her father, brother, and husband was an important theme and was developed both here and elsewhere. The next trait Eshtehardi developed was her diligence in worship, which, as mentioned earlier, was praised by Hoseyn himself as being unusual and exemplary. After discussing Zeynab's generosity, he stressed her close association with her brother. Her loyalty to her brother superseded even her duties as wife and mother. This was a more difficult issue than one might at first assume.

The fact that Zeynab accompanied her brother while her husband did not was an issue that was discussed in great detail in many of these narratives. There were several problems related to this fact that had to do with gender specifically. For example, was it possible for her husband not to have supported Hoseyn? If so, then how could she have married such a man? How could her family (i.e., her children) be viewed as just when the father was not? How could she disobey her husband? These issues, which often preoccupied many of these scholars, were dealt with in different ways in various texts. Eshtehardi addressed these issues by stressing that the husband was not able to accompany Hoseyn for good reasons. He said that her husband was a seventy-year-old blind man who needed to stay in the Hijaz in order to survive the massacre so that he could preserve and pass on the message of Hoseyn. It was also repeatedly stressed that he gave his enthusiastic support to Hoseyn by sending his sons to be martyred and by feeling pride that they were martyred alongside Hoseyn. The fact that Zeynab accompanied Hoseyn could thus be considered an endorsement of her actions by her husband. Her unusual closeness to her brother was also commented on by her mother, Fatemeh. The Prophet himself was quoted as saying, "This girl will go to Karbala with her brother."[28] She was said to have written into her marriage contract the condition that her husband must always allow her to see her brother at all times. Thus, her behavior was portrayed as not having been contrary to her husband's wishes, which would have raised all sorts of problematic issues concerning a husband's authority over his wife.

Eshtehardi's account was in sharp contrast to Bent al-Shate"s treatment of the same issue. Bent al-Shate' discussed at length the issue of Zeynab's husband and the question, "Why didn't he accompany Hoseyn to Karbala?" She argued that Zeynab must have been divorced by her husband, Abdollah, before Karbala. She quoted a historical source saying that Zeynab separated from him and was never reunited with him after the Battle of Karbala and, furthermore, that he married her sister Om Kolsum afterwards.[29] In the Persian translation circulated in Iran, her view was criticized by the Iranian translators/editors because of the implications of this series of events.

The second set of qualities Eshtehardi presented dealt with the details of Zeynab's actual involvement in the Battle of Karbala, which was arguably the most important of all her qualities. Eshtehardi summed it up in one line: "One of Zeynab's qualities was the fact that she was an active participant in the sacred uprising of Hoseyn."[30] He divided her involvement in Hoseyn's movement into three components: (1) protecting Hoseyn's only surviving son, Zeyn al-Abedin; (2) driving home the message of the fallen martyrs after the tragic event; and (3) caring for and supporting the martyrs and their families.

Eshtehardi began by calling her "Zeynab, the Lioness of Karbala." In his account, she served as the mother of the men in the group, taking care of them and calming their spirits (especially the young children). He then went on to describe the events of the night of *Ashura* when Hoseyn's son Zeyn al-Abedin became severely ill. He told Zeynab to take care of her sick nephew. When she realized that Hoseyn was going to be killed later that day, she said, "I wish I could die so that I would not see that this is the last night of your life."[31] Hoseyn consoled her by telling her to be patient and to persevere.

Zeynab also encouraged Abbas on the night of *Ashura* by reminding him of what her father, Ali, had said: "You need to be the reserves of Karbala. Just as I [i.e., Ali] was to the Prophet, you must be to Hoseyn."[32] Abbas confirmed this and swore to do so. Zeynab also protected Zeyn al-Abedin from being killed on several occasions. On the day of *Ashura,* she prevented Shemr from killing him while he was lying ill in his tent, and later, when the tents were set on fire, she rescued him by pulling him out from his burning tent. She also prevented Ebn-e Ziyad from executing him later on in Kufa.

Eshtehardi also gave a detailed description of Zeynab's involvement in the battle, which corresponded to the gender-specific roles discussed earlier. He said that Zeynab was not idle for a moment during the Battle of Karbala. She lent her support to the male *mojahedin* and took care of the women and children. She did this despite the fact that she herself was suffering from hardships and from the emotional strain of los-ing her sons, other relatives, and, of course, her brother Hoseyn. She was very active in this jihad and holy defense. She then went onto the battlefield at the moment when her brother fell and he was about to be killed, in order to lend him support with her speeches: "Oh Son of Sa'd, They wish to kill the son of the Prophet, while you are watching?!? Is there not one Muslim or decent person among you?!? If only the skies would be destroyed and the mountains of the Earth would be crumbled."[33]

Many of the enemy soldiers responded by crying, having felt a sense of shame. Hoseyn then ordered her to leave the battlefield and to return to the tents in order to care for the women and children, which she obediently did. There was one final element in Eshtehardi's portrayal of Zeynab's involvement in the battle. He described how she lent logistical support from her tent, which was positioned strategically between the battlefield and the rest of the camp. He then provided an account of her role as spokesperson for the cause after the tragedy. Below is one of the two speeches he quotes at length:

> Oh Yazid! You think that you have made the world difficult for us, and you are taking us from city to city as prisoners. Do you think that God holds contempt for us and honor for you? No, stop and think for a moment. Have you forgotten the words of God in the Qur'an, which says, "Let not the unbelievers think that Our respite to them is good for themselves; We grant them respite that they may grow in their iniquity, but they will have a shameful punishment" [Qur'an 3:178]. . . .
>
> Oh descendants of those whose ancestors were freed when the Prophet conquered Mecca, is it just to parade the women of the Prophet's family around from city to city for the public to watch, while the women and girls of your family sit in your palace hidden from view? Indulge in your trickery and strategies, and fire all the arrows you can, but know this, that lying to God will never succeed in destroying the memory of our presence in this event, nor do you have the power to put out the flame of revelation and prophecy. . . .
>
> Even though your actions come close to laying waste the heavens, and shattering the mountains, these actions on your part are no surprise to me, because you are the son of the very same woman who put the liver of the first martyrs of Islam between her teeth. And you are the son of those who raised their flag against the Prophet

himself and who had the blood of the martyrs on their hands. What can be expected from the offspring of such as these?!? . . .

You are not a human being, you are not human, you are an oppressor who inherited bloodthirsty oppression from your father! . . . Even though my heart is wounded, and wearied, and my tears are flowing, surely very soon the day of God's punishment will come and everyone will be subjected to God's justice, and this is sufficient for us. . . . If fate has brought me here to face you, this was not something which I wished to happen. But now that it is so, I count you as small and I reproach you. . . .

Do not be pleased that you have killed our dear ones. "Think not of those who are slain in God's way as dead. Nay they live, finding their sustenance in the presence of their Lord" [Qur'an 3:169]. But woe unto you! For God will be your judge, and the Prophet your enemy, and Gabriel will be our ally against you. On that day the person who placed you above the people will realize what a great sin he has committed, and what a worthless human being he has raised to a high status. . . . Oh God! Take revenge against our oppressors. . . . [34]

Like other social and political issues that were the subject of debate, the newly developing religious discourse on gender that became more pronounced in the 1950s and the 1960s was reflected in Karbala symbols and rituals. The Karbala narrative therefore became a vehicle for expressing a variety of different concepts related to gender. The Karbala narrative was used to promote several ideas, including the importance of hijab; the division of the political, economic, and social spheres of men and women; distinctions between male activities and female activities; the importance of male authority over women; and the corresponding subservience and loyalty of women to men. These models of behavior were usually promoted as alternatives to what was increasingly being portrayed as Western concepts of womanhood promoted by the Pahlavi regime. The new ideals of gender-specific behavior were often articulated as being both nontraditional and Islamic. Thus, they drew from the historical examples of women and men at Karbala in formulating and promoting new gender ideals for society.

8

The Islamic Republic

*T*here are numerous detailed accounts of the actual transfer of political power following the Islamic Revolution of 1978–79, so it is not necessary to recount this material. Here, the concern is the state's use of religious symbolism to promote its own legitimacy following the 1978–79 revolution. In relation to the transfer of power, it is sufficient for these purposes to keep in mind that the revolution, the roots of which went back for years or even decades, culminated in a massive movement including diverse groups with divergent ideological perspectives that shared little more than the desire to overthrow the shah. Once this basic common goal was achieved, these groups were not as united in purpose as they had been prior to the revolution itself. Unlike other groups, leaders, and ideological camps, Khomeini and the revolutionary religious leadership who supported him were able to sustain their movement on a large scale beyond the revolution itself and thereby succeeded in taking over the state apparatus. The effective use of Shi'i symbolism by the religious leadership surrounding Khomeini was a critically important factor in its success in taking over the state apparatus.

Upon taking power in 1979, Khomeini and his followers set out to consolidate their authority and to build a new government modeled on an abstract vision of Islamic government as articulated by Khomeini himself in his construction of the doctrine of "rule of the jurist consult" (*velayat-e faqih*). Shi'i symbols and rituals were central to this process. Just as Shi'i symbols and rituals had been used in the 1960s and 1970s to mobilize the masses to overthrow the shah, they were now used to construct a vision of the state and its place in the international political order. This role was articulated as being the defender of the oppressed masses of the world from imperialist domination and oppression. While this was clearly understood as an Islamic movement, it was allowed to extend to non-Muslims in certain ways.

Upon taking power, the revolutionaries were initially focused upon exporting the revolution and leading an Islamic, or even a "third world-ist," revolution. However, while the Islamic revolution was extremely influential in other countries, it did not lead to a series of similar Islamic revolutions. The leaders of the Islamic revolution believed that their ideology was universalistic in some ways. However, on a more practical level it functioned at a national level. Iran was not only the center and starting point of the revolution, it was increasingly virtually the only place where the ideals were implemented. Furthermore, Iranian nationalism was not fundamentally subverted by the revolutionary ideology. Rather, it was recast in a new light, rejecting the more extreme secular tendencies of some forms of Iranian nationalism and inserting into it a revolutionary component.[1]

While the policies of the new regime were sometimes dictated by idealism, at other times they were governed by pragmatism. However, when it came to the religious rhetoric of the regime, the revolutionary Karbala Paradigm continued to be used in new forms throughout the 1980s and 1990s. The shah, the United States, Israel, and Iraq (and sometimes other nations) were equated with Yazid, and the Islamic revolutionary regime and its supporters with Hoseyn and his followers. Michael Fischer recounts how Khomeini, when faced with the possibility of direct U.S. military intervention in Iran, said that all Iranians were ready and willing to become martyrs just as Hoseyn and his followers had done at Karbala in 680.[2] "Commanding the right and forbidding the wrong" continued to be a central dogma of the state. Numerous efforts at economic development and reconstruction were similarly referred to as *jahad-e sazandegi,* or "a sacred struggle for construction and development."

Throughout the 1980s and 1990s, the themes of the revolution were kept alive by shifting the focus away from opposition to the Pahlavi regime and toward opposition to the two great superpowers on the international stage, the United States and the Soviet Union. This was not a new direction, for the revolutionaries had been targeting the United States and communism during the revolution itself. However, now slogans like "Neither East nor West," which stressed Iran's independence, became part and parcel of the revolutionary regime's ideology, rhetoric, and policies. Hence, opposing the imperialist policies of the United States and the Soviet Union were portrayed as a jihad (religious struggle), and those killed in this endeavor were considered martyrs. The massive military power wielded by the United States and the Soviet Union was easily equated to the overwhelming military might of Yazid's army. Likewise, the consumerism and perceived economic excesses of the United States along with the communist materialism of the Soviet Union were equated with the worldliness and corruption of Yazid and his supporters.

As Iran became more politically isolated, facing economic hardships, diplomatic pressures, and foreign invasion, this model of struggle in the face of insurmountable odds fit well into the symbolic rhetoric of Karbala. Courage and self-sacrifice for the ideals of Islam were aggressively encouraged. For example, in 1980 Iraq invaded Iran, leading to a bloody eight-year war. During this war, Iraq was backed by the United States, several other Western nations, and most Arab regimes, with the notable exception of Syria. Iranians found themselves standing alone, not so far from Karbala, fighting for the survival of the Islamic revolution, for the Shi'i Muslims and holy shrines in southern Iraq, and for the independence of Iran itself. The symbolic language of jihad and martyrdom was used extensively and effectively to mobilize the masses of Iranians to fight against the Iraqi invasion. Because Iran was severely "outgunned" by Iraq and its supporters, Iranian casualties were particularly high, and "martyrdom" was especially commonplace.

The Friday sermon became a major vehicle for reinforcing the revolutionary ideology and legitimacy of the state. Ulama began to hold machine guns at their sides while giving the Friday sermon, a symbol of the connection between "the war of words" and armed struggle in the path of God. The strongest supporters of the state have usually attended the large Friday prayer gatherings held in each city, especially in Tehran, where the prayer is conducted at the University of Tehran. While not everyone has regularly attended these Friday sermons, they have been particularly important in spreading the government's message, because they have been televised, played on the radio, published in newspapers, and even collected and published in books. The contents of these sermons have been analyzed elsewhere, so they need not be repeated in detail here.[3]

In relation to the specific themes of *Moharram*, these sermons, especially during the ritual season, have stressed the revolutionary message of Hoseyn's movement, which is covered in some detail in previous chapters. Many of these sermons stressed the abstract ideals of the Karbala Paradigm, followed by words intended to encourage the believers to act in accordance with those ideals. For example, on October 18, 1983, Ayatollah Khamenei gave a Friday sermon in which he recounted a somewhat typical story about Karbala:

On the day of *Ashura*, after his companions with both tears and insistence asked for permission and entered the battlefield and fought and were martyred, and nobody other than the youth of the Bani Hashem remained—the group devoted to Hoseyn Ebn-e Ali (AS)—Ali Akbar was the first youth to approach Imam Hoseyn (AS) and asked for permission to enter the battlefield. He came to Imam Hoseyn, who—and here is the remarkable thing—Imam Hoseyn, without the slightest hesitation, gave Ali Akbar permission to go to the battlefield. . . .

He went to the battlefield and fought until he was exhausted, and being a brave youth he was able to fight his way through the ranks of the enemy and return to his father. He said to Imam Hoseyn (AS) "O father, I am dying of thirst." Clearly there was no water in the camp of Imam Hoseyn Ebn-e Ali (AS). Therefore, he said "My son, go and continue fighting in the path of God! Soon you will be drinking from the hand of the Prophet (SAS)." Shortly thereafter everyone heard Ali Akbar's voice from the middle of the battlefield saying "Father, peace be unto you." "Goodbye my father." "This is my grandfather the Prophet of God."[4]

Khamenei concluded this part of his sermon with the following appeal to the audience and two supplications to God:

Brothers and sisters [who have gathered here for prayer]! Make pious faith in God your calling, as you follow [the example of] Hoseyn Ebn-e Ali (AS), and his companions, and his youthful supporters, and his children. "O Creator! Cause us to be among his companions and supporters. (Amen from those congregated for prayer)." "O Creator! Cause us to be among the people of Karbala. (Amen from those congregated for prayer)."[5]

Many of these sermons had a more immediate and functional message, such as encouraging family planning, discouraging drug use, mobilizing the people for defense of the country, discouraging violations of hijab regulations, and so forth. For example, in a Friday sermon I observed in Shahreza during the first Friday of *Moharram* in 1997, the imam spoke of political activism as being in the best traditions of Hoseyn's movement. He then encouraged everyone to vote in the national presidential elections, stating that participation in government elections was one of the best ways to carry on the sort of activism envisioned by Imam Hoseyn and the revolutionaries surrounding Khomeini. He then proceeded with lamentations for the martyrs of Karbala, which inspired passionate displays of crying and wailing on the part of the listeners.

The state has promoted religious culture in diverse ways. Religious programming on radio and television was expanded. More important, religious programming was infused with revolutionary content, and political programming was infused with religious rhetoric. Much of this religious programming consisted of basic religious education, Qur'anic recitation, and sermons. However, during the month of *Moharram* the number of programs devoted to Hoseyn and Karbala dramatically increased. Programs included *ta'ziyeh* performances, recitation of ritual chants and poetry, montages of Karbala imagery, film clips from ritual performances around the country, and interviews with ritual participants and organizers. The state has also encouraged ritual events in public schools and in other public venues.

The *Vezarat-e Farhang va Ershad-e Eslami* (Ministry of Culture and Religious Guidance) sponsors a wide variety of religious events and rituals every year. In 1998–99, it sponsored hundreds of religious events, many commemorating the birth or death of Shi'i religious figures, such as the Prophet, the imams, and their families. Many were celebrations of religiously significant historical events, like the Prophet Mohammad's speech at Ghadir Khom, in which he reportedly announced Ali as his successor. A large number of these events were devoted to mourning rituals of all sorts, including sermons and speeches, *rowzeh khanis*, *ta'ziyeh* performances, and so forth. The fact that these ritual events were scattered all over the nation, including virtually every province, is a good indication of the efforts of the government to reach the broadest national audience possible. Most of these events were attended by a few hundred or a few thousand participants, but some included tens of thousands of participants. One *ta'ziyeh* performance, which was held in Hamadan during the month of *Moharram*, was reportedly attended by more than twenty thousand people. Another ritual mourning event for Hoseyn that was held on the ninth and tenth of *Moharram* in the province of Chaharmahal va Bakhtiyar was attended by one hundred thousand people.[6]

The Ministry of Pious Endowments (*Vezarat-e Owqaf*), and its local equivalents (e.g., *Edareh-e Koll-e Owqaf va Omur-e Khayriyeh-e Ostan-e Tehran*), has also been extremely active in sponsoring religious rituals. For example, in *Moharram* of 2002 the Office of Pious Endowments for Tehran announced two hundred religious rituals that were sponsored under its auspices in Tehran and the surrounding area. These rituals were held at sites that were registered as *vaqf* properties, such as mosques and *hoseyniyeh*s. Most of these events consisted of a *rowzeh khani* ritual, a sermon or lecture, and dinner.[7] Cultural centers funded by the state or local community organizations have also worked hard to keep the performing tradition of *taʿziyeh* alive by sponsoring local performances.[8] This has been accompanied by periodic articles and discussions in newspapers and other publications of the historical roots of this ritual drama, as well as issues related to its perceived decline.[9]

Cemeteries provide an excellent example of how the revolutionary regime stressed the importance of jihad and martyrdom, modeled after Hoseyn and his followers at Karbala. In most cities around the country, small and large cemeteries became the symbolic "gardens of martyrs." *Behesht-e Zahra*, located just south of Tehran, is the most famous of these sites. Khomeini made a symbolic visit to the graves of the martyrs upon his return to Iran in February 1979, thus ending his sixteen-year exile. Usually, these special graveyards were placed in separate sections, fenced off from the regular graveyards. As Faegheh Shirazi has pointed out in her forthcoming research, in sharp contrast to the traditional terms for graveyards, which were often derived from terms for graves or dirt, the names of many of these new graveyards contain the name of a member of Hoseyn's family, such as Ali, along with a term for heaven, paradise, or garden. The names of his female relatives, such as Fatemeh and Zeynab, were particularly common. Numerous statements and images of Fatemeh and Zeynab were usually placed all over these sites.

Martyrs' cemeteries were decorated with banners and signs containing revolutionary slogans, posters of Khomeini and other revolutionary leaders, pictures of soldiers fighting courageously, quotations from Khomeini's speeches and the Qur'an, images of women and children mourning the loss of their loved ones, and depictions of martyrs praying for salvation. Above the entrance to *Behesht-e Zahra* is the following quotation, in Arabic, Persian, and English, from verse 169 of the third Surah (*al Imran*) of the Qur'an: "Do not think that those who were slain in the path of Allah are dead. They are alive and well provided for by Allah."

There are also numerous quotations from Khomeini's speeches praising the martyrs. In 2001, the following quotes were posted in the main martyrs' cemetery in Isfahan, named *Behesht-e Zeynab*: "God's peace be upon those *mojahedin* of great dignity, whose martyrdom ensures the success of Islam"; "It is the pure graves of the martyrs that will remain the object of pilgrimage and the source of blessings for mystics, lovers of God, and the free, until the day of judgment"; and "History shall not forget the sacrifice of these zealous youth [who accepted martyrdom as an obligation]." Also liberally posted around the graveyards were revolutionary slogans, such as "Death to America" and "We are honored to implement the tenets of the Qur'an and the Sunna." In the martyrs' cemetery in Tehran, *Behesht-e Zahra*, there was a banner stating, "We shall continue [on] the path of the Imam (RA) and the martyrs," and another with the statement, "The blood-red path of martyrdom is the path of the family of Mohammad and Ali." Rural areas and small towns were no exception to this general practice. In the main martyrs' cemetery in Shahreza, a small town south of Isfahan, right next to the main saint shrine of Shahreza, a sign quoted Khomeini's praising of the martyrs.

The cemetery planners usually borrowed from the symbolic vocabulary of *Moharram* artistic representations combined with revolutionary imagery.[10] For example, the scenes of battle and martyrdom are reminiscent of the coffeehouse paintings used as visual aids by professional storytellers who narrated the stories of Karbala. When this narrative tradition declined in the 1960s and 1970s, these paintings became museum pieces and decorative features of *hoseyniyeh*s. They were also used to decorate certain types of funeral biers or floats that are carried in ritual processions.[11] Posters, stamps, and other forms of state-sponsored art followed this general trend as well.

A new practice emerged of erecting memorials to the fallen martyrs. Of course, the graveyards themselves served as a massive memorial, but there were also more personal and individual memorials. In addition to the traditional gravestones containing religious calligraphy, the newly styled graves of the martyrs often had glass display cases containing pictures of each martyr, often both from the war front and in their civilian life, such as when they were young boys. An account of the details of their martyrdom was often included. Many also contained miscellaneous personal touches such as poetry, prayers, personal letters, plastic flowers in little vases, prayer beads, or other small objects with either sentimental or religious value. These memorials, which served to keep the memory of the martyrs alive, also served as an expression of piety and devotion on the part of the families of the martyrs. Memorials could also be motivated primarily by political beliefs. Thus, graves were transformed from relatively anonymous sites into memorials for the revolutionary ideology, in which the martyr (and hence the act of martyrdom) was glorified.

Memorials of martyrdom also emerged in other forms. Images of martyrs like Motahhari and Beheshti were placed on stamps and posters and were often painted in the form of huge murals at cemeteries or on the sides of prominent buildings. Symbols of struggle and martyrdom also became centerpieces of *meydan*s, or squares at major intersections. Special newspaper and magazine articles and radio and television programs memorialized the sacrifices of the fallen martyrs. Streets, parks, schools, mosques, and other sites were routinely named after martyrs. For the families of martyrs and those wounded in the war, who were often described as having "martyred their bodies," foundations were also created. There were also religious gatherings devoted specifically to honoring the families of martyrs. It should be kept in mind that while martyrdom could have an overtly political aspect, it could also be a deeply personal expression of either piety or patriotism. Sometimes the most significant aspect of martyrdom was also the simplest and most personal. The emotional, religious, and moral meaning invested in the sacrifice of martyrdom helped families work through the emotional pain of having lost a beloved family member in the bloody Iran-Iraq war.

One interesting ritual practice (i.e., since the interest here is in rituals in particular) that emerged following Khomeini's death in 1989 was a series of annual mourning rituals in his honor. Following his death a massive shrine was built in his honor southwest of Tehran, not far from *Behesht-e Zahra*. Because of the large scale of this shrine complex, it is still not complete after more than a decade of construction. This shrine has become a site for pilgrimage by believers from all over Iran and the rest of the Shi'i world. Each year during the nights of *Moharram*, mourning rituals have taken place at Khomeini's shrine complex. These mourning rituals, organized by different *hey'at*s, have included *rowzeh* sermons, processions, chants, *sineh zani* (flagellation of the chest), and even *zanjir zani* (flagellation with chains). In addition, speeches and sermons have been given honoring Khomeini, the martyrs of the revolution and the war, and other followers of Khomeini's message. These rituals have had the effect of preserving Khomeini's political message while at the same time allowing a means for believers to express their piety and devotion to the Shi'i imams. These rituals have been mirrored by similar events held across the country.[12]

Ashura rituals, in all their diverse forms, continued to be central to the government's efforts to mobilize the masses in support of the regime's ideology and policies. The revolutionaries had perfected the method of combining religious mourning rituals with political protests in the 1960s and 1970s. Many of the ritual organizers were associated with the state. Others were mobilized independently by religious associations (*hey'at*s) or autonomous local community groups called *komiteh*s. These rallies contained traditional ritual components, but the focus was usually on chanting political slogans, carrying banners and poster boards with political slogans, and giving or listening to explicitly political speeches.

Every year during the month of *Moharram*, at least one major ritual protest was usually organized by a coalition of groups and organizations devoted to the ideals of the revolution. One typical large-scale ritual demonstration was held on the tenth of *Moharram* of 1979, in Tehran. This event was sponsored by a coalition including the following organizations: the Revolutionary Ulama, the Revolutionary Societies of Teachers, the Islamic Revolutionary *Mojahedin,* the Revolutionary Guard, the Islamic Revolutionary Party, the Association of Educators, the Interim Revolutionary Committee, the Committee of Guild Affairs, the Committee of Supporters of the Imam, the Association for the *jahad-e sazandegi* (construction jihad), the Foundation for the Oppressed, and the Engineers Association of the Islamic Republic of Iran. *Hey'at*s and other organizations and individuals from all twelve districts of the city of Tehran were encouraged to congregate at specific locations in their districts. From there they were to travel in ritual procession along a predetermined route that took them eventually to Independence Square and the University of Tehran. Once they arrived at the final destination, they participated in mourning rituals and political chants, while listening to Qur'anic recitation, religious sermons, and political speeches by such speakers as the prominent revolutionary ideologue Dr. Beheshti. This event coincided with the Friday prayer service given at the university.[13] Similar events were planned annually during the month of *Moharram*, with Khomeini, his successor Khamenei, or other high-level government representatives in attendance.

These sorts of events had both religious and political tones. In 1979, for example, ritual processions, which had been planned in advance, passed by the American Embassy while chanting revolutionary slogans. It was reported that many of the participants, both soldiers and civilians, wore burial shrouds (*kafan push*), which have traditionally been a common feature of *Moharram* religious rituals, as symbols of martyrdom. They had slogans painted on their chests, proclaiming, "We have come to be martyred" and "We prefer death to disgrace." Women and girls wearing shrouds (*kafan push*), interestingly, were also reported to have been present in this demonstration and were chanting, "Aircraft-carriers no longer have any affect; Carter is unaware of jihad and martyrdom." Also worth noting was the fact that there was a large contingent of Azerbaijani Turks (resident in Tehran) in the demonstrations. They chanted in Turkish, and their elaborate displays were reported to have drawn the full attention of the onlookers. All this took place in front of a large number of foreign reporters, who broadcast their impressions across the global media.[14]

These political rallies, which included various elements of religious mourning rituals, should not be confused with the far more common religious rituals, which continued to be sponsored by the state and by others in Iranian society. As a general rule of thumb, religious rituals that were sponsored by the state and its supporters tended also to contain revolutionary political rhetoric. Rituals sponsored by others were generally less focused upon issues related to the state, the revolution, imperialism, or the West. These rituals tended to stress the abstract political aspects of Hoseyn's movement, along with religious ethics, social justice, and salvation.

One of the most significant trends in relation to the Islamic regime's use of Shi'i symbols and rituals is the fact that, in sharp contrast to portions of the Qajar and Pahlavi periods, there has not been any major opposition movement centered around these symbols and rituals since the Islamic Revolution. This lends credence to Mansoor Moaddel's argument that one of the most important factors contributing to the shah's crisis of legitimacy was his failure to participate effectively in the Shi'i discourses that were increasingly dominated by the religious opposition.[15] The case of the Islamic regime demonstrates a similar point in reverse. The regime's effective use of these symbols has been part of the reason an opposition discourse centered on the Karbala Paradigm has not emerged since the 1970s. The state, by claiming a certain type of authority over these symbols and rituals, has effectively taken this powerful tool away from any potential opposition groups. The fact that these rituals have not been used to challenge the state's legitimacy on a mass scale is indicative of the degree to which the public accepts the state's relative legitimacy within the realm of Shi'i symbols and rituals. This indicates that the state's interpretations of Karbala symbolism have not yet provoked broad-based challenges or hostile revisionism of its vision of the Karbala Paradigm.

It should also be pointed out that the most dominant trends in relation to Shi'i rituals were not those strains directly controlled by the state. The state-sponsored rituals were generally isolated events, sometimes with large attendance, sometimes with more limited attendance. They were important politically. However, the vast majority of religious rituals were organized by individuals and groups in the society for a wide variety of purposes. Furthermore, Shi'i rituals continued to evolve independently from state control. Hence, it can be said that while the state was quite effective in influencing Shi'i rituals, the greatest influences came from the society and culture as a whole. Broad-based changes (and continuities) in Iranian society and culture ultimately determined the path of evolution of these rituals.

Before the discussion proceeds to the specifics of these ritual performances, the broad trends in relation to religious institutions in Tehran are to be addressed first. As previously stated, the focus on Tehran is due entirely to practical considerations. It would be virtually impossible here to include all the regional trends in Iran, which are remarkably diverse. That will need to be undertaken in future research projects. Tehran, however, does need to be contextualized within broader national and regional trends.

One long-term trend that continued following the Islamic Revolution was the trend toward class and regional variation with regard to religious culture. For Tehran, the trend that began during the Pahlavi era and had roots in the late Qajar period involved at least five general axes: south versus north, center versus periphery, east versus west, traditional versus Westernized, and poor versus wealthy. Shi'i cultural practices were most prevalent in the southern portions of Tehran, toward the center, among the poorer groups, or in communities with stronger ties to traditional sectors in the society, such as the bazaar, or to traditional modes of production or to immigrants from other regions of Iran.

In 1994–95, there were 1,400 mosques and 159 *takyeh*s or permanent *hoseyniyeh*s registered in Tehran. The concentrations of mosques and permanent *takyeh*s or *hoseyniyeh*s in different districts are one indicator of citywide trends. Of the city's mosques, 51 percent were located in six districts (out of a total of twenty city districts). Two of these districts were in the center of the city, three were in the south, and only one was in the north (more specifically, the northeast). The seven districts with the highest concentrations of mosques included the central district 12 (with 196, or 14 percent of the total), which comprises the old bazaar quarter, dating back to the Qajar period. Next to the bazaar district were the three southern districts 17, 20, and 15, which had 116, 111, and 103 mosques, respectively, or a combined total of 23 percent of all of Tehran's mosques. The only northern district with comparable numbers was the northeastern district 4, which had 109 mosques, or 13 percent of the total.[16] *Hoseyniyeh*s followed a similar pattern with seven districts accounting for 75 percent of the city's total. Of these seven districts, two were in the north and northeast of the city, four were in the central and east-central areas, and one was in the southeast. The north and northeastern districts 3 and 4 had a combined total of 31 permanent *hoseyniyeh*s or *takyeh*s, or 19 percent of the city's total. The central and eastern districts 8, 11, 12, and 14 accounted for 76 *hoseyniyeh*s, or 41 percent of the total. Finally, the southern district 15 contained 24 *hoseyniyeh*s, or 15 percent of the total.[17]

These figures indicate a strong correlation between location and the prevalence of mosques and *hoseyniyeh*s. The general pattern was that the concentration tended to be highest in the center as compared to the periphery, in the south as compared to the north, and in the east as compared to the west. These trends also correlate well with income gaps, class grouping, population density, property costs, and access to public services. More affluent groups were more concentrated in the north as compared to the south, at the center as opposed to the select regions located on the periphery, and, to a lesser extent, in the west as opposed to the east.[18]

Kashani identifies similar trends in relation to *hey'at*s, or religious associations. He quotes census figures from the *Sazman-e Tablighat-e Eslami-e Tehran*, which collected data on the number of *hey'at*s in Tehran in 1997–98. According to its data, the distribution of *hey'at*s throughout Tehran was 2,450 in the southeast (40 percent of the total), 1,850 in the southwest (30 percent of the total), 1,000 in the northeast (16 percent of the total), and 900 in the northwest (15 percent of the total).[19] The numbers for the south of the city are more than twice that of the north, and the numbers for the east are higher than the west. He goes on to estimate tentatively that there were 10,000 *majales* ritual events in Tehran during that year. Given the popularity of these rituals, this is a reasonable estimate.

The growth trends in religious institutions in Tehran from the 1970s to the 1980s show interesting changes, especially when compared to national trends. This can be illustrated by comparing the rates of growth in the numbers of religious institutions from 1974–75 through 1984–85.[20] The broadest trend during this period was that the number of religious institutions grew at a relatively slower rate in Tehran than it did in the rest of Iran. For example, in Tehran the total number of religious institutions increased by 6 percent (from 1,283 to 1,363). Throughout the rest of Iran it increased at a rate of 19 percent (from 8,512 to 1,096), which is more that three times the rate of growth for Tehran. Furthermore, while the number of mosques in Tehran increased by 39 percent, the number of mosques outside Tehran increased by 51 percent.

*Takyeh*s or permanent *hoseyniyeh*s provide an even clearer example of this difference in growth. From 1974 to 1985, the number of permanent *hoseyniyeh*s in Tehran increased by 14 percent (from 86 to 98), while the number of permanent *hoseyniyeh*s in the rest of the country increased by 57 percent (from 1,235 to 1,941). Statistics from other years also support this general pattern. This trend is particularly striking when one considers that Tehran has had an extraordinarily fast rate of growth in its population during this period.

These trends also illustrate how the permanent *hoseyniyeh* as a religious institution was becoming relatively less prevalent than the mosque. It also shows that this trend was more pronounced in Tehran than it was in the rest of Iran. Another indication is that in 1985 *hoseyniyeh*s made up 7 percent of the religious institutions in Tehran, while throughout the rest of Iran *hoseyniyeh*s made up 19 percent of all religious institutions. This implies that the permanent *hoseyniyeh* was more prevalent in regions outside Tehran, as compared to Tehran.

According to data from 1974–76 and 1996, the provinces with the most numerous permanent *hoseyniyeh*s or *takyeh*s were Khorasan, Mazandaran, Yazd, Semnan, Khuzestan, Isfahan, Tehran, and the Central Province (i.e., Markazi).[21] It is also noteworthy that Mazandaran province had an unusually high percentage of permanent *takyeh*s. In 1996 the number of permanent *takyeh*s registered was almost equal to the number of *hoseyniyeh*s. This is an excellent example of the tremendous regional diversity of religious practices in Iran and warrants further study.[22]

By contrast, in both Tehran and the rest of Iran, the numbers of both mosques and permanent *hoseyniyeh*s increased at higher rates than most other religious institutions. This indicates that, while the mosque was becoming relatively more prevalent than the permanent *hoseyniyeh*, the importance of these two religious and cultural institutions was still paramount. These figures also do not take into account temporary or informal religious sites, which have always constituted the vast majority of ritual sites. For example, according to statistics gathered in 1996, permanent *takyeh*s made up a mere 16 percent of the registered ritual institutions, while *hoseyniyeh*s of various sorts made up 84 percent of the total.[23] In 1996, approximately two-thirds of the *hoseyniyeh*s and permanent *takyeh*s in Iran were established as pious endowments (*vaqf*), which means that while they were less numerous than informal institutions, they were relatively more permanent. Yet this was lower than the average for all religious institutions, 95 percent of which were *vaqf* properties. However, this is partly explained by the fact that all mosques were considered *vaqf* properties. These figures still do not include the far more numerous informal ritual gatherings, which would not be included in such statistics and are nearly impossible to quantify or document accurately because they are generally unregistered, temporary, and informal.

Many factors have contributed to the different trends in Tehran versus the rest of Iran. For example, these figures include shrine cities such as Mashhad and Qom, which have always had a far higher concentration of religions buildings, institutions, and activities, as compared to the rest of the country. They also include areas that may be relatively less urbanized, such as Sistan, Mazandaran, or parts of Azerbaijan, which have relatively lower overall growth rates than the large metropolis of Tehran and have not witnessed the same degree of rapid change that took place in Tehran and other larger cities during the twentieth century. Some of these rural regions, such as parts of Azerbaijan and Mazandaran, may have relatively fewer large cities or have very high population densities. These figures also include other large cities that have had a relatively slower growth rate than Tehran. This is significant because one factor contributing to the relative decline in prevalence of the *hoseyniyeh* and permanent *takyeh* in Tehran has been the dramatic expansion of the city's population and the resulting informal networks and social institutions that emerged to meet the rapidly increasing needs of this metropolis.

The fact that Tehran has been the capital city for the past two centuries has also been a contributing factor. Elite patronage of religious institutions during the Qajar period is sharply contrasted with the relative lack of patronage by many of the new elites who emerged in Tehran during the Pahlavi era. These new elites, especially those closely associated with the state, were less enthusiastic patrons of large-scale rituals. Tehran is also unique in that it is the city where the government has historically had the greatest influence over these rituals because the state's authority was rather limited in many other provinces, especially during the early Pahlavi reign. Therefore, Reza Shah's ban on these rituals was most rigorously enforced in Tehran. Similarly, the postrevolutionary regime's ban on the controversial *qameh zani* (flagellation with a blade) ritual was most effectively enforced in Tehran.

The focus now turns to the rituals themselves. Throughout this period, community identities, professional or corporatist relationships, and social bonds were important in forming religious associations, such as *hey'ats*, which in turn were the primary organizers of ritual performances. The majority of ritual gatherings continued to be performed in homes, mosques, businesses, social and cultural institutions, and a variety of other temporary ritual sites. Rituals were usually organized by families, traditional guilds, professional associations, groups with ethnic or regional affiliations, and virtually any other social grouping one can imagine.

The religious associations known as *hey'ats* remained particularly strong throughout this period. These ritual performances were usually not explicitly political in that they were not organized by the state or by political parties. Nor were they intended to target specific revolutionary or antirevolutionary political issues such as imperialism, global revolution, or domestic political or economic problems. These rituals served a variety of personal and social functions simultaneously. One of the most important functions was soteriological. In other words, rituals served as expressions of piety as believers mourned the tragic events of Karbala, both to keep alive the memory of Hoseyn and the other martyrs and in the hopes to achieve salvation through devotion to the imams. They also could serve other more immediate personal purposes such as relieving stress, anxiety, frustration, or depression through public or physical mourning. For many participants and observers the grand spectacle of the ritual performances served even as a sort of amusement or entertainment. For some, such as girls and young women, it could even be a welcome excuse to spend time outside in the city streets with family or friends, unhindered by social conventions that encouraged women to stay in the home.

These rituals also served a variety of social functions. Most neighborhoods had a host of *hey'ats* that organized rituals. While many of these were associated with specific ritual sites or buildings like mosques, *hoseyniyeh*s, or *takyeh*s, the vast majority were less formal organizations centered on neighborhoods, corporatist associations, ethnic groups, guilds or professional associations, social networks, or families. The traditional professional guilds such as the goldsmiths guild or the clothiers guild continued to sponsor rituals. The emergence of new professional associations and groups continued as coworkers in all sorts of different professions such as electricians, engineers, cab drivers, truckers, and so on organized ritual events. Ethnic groups tended to congregate in religious centers and perform rituals together. Women also gathered in women's groups to perform female-only mourning rituals, such as *rowzeh khani*s or *sofreh*s, religious dinners dedicated to honoring a religious figure or held for some other pious purpose. Ritual participation also served as a vehicle for socializing youth and promoting social and cultural ideals. The majority of these rituals, however, were performed on a small scale and were organized by informal social networks centered around families, friends, and neighbors.

In most districts of Tehran there have always been *hoseyniyeh*s that cater to communities with regional affiliations. For example, there are *hoseyniyeh*s for immigrants from regions such as Sabzivar, Yazd, Zarabad, Shiraz, Zanjan, Isfahan, Bakhtiyari territories, and Zanjan, just to name a few. Some of them are from other regions of Iran, but others constitute foreign immigrants or ethnic minorities such as the Azerbaijani Turks, Kurds, and Arabs. There are also mosques associated with most of these groups, such as the Yazdi mosque in Qolhak or the Azerbaijani mosque located on Khayyam Street.[24] While these mosques and *hoseyniyeh*s constitute a small minority, they also indicate the degree to which these religious institutions continue to serve the function of reinforcing regional and ethnic identities.

It should be pointed out that these "permanent" religious institutions represent only a tiny fraction of the total religious associations or groups that have existed in Tehran. Most immigrant groups, often being recent arrivals with limited resources, have not been able to establish permanent associations. Instead, they have generally formed less permanent associations, such as *hey'at*s, which serve essentially the same purpose. These groups often perform minor variations on the same rituals, including distinctive displays of clothing, ritual devices, banners, and so on. For example, the Azerbaijani immigrants from Ardebil often use a brass-handled chain for striking their backs, and at least one Kashani *hey'at* observed for this study formed a procession of water bearers, which is a traditional ritual procession that is currently relatively less common in other regions. Arabs often use hexagonal drums, and their banners and funeral biers are usually distinctive. Some groups from the rural areas south of Isfahan often strike together two pieces of wood (shaped roughly like a sphere chopped into two pieces), producing a loud noise. Groups that speak other languages, such as Turks, Arabs, and Kurds, usually also hold at least part of their sermons and chants in their native languages. There is usually a great deal of pride and good-natured competition between different identity groups as they try to outdo one another in terms of their religious enthusiasm and ritual piety. Ritual participants often make the claim that the best rituals are performed in their hometown or among their kinsmen.

Below is a generalized description of selected aspects of typical ritual performances. Because of the diversity of regional practices, it would be impossible in the space allowed here to describe the rituals completely or to provide for all variant patterns one is likely to encounter. The selected aspects of the rituals described here were observed while I was conducting research during the springs and summers of the years 1993, 1997, and 2001 in Tehran, Ray, Qom, Isfahan, Shahreza, and Mashhad.[25]

Most neighborhood *hey'at*s began performing rituals on the first of *Moharram*, but the larger performances usually started after the fifth of *Moharram*. The neighborhood *hey'at* performed rituals primarily at night, and in some cases they lasted until the following morning. A typical routine began with people from the neighborhood gathering in the *hey'at* and chatting over tea as they waited for the program to begin. The environment was social and had both a somber, tragic atmosphere and a lighter, more festive mood. Eventually, the orator, or *rowzeh* preacher, sat behind the microphone and began the sermon. Lessons to be drawn from Karbala were woven into the narrative; in some cases, political ideals such as opposing the "imperialist West" or even voting in the upcoming presidential elections were also integrated into the central narrative.

Two main types of sermons or lectures were given. The mourning sermons were usually conducted by professional *rowzeh* preachers or by lower-ranking ulama. Often a lecture was given as well, sometimes by higher-ranking ulama and occasionally by other scholars or leaders. Once the sermon began, the tone changed quickly to one of tragic mourning as the listeners often cried and performed symbolic self-flagellation, in the form of chest beating. The terms "symbolic self-flagellation" and "symbolic chest beating" are used here to distinguish them from "ritual self-flagellation," which was performed elsewhere in the rituals.

At this point, however, there were still many people who simply sat and talked quietly in the corner, thus not fully participating in the mourning. Children were often running around as they anxiously waited for the more physical and dramatic phase in the ritual. Listening to the sermon led slowly to real self-mortification in the form of structured chest beating or the striking of chains against the back. Not everyone took part in this phase of the ritual, especially not women, but also others who simply chose to refrain from participating. Many others simply sat and mourned quietly.

At a certain point it was announced that the *dasteh*, or procession, would move into the street. In most cases, the *hey'at* had been invited to another neighborhood *hey'at*, but in some cases they simply traveled through a predetermined path, perhaps visiting a major shrine or mosque along the way, and returned to their *hey'at* location. The ritual processions comprised anywhere from several dozen to several hundred men and boys. Severalfold more men, women, and children followed behind, flanking both sides, and for some of the larger processions there were often numerous onlookers, not affiliated with the *hey'at*. The procession, or *dasteh*, itself usually consisted of two rows, with an individual leading the chants over a loudspeaker attached to an electric generator that was placed either on a wagon or a car. Drummers beating basic rhythms in unison accompanied the chant leader. In the front were held large and often heavy banners, such as the *alamat*, a symbolic military standard of Hoseyn. There was usually a cloth banner with the name of the *hey'at* sewn onto it and black flags with religious phrases related to the family of the Prophet written on them.

The social function of visiting other *hey'ats* was usually an extremely important aspect of these religious events. Once the procession arrived at the hosting *hey'at*, several things happened. First, there was a greeting given by the banner holders, who bowed to each other and spun around in circles, holding the heavy steel banners. These banners often weighed several hundred pounds, allowing the men to demonstrate their prowess and strength in front of their neighbors. A lamb was often ritually slaughtered as the hosts chanted rhythmically, "Welcome, welcome." Once inside the *hey'at*, the "indoor ritual" was performed in the same fashion as it was earlier in the visiting *hey'at*'s own *takyeh*, or ritual site, and tea or food was served. The men sat in the central space, while the women usually entered the house from a separate entrance. Women often accompanied the *dasteh* throughout the night, lending moral support (by shouting or bearing witness to the efforts of the men), as well as mourning (in the form of crying) and occasionally performing "symbolic beating" of the chest or head. Eventually the procession left and continued along a designated path. If it passed another *takyeh*, as was usually the case, the participants performed the same rituals at the door, but would not enter, or they entered and only took tea. Upon returning to their *hey'at*, the procession continued with the sermons and the self-flagellation rituals late into the night, sometimes continuing until morning.

In most major cities in Iran there is usually at least one central location, and typically many separate locations, at which the different *hey'ats* gather to participate in a massive ritual involving, in the case of Tehran, hundreds of *hey'ats* and tens of thousands of people.[26] This ritual generally takes place on the ninth and tenth days of *Moharram,* although it can also take place at other times such as the third and for-tieth days after Hoseyn's death. In Tehran during the 1990s, this ritual was performed in several locations, one of the most important of which was in front of the central bazaar on the commemoration of the *sevvom*, or the honoring of the anniversary of the third day after Hoseyn's death.

This event differed from the "neighborhood ritual" in that it was much larger and far more elaborate, it was localized but conducted outdoors, and it often included additional types of processions. This ritual consisted of a large number of the local processions participating together in a massive parade. In this capacity the central processions were the same as those in the neighborhood rituals, and the mourners behaved in a similar manner, except that they did not usually follow behind each procession. Some informants stated that to do so would have broken up the continuity of the chain of processions. Another important distinction between the mass ritual and the neighborhood ritual was that the state was able to influence the mass event much more easily, thereby enforcing whatever policies had been decreed regarding *Ashura* rituals. Many of the women interviewed, who had followed the procession in the neighborhood ritual, stated that they did not follow behind the processions in the mass ritual because the state had forbidden it.[27] This example was relatively unusual, in that the state was able to influence the pattern of women's participation in these rituals.

This large scale was particularly important in relation to the incorporation of women's roles in the ritual because women were much more likely to take part in the two types of processions that were uniquely female in their makeup and were part of the central procession. These components of the processions were observed more often in the larger gatherings than they were in the much smaller neighborhood performances. The first was called the procession of the *osara*, or prisoners, and the second was the *dasteh-e Bani Asad*, or the procession of the tribe of *Asad*. These two processions were actually part of a more elaborate performance of the Battle of Karbala that was referred to as *shabih khani*, or reenactment in full costume. Both men and women (and, of course, men wearing the costumes of the female characters) participated in this procession, which usually followed at the end of the long chain of processions.

There were components of the procession that were uniquely female in character. *Shabih khani* involved men, who, dressed in Arab military garb, usually on horseback, wearing full armor and carrying swords, represented the armies of Hoseyn and his enemies. They rode by in procession, followed by the victims of the battle, which included the dead and arrow-riddled bodies of Hoseyn and his infant son, Ali Asghar, as well as the prisoners (*osara*). The prisoners included his ill son, Zeyn al-Abedin, as well as women and children who were led either in chains by soldiers cracking whips behind them or on the backs of camels. This scene of the *Bani Asad* was a particularly tragic depiction of the aftermath of the martyrdom of Hoseyn and his followers and was named after the Arab tribe that is supposed to have arrived at the scene to bury the mutilated corpses that were left on the battlefield. The women carried water, shovels, and corpses. Because the prisoners were mainly women and children, the costumed characters were sometimes also women, although throughout the centuries this procession was most often made up of men dressed up as women (men who frequently did not bother to shave their beards and mustaches).

In front of the Tehran bazaar in 1997, women carried banners with statements such as "Fatemeh Zahra, who, if she had been a man [she] would have been a prophet; therefore, sisters we should follow her example," or "Peace be upon you, O, daughter of the Prophet of Allah [Mohammad]."[28] At times, they even carried the procession's banners or military standards that were sometimes placed on the tops of the funeral bier (called a *nakhl*) in which the bodies of Hoseyn and his son were supposedly carried. This was particularly significant because these banners were the symbolic military standards of the procession and under normal circumstances would have been quite off limits to women. Furthermore, the *alamat*s used in the procession were usually extremely heavy and were carried by the largest and strongest men in each *hey'at*. Therefore, it is significant that a smaller *alamat* was positioned on the funeral bier for the women to carry.

This large-scale ritual demonstrates diverse ways in which women could participate in the central procession. However, their roles were still heavily gendered within this ritual as well. While women were not often as heavily involved in the central procession, when they were it tended to be in association with specific activities. These activities roughly coincided with the activities outlined for women in the historical narratives presented in the accounts of Karbala. They participated in the role of the humiliated captives. In some cases, women played the role of captive, while in other cases men played this role, dressed up as women.[29] In either circumstance, female characters were present, played by either men or women. In addition, women were involved in carrying the dead bodies of martyrs, in particular the dead body of Hoseyn and his infant son. Women were also involved in activities associated with being the spokespersons for the cause. For example, women could sometimes be seen holding banners with slogans or shouting chants.

In conclusion, reviewing selected aspects of Shi'i symbols and rituals during the years following the Islamic Revolution of 1978–79 reveals several general trends. The new Islamic regime was quite effective in using the revolutionary symbolism of Karbala to articulate the state's ideology. It was not a forgone conclusion that the revolutionary model, which proved to be so effective during the revolution itself, would continue to be effective in the hands of a new regime. This success is one of the primary reasons an opposition discourse centered on *Ashura* symbols and rituals did not emerge.

The state was also able to influence some aspects of ritual performances by sponsoring rituals and by exerting control over other rituals. However, the dominant trends in religious culture, namely, the popular rituals themselves, were largely outside the direct control of the state. For example, the regime banned the controversial ritual *qameh zani,* in which mourners strike their heads with swords, producing blood and injuries. Ayatollah Khamenei, the successor to Ayatollah Khomeini as spiritual leader of the Islamic Republic of Iran, in a speech to an audience of religious scholars said that "this practice [*qameh zani*] is wrong. . . . This is ignorance. These things are contrary to religion."[30] However, in 1997 many groups were still performing this ritual in private. This should not be understood as an act of political protest. Rather, it should be viewed as just another case where people's actions take place outside the realm of the state's control. Therefore, while the ritual participants may consciously be flaunting state-imposed restrictions, they are not necessarily challenging the state's legitimacy or broader authority.

Ashura rituals continued to evolve independently of the state in accordance with broader societal and cultural trends, such as the declining role of the permanent *takyeh* and the continued importance of social bonds, ethnic and family ties, and corporatist associations in governing patterns of ritual participation. Many of the trends that began during the Pahlavi period continued after the revolution, because many of the demographic and social changes underway in society were not fundamentally altered by the shift in government ideology. These patterns of change and continuity become particularly interesting when one looks at them over the course of the past century and a half.

9

Conclusion

Karbala symbols and rituals have been influenced in significant ways by the policies and agendas of the various regimes ruling Iran. However, while the state has been able to influence these symbols and rituals, it has not often been able to control them. The state's ability to make use of Karbala symbols and rituals has been an important factor in the state's ability to maintain its legitimacy and at least some degree of integration with the broader society. The state's failure to incorporate these symbols and rituals adequately into its program and ideology, particularly in the later decades of Pahlavi rule, contributed in part to the state's crisis of legitimacy.

During the nineteenth and twentieth centuries, Shi'i symbols and rituals were used by the state to bolster its legitimacy in Iran. This use can clearly be seen in the policies of three radically different regimes: the Qajars (1796–1925), the Pahlavis (1925–1979), and the Islamic Republic (1979–present). During this period of rapid change, government attitudes and policies regarding Shi'i (*Moharram*) rituals underwent important changes with each successive government. Although they used them in different ways, the Qajars and the leaders of the Islamic Republic relied heavily on Shi'i symbols and rituals. The main difference between these two regimes was the fact that the Islamic Republic was essentially a modern nation-state. The Pahlavis, by contrast, worked diligently to weaken the political influence of these religious traditions.

The Qajars reinforced their political legitimacy by enthusiastically supporting Shi'i rituals. They sponsored *Ashura* rituals, called *rowzeh khanis*, or *majales*, in their palaces and built large amphitheaters, or *takyehs*, in which *Moharram* rituals such as *ta'ziyeh* were regularly performed. The Qajars positioned themselves at the top of a hierarchy of patronage that descended to the lowest levels of society. The social hierarchy, and, most important, the paramount position of the Qajars, was reinforced with these rituals in several ways. For example, participants were seated according to status. In addition, servants of the shah sometimes led processions, and the shah's troops marched in these rituals. Ritual participants made frequent references to the generosity of the royal patrons, and prayers were regularly offered for the shah. Provincial governors, military generals, and other government officials emulated this pattern of patronage.

On occasion, bonds of loyalty between the Qajar shah and his subjects were strengthened by temporarily reversing the patterns of social hierarchy. For example, during *Moharram* (the primary month of ritual performances), descendents of the Prophet (*sayyed*s), who were sometimes very poor or indigent, were usually treated as virtual royalty. The elite associated with the state (although not the shah himself) made public displays of humility by dressing in the clothes of a commoner or even in rags. At such times, they often appeared without headdress, even though this violated standards of behavior for people of high status. The children of upper-class families further deviated from social norms by serving food or drinks to the audience, the *sayyed*s, and the poor. They also joined children of lower-class families in performing as characters in the ritual reenactments.

Patterns of patronage could also be reversed as the shah interrupted the ritual performance to make a public show of receiving donations for the ritual from other members of society, such as merchants, guild leaders, and landowners. This act reinforced the status of elite members of society. All the aforementioned expositions fortified social and political bonds between the ruler and the ruled in Qajar society. For the Qajar rulers and their subjects, *Moharram* symbols and rituals provided a common vocabulary that rendered some degree of mediation or integration between the state and society. Political issues of the day were routinely debated in sermons given at these ritual events. These rituals, therefore, served both to bolster the legitimacy and policies of the state and as a vehicle for expressing other views that were sometimes critical of the state or other elites. Hence, both supporters and critics of state policies took part in these debates.

Contrary to the Qajars, the Pahlavis did not utilize *Moharram* symbols and rituals as one of the principal means for reinforcing their political legitimacy. Reza Shah was quite hostile to most of these rituals, outlawing many of them. His son Mohammad Reza Shah tacitly accepted only the more politically moderate rituals. The negative disposition of the Pahlavis toward *Ashura* rituals was motivated by several factors. Many Iranians were concerned that *Moharram* rituals could undermine Iran's international image as a modern and civilized nation. Modernizing elites in Iran increasingly rejected these rituals as barbaric and backward components of Iran's culture. Instead, the new elites stressed aspects of Iran's heritage that were more in line with Western tastes and sentiments, such as Iran's imperial heritage and its historical contributions to science, philosophy, technology, literature, and the arts. The new elites often stressed the point that Iranians were members of the Aryan race, which fit nicely into race theories that were still prevalent in some European circles.

The Pahlavis were also concerned that *Moharram* rituals had the potential to challenge the nationalist ideology and modernization program promoted by the state. The Pahlavi modernization program, which was largely derived from Western models, included industrialization, urbanization, nationalism, secularism, and a strong monarchy. Pahlavi leaders placed primary stress upon their legitimacy as Iranian monarchs and promoted a secular Iranian national identity that usually excluded any substantial Islamic referents. There was little room for Shi'i symbols and rituals within this program. Many of the ideas promoted by the Pahlavis were in line with the beliefs espoused by secular nationalists, with the notable exception of anti-imperialism, democracy, constitutionalism, and various Marxist concepts. The common symbolic vocabulary of *Ashura* maintained its salience among the majority of Iranians but was rejected by the state and secular nationalist elites. Subsequently, a discord was created between the state and secular nationalists, on the one hand, and much of Iranian society, on the other hand.

Following the Khomeini-led revolution of 1978–79, *Moharram* symbols and rituals were once again used as one of the primary means for promoting the legitimacy and revolutionary program of the new state. Since its inception, the government of the Islamic Republic has increasingly promoted an Iranian national identity that included rejecting direct foreign political and economic influence, resisting international imperialism led by the United States and the Soviet Union, and curtailing Western "cultural imperialism." This identity also established Islamic ideals as the norm of Iranian society. *Ashura* rituals have proven to be effective in mobilizing the masses. The concepts of jihad and martyrdom were employed quite effectively to motivate a sense of moral courage among the Iranian troops fighting in the war with Iraq. During the war, almost every city in Iran built special cemeteries for its fallen martyrs. Like the Qajar era, the postrevolutionary era was characterized by extensive use of *Moharram* symbols and rituals as one of the principal vehicles for expressing and promoting bonds between the state and the populace. However, this period was fundamentally different from the Qajar era. The Qajars were attempting to maintain and preserve a social ideal that endorsed the shahs as rulers and criticized Sunnis, like the Ottomans, as hypocrites. The government of the Islamic Republic used *Ashura* symbols and rituals to reject some patterns of social and economic change brought on by rapid modernization, while at the same time promoting other modernist transformations. Unlike the Qajars, the postrevolutionary regime was an Islamic variant of the modern nation-state. In this capacity, it advocated a substantially new social and political vision of Iran's place in the postcolonial era.

In comparing the three successive regimes that ruled Iran in the nineteenth and twentieth centuries, it is clear that the patterns of ritual patronage and manipulation of Shi'i symbols have changed dramatically. During the Qajar period these trends provided a compendium of standards that served to maintain social and political bonds between the state and society, thereby creating a measure of mediation and integration between them. This connection was severed during the Pahlavi period as the nationalist discourse developed a new set of symbols and referents aimed at transforming Iranian society along Western, secular, and nationalistic lines. This dominant state-led secular discourse did not substantially change during the remainder of the Pahlavi era, including the period between Reza Shah's forced abdication in 1941 and the 1953 coup that replaced the liberal nationalist government of Mosaddeq with that of the returning shah, Mohammad Reza. Preexisting economic and social classes were transformed and new ones emerged.

Ashura symbols and rituals were central to the religious oppositional discourse that developed and gained greater influence during the reign of Mohammad Reza Shah (especially in the 1960s and 1970s). Leaders from a variety of ideological orientations, such as liberals, leftists, conservatives, reactionaries, and revolutionaries, all used *Moharram* symbols and rituals to promote their social and political ideals. *Ashura* rituals were among the most popular events in Iranian society and, therefore, served as an ideal vehicle for reaching the masses of Iranians. This pragmatism does not necessarily imply that they did not sincerely believe in the symbols of Karbala. The appeals to the symbols of Karbala allowed such leaders as ʿAli Shariʿati, Morteza Motahhari, Ahmad Rezaʾi, and Ayatollah Khomeini to reach a very broad audience and to popularize their ideas on a mass scale. Speeches given at *Moharram* rituals were further publicized through the circulation of recordings and transcriptions.

The Karbala narrative was reinterpreted in the 1960s and 1970s to stress active political opposition to the shah. The process of reinterpretation rejected the Pahlavi regime, political and economic dependence on the West, and social ideals imported from the West. The Karbala narrative proved to be very adaptable to a changing political environment, but this flexibility had limits as well. The more successful narratives restricted their reinterpretations to selected key symbols, leaving the core-narrative essentially intact, while inserting important elements into the story. They also changed the definition of the "self" and the "other." They redefined the "self" to include all victims of imperialism (Shiʿis, Sunnis, and even non-Muslims). They likewise redefined the "other" so that instead of referring exclusively to the Sunnis, it referred primarily to Western imperialists, corrupt rulers, and the shah. The overall effect was to place a new stress upon the idea of active rebellion against the shah and the imperialist powers.

Beginning with the reign of Mohammad Reza Shah, Karbala symbols also increasingly became a means for debating issues of gender within newly emerging discourses on gender in Iranian society. The religious opposition to the shah, and later on the Islamic Republic, used Zeynab and Fatemeh as role models to challenge the Western-oriented models of womanhood promoted by the Pahlavi regime. The liberated Western woman was replaced by the pious and revolutionary personalities of Zeynab and Fatemeh. The symbols stressed differences between males and females, the authority of men over women, the subordination of gender issues to national concerns, the loyalty of women to the greater national good, and the restriction of female gender roles to those of nurturing and supporting men and children. *Ashura* rituals served as a means for promoting and enforcing gender-coded space and activities. Rituals became the sites of contention regarding the gender ideals promoted by the state and by members of Iranian society as a whole.

Karbala symbols and rituals have been one of the primary means for expressing social and political ideals on a broad societal level. In some cases this took the form of direct opposition to the state. In other cases it served as a means for maintaining social bonds, ideals, and identities independently of the agendas and policies of the state. Patterns of social change have been influenced by economic forces that transformed both preexisting and newly emerging political relationships, as well as social institutions, groupings, and identities. Discourses on contemporary social and political crises have also found expression in Karbala symbols and rituals. Changes in interpretations and expressions of these symbols and rituals demonstrate how Iranian society changed during the nineteenth and twentieth centuries both in response to and independently of state-led modernization and social transformation programs. During the Qajar period, for example, *Moharram* rituals served as one of the primary means for expressing and reinforcing social relationships, including ethnic, occupational, regional, family, and tribal bonds. This continued into the twentieth century, as the Pahlavi modernization program and modern economic forces transformed Iranian society. Preexisting economic and social classes were transformed and new ones emerged.

During the nineteenth and twentieth centuries, *Ashura* rituals evolved somewhat independently of, or in some cases in opposition to, the policies of the successive regimes. *Moharram* rituals served as one of the primary means for expressing and reinforcing a variety of identities, social bonds, and social ideals. During the Qajar period, for example, *Ashura* rituals served as one of the primary means for expressing and reinforcing social relationships including ethnic, occupational, regional, family, and tribal bonds. This continued throughout the twentieth century, as the Pahlavi modernization program and modern economic forces transformed Iranian society. *Moharram* rituals served as one of the primary expressions of alternative identities based on ethnicity, regional affiliations, ideological orientation, cohort, guild, occupation, family ties, and neighborhood. During the rule of the Pahlavis and the Islamic Republic, as society itself transformed, these identities continued to survive, evolving in new directions and expanding to include new identities.

Families and social networks were promoted through participation in rituals, as the host provided a venue for socializing by having a ritual performance at his or her home. For example, women gathered in groups with their close friends to socialize and perform pious acts. Extended family worked together to carry off large religious events. Rituals have always been an important vehicle for socializing, meeting new people, and promoting one's image in front of friends and family. Business relationships could also be strengthened through this sort of social interaction. In particular, the cohesion of professional guilds, unions, and associations was preserved through sponsorship of mass events for its members. As new professions emerged in the twentieth century, the old patterns of using religious culture to promote unity and cohesion were often employed. Patron-client relationship was reinforced as elites and non-elites cooperated in organizing these group events, each offering his or her time, money, or home.

Various sorts of identities were also preserved through these ritual events. Neighborhoods were the most common unit of organization for rituals, but other identities like ethnicity, tribe, and regional affiliations were also extremely common. There has always been a pronounced tendency for such groups as Arabs, Turks, and Kurds to form their own *hey'at*s, *hoseyniyeh*s, or *takyeh*s. These rituals were usually performed at least partly in their native languages. They took pride in their regional variations in ritual practices and showed a healthy sense of inward-looking camaraderie and outward-looking competition with other ethnic groups. Immigrants from other regions followed similar patterns. Tehrani residents, who were originally from places such as Qom, Isfahan, Shirazi, or Hamadan, tended to form religious associations based on regional affiliations. Their ties could sometimes last for generations after they moved to a new city. Hence, it can be said that the rituals of Karbala have served as a "glue" of sorts helping to hold various types of social, familial, professional, corporatist, or identity groups together.

The rituals themselves also changed over time. The *ta'ziyeh* became less extravagant and more associated with rural areas and traditional sectors in the society. With increased transportation opportunities, it also became easier for people to travel either to their hometowns or to shrine cities as part of their religious ritual performances. Other arts, like the popular story-telling tradition of *pardeh khani,* were slowly supplanted by newer forms of religious expression. New entertainment media, along with increased education, and changing aesthetics also contributed to these transformations. For example, *rowzeh* sermons were increasingly available on audiotapes that could easily be purchased. Films, plays, television programs, and other media productions based on Karbala themes became commonplace. Eventually, computer programs and Internet sites served as vehicles for pious expression. The large permanent *takyeh* became less central to religious rituals, especially in large cities like Tehran. *Hey'ats* and informal ritual gatherings increased in relative importance. All these patterns of change varied from region to region and across class lines.

The symbols and rituals of Karbala illustrate how, over the course of the nineteenth and twentieth centuries, Iranian society changed in response to, and independently of, the state's modernization program. International influences changed Iran's relationship to foreign states and transformed social, economic, and political relationships within Iran. As the state adopted a social and political model derived primarily from Western societies, Iranian society adapted in very different ways. Nationalist identities failed to supplant alternative social identities, Western cultural values were not adopted wholesale, and the state was unable to control or to change fundamentally popular understandings and expressions of Karbala. Karbala could have been used by the Pahlavis to promote stronger ties between the state and Iranian society, as the Qajars and the government of the Islamic Republic did. Instead, *Ashura* rituals increasingly became vehicles for opposition to the state's program. By the 1970s, the failure of the Pahlavis and the secular nationalists to accommodate successfully the Karbala Paradigm into their rhetoric and beliefs contributed to a crisis of legitimacy for both the state and the nationalist project in Iran. Society had evolved independently of the state, while the state continued in its efforts to transform Iranian society along Western lines. Karbala proved to be the primary site of political discourse during much of the Pahlavi period. The diverse manifestations of Karbala symbols and rituals, which varied across time, region, and class groupings, illustrate the limits of the state's role in the process of social and cultural transformation underway in modern Iran. Stated differently, these trends illustrate the relative dynamism, resilience, flexibility, and continuity one encounters when looking at Iranian religious culture during the modern period.

Notes

Preface

1. The term Karbala Paradigm is used in accordance with Michael Fischer's usage in *Iran: From Religious Dispute to Revolution* (Cambridge, Mass.: Harvard University Press, 1980).

1. A Brief Historical Background of Shiʿism and Moharram

1. This hadith is reported by the famous Sunni traditionalist Ahmad Ibn Hanbal in his collection *Musnad*. This translation is provided by Moojan Momen, *An Introduction to Shiʿi Islam* (New Haven, Conn.: Yale University Press, 1985), 14.

2. Ibid., 17.

3. The Karbala narrative is an excellent example of what Victor Turner and Stephen Pepper call a "root metaphor" and Max Black calls a "conceptual archetype." (For a discussion of "Root Metaphor," see Stephen Pepper, *World Hypotheses* [Berkeley and Los Angeles: University of California Press, 1942], and Victor Turner, *Dramas, Fields, and Metaphors* [Ithaca, N.Y.: Cornell University Press, 1974]. For a discussion of Max Black's conceptualization of "conceptual archetypes" see Black, *Models and Metaphors: Studies in Language and Philosophy* [Ithaca, N.Y.: Cornell University Press, 1962]). According to these approaches, symbolic interpretation is understood as a process of giving meaning to an unknown subject by making reference, either consciously or unconsciously, to a known and familiar conceptual reference point. This reference point can be a historic event, real or imagined, that has a well-developed and articulated meaning in a given society. Therefore, the symbols can provide a set of categories for understanding other aspects of experience. This process of analogy allows meaning to be derived concerning a contemporary reality, which may otherwise cause confusion or even anxiety.

4. Ibn al-Kathir, *al-Bidaya wa al-nihaya* (Cairo: Matbaʿah al-Saʿada, AH 1358). This translation is from Michel M. Mazzaoui, "Shiʿism and Ashura in South Lebanon," in *Taʿziyeh: Ritual and Drama in Iran*, ed. Peter J. Chelkowski (New York: New York University Press, 1979), 231.

5. From Abu Bakr al-Khwarazmi's *Maqtal al-Hoseyn*. This translation

is from Mayel Baktash, "Ta'ziyeh and Its Philosophy," in Chelkowski, ed., *Ta'ziyeh*, 97.

6. For detailed analysis of the core basic beliefs associated with the Karbala symbolism, as well as the historical development of these beliefs and practices, see the following two books: Mahmoud Ayoub, *Redemptive Suffering in Islam: A Study of the Devotional Aspects of 'Ashura' in Twelver Shi'ism* (New York: Mouton Publishers, 1978); and Momen, *Introduction to Shi'i Islam.*

7. For a thorough treatment of the emergence and historical development of *ta'ziyeh* rituals from the Safavid through the Qajar periods, see Enayatollah Shahidi and Ali Bolukbashi, *Pazhuheshi dar ta'ziyeh va ta'ziyeh khani az aghaz ta payan-e dowreh-e Qajar dar Tehran* (Tehran: Daftar-e Pazhuheshha-e Farhangi, Komisiyon-e Melli-e Yunesko dar Iran, 2001).

8. *Rowzeh* preachers were usually men, although female orators sometimes gave the sermon in private *rowzeh khani*s attended exclusively by women.

9. Jean Calmard, "Le Patronage des Ta'ziyeh: Elements pour une Etude Globale," in Chelkowski, ed., *Ta'ziyeh*, 122. For a detailed study of Shi'i rituals and state patronage leading up to the Safavid period, see the unpublished dissertation by Jean Calmard, "Le culte de l'Imam Husayn. Etudes sur la commémoration du Drame de Karbala dans l'Iran pré-safavide" (dissertation, University of Paris III, 1975).

10. For detailed discussions of the *ta'ziyeh* traditions in Iran, please refer to the following books: Chelkowski, ed., *Ta'ziyeh*; Sadeq Homayuni, *Ta'ziyeh dar Iran* (Shirazi, Iran: Entesharat-e Navid, 1989); Shahidi, and Bolukbashi, *Pazhuheshi dar ta'ziyeh va ta'ziyeh khani az aghaz ta payan-e dowreh-e Qajar dar Tehran;* Samuel Peterson, ed., *Ta'ziyeh: Ritual and Popular Beliefs in Iran* (Hartford, Conn.: Trinity College, 1988); Jaber Anasori, ed., *Shabih khani, kohan olgu-e nemayeshha-e Irani* (Tehran: Chapkhaneh-e Ramin, 1992); Mohammad Ebrahim Ayati, *Barresi-e tarikh-e Ashura,* 9th ed. (Tehran: Nashr-e Sadduq, 1996); and Laleh Taqiyan, *Ta'ziyeh va te'atr dar Iran* (Tehran: Nashr-e Markaz, 1995).

11. For Shi'i rituals outside Iran, please refer to the following studies: Vernon James Schubel, *Religious Performance in Contemporary Islam: Shi'i Devotional Rituals in South Asia* (Columbia: University of South Carolina Press, 1993); Augustus Richard Norton, *Shi'ism and the Ashura Ritual in Lebanon* (New York: Al-Saqi, 2003); Juan R. I. Cole, *The Roots of North Indian Shi'ism in Iran and Iraq: Religion and State in Awadh, 1722–1859* (Berkeley and Los Angeles: University of California Press, 1988); Yitzhak Nakash, *The Shi'is of Iraq* (Princeton, N.J.: Princeton University Press, 1994); David Pinault, *The Horse of Karbala: Muslim Devotional Life in India* (New York: Palgrave, 2001); David Pinault, *The Shi'ites, Ritual, and Popular Piety in a Muslim Community* (New York: St. Martin's Press, 1992); Frederic Maatouk, *La representation de la mort de l'imam Hussein a Nabatieh* (Beirut: Université libanaise, Institut des sciences sociales, Centre de recherches, 1974); and

Waddah Shararah, *Transformations d'une manifestation religieuse dans un village du Liban-Sud (Asura)* (Beirut: al-Jami'ah al-Lubnaniyyah, Ma'had al-'Ulum al-Ijtima'iyah, 1968).

2. The Qajar Elites and Religious Patronage (1796–1925)

1. Portions of the above analysis of the Qajar period are based on a conference paper titled "Muharram Rituals, Social Identities, and Political Relationships under Qajar Rule: 1850s–1930s," which was presented in September 2000 at a conference sponsored by the University of Bristol and the British Institute of Persian Studies, in Bristol, England. The conference was titled "Religion and Society in Qajar Iran." A version of that conference paper is currently scheduled to be published, along with the other conference papers, in a forthcoming book edited by Robert Gleave.

2. Said Amir Arjomand, *The Shadow of God and the Hidden Imam* (Chicago: University of Chicago Press, 1984), 223.

3. Mayel Baktash, "Ta'ziyeh and Its Philosophy," in *Ta'ziyeh: Ritual and Drama in Iran*, ed. Peter J. Chelkowski (New York: New York University Press, 1979), 107–9.

4. Aniseh Sheykh Reza'i and Shahla Azari, eds., *Gozareshha-e nazmiyeh-e mahallat-e Tehran* (n.p.: Entesharat-e Sazman-e Asnad-e Melli-e Iran, 1998), 282.

5. Sayyed Hoseyn Mo'tamedi Kashani, *Azadari-e sunnati-e shi'ayan dar boyut-e olama va howzehha-e elmiyyeh va keshvarha-e jahan*, 2 vols. (Qom, Iran: Chapkhaneh-e E'temad, 2000), 2:250.

6. Ibid., 2:252–55.

7. Ibid., 2:256.

8. Ibid., 2:258–94.

9. Abdollah Mostowfi, *The Administrative and Social History of the Qajar Period*, trans. Nayer Mostofi Glenn (Costa Mesa, Calif.: Mazda Publishers, 1997), 1:158.

10. Sven Hedin, *Overland to India* (London: Macmillan and Co., 1910), 2:48.

11. Charles James Wills, *In the Land of the Lion and Sun, or Modern Persia* (London: Macmillan and Co., 1883), 283.

12. See Eugène Abin, *La Perse d'aujourd'hui—eran. Mésopotamie—avec une carte en couleur hors texte* (Paris: A. Colin, 1908).

13. Enayatollah Shahidi and Ali Bolukbashi, *Pazhuheshi dar ta'ziyeh va ta'ziyeh khani az aghaz ta payan-e dowreh-e Qajar dar Tehran* (Tehran: Daftar-e Pazhuheshha-e Farhangi, Komisiyon-e Melli-e Yunesko dar Iran, 2001), 112.

14. Farrokh Ghaffary, "Theatrical Buildings and Performances in Tehran," included in Nikki R. Keddie, *Qajar Iran and the Rise of Reza Khan, 1796–1925* (Costa Mesa, Calif.: Mazda Publishers, 1999), 97.

15. Wills, *Land of the Lion and Sun*, 282.

16. Eustache De Lorey and Douglas Sladen, *Queer Things about Persia* (London: Evelein Nash, 1907), 286–87.

17. Augustus H. Mounsey, *A Journey through the Caucasus and the Interior of Persia* (London: Smith, Elder, and Co., 1872).

18. Lady Sheil, *Glimpses of Life and Manners in Persia* (London: John Murray, 1856), 127–28.

19. Ibid., 127.

20. For a full account, see chap. 13 of Samuel G. W. Benjamin, *Persia and the Persians* (Boston: Ticknor and Company, 1887).

21. Jean Calmard, "Muharram Ceremonies and Diplomacy (A Preliminary Study)," in *Qajar Iran: Political, Social, and Cultural Change*, ed. Edmund Bosworth and Carole Hillenbrand (Edinburgh: Edinburgh University Press, 1983).

22. Nikki R. Keddie, *Roots of Revolution* (New Haven, Conn.: Yale University Press, 1981), 58–59.

23. Ahmad Kasravi, *Shi'ehgari* (Tehran: Chapkhaneh-e Peyman, 1943). Translated in Ahmad Kasravi, *On Islam and Shi'ism*, trans. M. R. Ghanoonparvar (Costa Mesa, Calif.: Mazda Publishers, 1990), 178.

24. Ivar Lassy, "The Muharram Mysteries among the Azerbeijan Turks of Caucasia: An Academical Dissertation" (dissertation, Helsingfors University, 1916), 60.

25. Reza'i and Azari, eds., *Gozareshha*, 213.

26. Dorothy De Warzee, *Peeps into Persia* (London: Hurst and Blackett Ltd., 1913), 82.

27. See Heinrich Karl Brugsch, *Reise der K. preussischen Gesandtschaft nach Persien 1860 und 1861 (Safarnameh-e ilchi-e Prus dar Iran: safari beh darbar-e soltan sahebqeran 1859–1861)*, trans. Mohandes Kordbcheh (Tehran: Entesharat-e Ettela'at, 1988), 227

28. Reza'i and Azari, eds., *Gozareshha*, 734.

29. Sven Hedin reports that "even in such an insignificant place as Chahardeh there is a tekkieh." Hedin, *Overland to India*, 2:41.

30. Wills, *Land of the Lion and Sun*, 279.

31. Ibid., 280.

32. De Lorey and Sladen, *Queer Things about Persia*, 282.

33. Mostowfi, *Administrative and Social History*, 175–76.

34. Samuel K. Nweeya, *Persia: The Land of the Magi, or Home of the Wise Men* (Philadelphia: Press of the John C. Winston Co., 1910), 105.

35. Ella Sykes, *Persia and Its People* (London: Methuenn and Co., Ltd., 1910), 153.

3. Qajar Society and Religious Culture

1. This is based on the figures registered in the official census of Tehran conducted by city officials in 1869; the survey included those living out-

side the city walls, but no military personnel. See Sirus Sa'dvandiyan and Mansureh Ettehadiyeh, eds., *Amar-e Dar al-Khalafeh-e Tehran: asnadi az tarikh-e ejtema'i-e Tehran dar asr-e Qajar* (Tehran: Nashr-e Tarikh-e Iran, 1989), 345. This population figure is used as an average for the last half of the nineteenth century, despite the fact that Tehran was growing very rapidly throughout this period. It has been estimated that Tehran's population grew from as low as 60,000 in the early nineteenth century to as high as 250,000 at the beginning of the twentieth century. See H. Bahrambeygui, *Tehran: An Urban Analysis* (Tehran: Sahab Books Institute, 1977), 19 and 23.

2. See Sa'dvandiyan and Ettehadiyeh, eds., *Amar-e Dar al-Khalafeh.*

3. Aniseh Sheykh Reza'i and Shahla Azari, ed., *Gozareshha-e nazmiyeh-e mahallat-e Tehran* (n.p.: Entesharat-e Sazman-e Asnad-e Melli-e Iran, 1998). See any of the nights on 197–235.

4. Abdollah Mostowfi, *The Administrative and Social History of the Qajar Period,* trans. Nayer Mostofi Glenn (Costa Mesa, Calif.: Mazda Publishers, 1997), 1:158.

5. The data on *takyeh*s are from 1852, while the population figures are from the 1869 census. See Sa'dvandiyan and Ettehadiyeh, eds., *Amar-e Dar al-Khalafeh.*

6. Mostowfi, *Administrative and Social History,* 170.

7. For a general account of processions, see Samuel K. Nweeya, *Persia: The Land of the Magi, or Home of the Wise Men* (Philadelphia: Press of the John C. Winston Co., 1910), 103–7. Also see Reza'i and Azari, eds., *Gozareshha,* 686–87.

8. Mostowfi, *Administrative and Social History,* 159–60.

9. Ella Sykes, *Persia and Its People* (London: Methuen and Co., Ltd., 1910), 150. See also Reza'i and Azari, eds., *Gozareshha,* 661.

10. Reza'i and Azari, eds., *Gozareshha,* 684.

11. Ibid., 301.

12. Sykes, *Persia and Its People,* 150.

13. For a few examples, see Reza'i and Azari, eds., *Gozareshha,* 197–235.

14. Nweeya, *Land of the Magi,* 105–6.

15. Lady Sheil, *Glimpses of Life and Manners in Persia* (London: John Murray, 1856), 129. See also Sven Hedin, *Overland to India* (London: Macmillan and Co., 1910), 2:42–43 for reports of a similar scene.

16. Charles James Wills, *In the Land of the Lion and Sun, or Modern Persia* (London: Macmillan and Co., 1883), 282.

17. Eustache De Lorey and Douglas Sladen, *Queer Things about Persia* (London: Evelein Nash, 1907), 290.

18. Hedin, *Overland to India,* 2:51.

19. Ibid., 43 and 48.

20. Dorothy De Warzee, *Peeps into Persia* (London: Hurst and Blackett Ltd., 1913), 79; and H. G. Winter, *Persian Miniature* (Garden City, N.J.: Doubleday Page and Co., 1917), 131, 137, and 140.

21. Reza'i and Azari, eds., *Gozareshha*, 731.

22. Wills, *Land of the Lion and Sun*, 281.

23. Enayatollah Shahidi and Ali Bolukbashi, *Pazhuheshi dar ta'ziyeh va ta'ziyeh khani az aghaz ta payan-e dowreh-e Qajar dar Tehran* (Tehran: Daftar-e Pazhuheshha-e Farhangi, Komisiyon-e Melli-e Yunesko dar Iran, 2001), 110, 204.

24. Reza'i and Azari, eds., *Gozareshha*, 213 and 248, respectively.

25. Shahidi and Bolukbashi, *Pazhuheshi dar ta'ziyeh va ta'ziyeh khani az aghaz ta payan-e dowreh-e Qajar dar Tehran*, 110.

26. Naser Najmi, *Tehran-e ahd-e Naseri*, 2d ed. (Tehran: Entesharat-e Attar, 1988), 265.

27. Mostowfi, *Administrative and Social History*, 169–70.

28. Molla Aqa Khansari, *Kolsum naneh* (Tehran: Entesharat-e Mor-varid, n.d.), 125–26.

29. Sheil, *Glimpses of Life*, 127–28; and Reza'i and Azari, eds., *Gozareshha*, 201.

30. Reza'i and Azari, eds., *Gozareshha*, 154, 164, 178, 184, 664, and 676.

31. Ibid., 178.

32. Ibid., 184.

33. Ibid., 208.

34. Ibid., 735.

35. Ibid., 731.

36. Ibid., 282.

37. Ibid., 278–79. References to the West or to Westerners were not uncommon. For example, Bismarck is discussed in another sermon (see 723).

38. Ibid., 232.

39. Ibid., 724.

40. Ibid., 733.

41. Ibid., 214–15.

42. Ibid., 734.

43. Ibid., 724.

44. Ibid., 740.

45. Ibid., 726.

46. Ibid., 728.

4. The Pahlavi Regime and the Emergence of Secular Modernism (1925–1979)

1. Mohammad Taqi (Malek al-Sho'ara) Bahar, *Tarikh-e mokhtasar-e ahzab-e siyasi-e Iran* (Tehran: Chapkhaneh-e Sepehr, 1943), 1:183–84.

2. Ja'far Shahri, *Tehran-e qadim* (Tehran: Entesharat-e Mo'in, 1990), 387. While he does not give a precise date for this account, he states that it is based on his personal observation while as a child during the final decades of Qajar rule.

3. Shahrough Akhavi, "State Formation and Consolidation in Twentieth-Century Iran: The Reza Shah Period and the Islamic Republic," in *The State, Religion, and Ethnic Politics: Afghanistan, Iran, and Pakistan,* ed. Ali Banuazizi and Myron Weiner (Syracuse, N.Y.: Syracuse University Press, 1986), 29.

4. Rosalie Slaughter Morton, *A Doctor's Holiday in Iran* (New York: Funk and Wagnalls Co., 1940), 196.

5. Enayatollah Shahidi and Ali Bolukbashi, *Pazhuheshi dar ta'ziyeh va ta'ziyeh khani az aghaz ta payan-e dowreh-e Qajar dar Tehran* (Tehran: Daftar-e Pazhuheshha-e Farhangi, Komisiyon-e Melli-e Yunesko dar Iran, 2001), 116–17.

6. According to W. V. Emanuel they were banned in 1935. See W. V. Emanuel, *The Wild Asses: A Journey through Persia* (London: Jonathan Cape, 1939), 262.

7. H. G. Winter, *Persian Miniature* (Garden City, N.J.: Doubleday Page and Co., 1917), 150.

8. Fred Richards, *A Persian Journey: Being an Etcher's Impressions of the Middle East* (London: Jonathan Cape, 1931), 166.

9. Javad Mohaddesi, ed., *Farhang-e 'Ashura* (Qom, Iran: Nashr-e Ma'ruf, 1996), 358.

10. "Azadari," *Ettela'at,* 1 June 1931.

11. For a detailed discussion of this trend, see Shahrough Akhavi, *Religion and Politics in Contemporary Iran: Clergy-State Relations in the Pahlavi Period* (Albany: State University of New York Press, 1980).

12. *Ettela'at,* 24 June 1928, 3, ad no. 39.

13. Ibid., 2 July 1927, ad no. 1. His title is *na'eb ra'is-e majles-e showra-e melli.* See also ibid., 22 June 1928, ad no. 27.

14. For an example, see ibid, 30 April 1933, 2, ad no. 300.

15. For a detailed discussion of the role of religion in Iranian nationalism during this period, see Kamran Aghaie, "Islam and Nationalist Historiography: Competing Historical Narratives of Iran in the Pahlavi Period," *Studies on Contemporary Islam* 2, no. 2 (2000): 20–46.

16. Abd al-Hosayn Zarrinkub, *Do qarn-e sokut. chap-e 2, ba tajdid-e nazar va ezafat va-tashihat* (Tehran: Amir Kabir, 1957), 70–74.

17. Ibid., 75.

18. Ibid., 83.

19. Ibid., 86.

20. Ahmad Karimi, "Imam-e napeyda, ya dastaviz-e tambalan?" *Parcham,* 1943, 2.

21. Ahmad Kasravi, *Shi'ehgari* (Tehran: Chapkhaneh-e Peyman, 1943). Translation from Ahmad Kasravi, *On Islam and Shi'ism,* trans. M. R. Ghanoonparvar (Costa Mesa, Calif.: Mazda Publishers, 1990), 169–73.

22. *Ettela'at,* 4 March 1938, 2.

23. Akhavi, *Religion and Politics,* 61.

24. *Ettelaʿat,* 24 October 1950. This banning of *qameh zani* and *taʿziyeh khani* was reiterated over the years (e.g., in *Moharram* of 1970). See also *Ettelaʿat,* 8 March 1970.

25. Michael M. J. Fischer, *Iran: From Religious Dispute to Revolution* (Cambridge, Mass.: Harvard University Press, 1980), 134.

26. *Ettelaʿat,* 8 October 1951.

27. Ibid., 14 October 1951. He hired several of the most famous reciters/speakers to perform in this event, including Agha-e Haj Mirza Abd Allah, Agha-e Sadr Balaghi, and Agha-e Falsafi.

28. Ibid., 22 September 1953, 4.

29. The independence brigade of Gilan did the same thing in their *majles* that they held in the Haj Samiʿi Mosque during the same year. See ibid., 22 September 1953, 4.

30. Ibid., 24 October 1950.

31. Ibid., 22 and 23 September 1953.

32. Akhavi, *Religion and Politics,* 23.

33. A speech by Mohammad Reza Shah given in 1971. See Vezarat-e Ettelaʿat Markaz-e Barresi-e Asnad-e Tarikhi, *Jashnha-e 2500 saleh-e shahanshahi beh revayat-e asnad-e SAVAK,* 2 vols. (Tehran: Markaz-e Barresi-e Asnad-e Tarikhi, Vezarat-e Ettelaʿat, 1998), 1:8. For a government account of the state-sponsored activities associated with the event, see *Gozaresh-e kolli-e faʿaliyatha-e marbut beh jashn-e do hezar va pansadomin sal-e bonyangozari-e Shahanshahi-e Iran dar dakheleh-e keshvar* (Tehran: Nashriyeh-e Komiteh-e Omur-e Beyn al-Melali-e Jashn-e Shahanshahi-e Iran, 196?)

34. SAVAK document no. 4157, dated 6/18, 1350. Vezarat-e Ettelaʿat Markaz-e Barresi-e Asnad-e Tarikhi, *Jashnha-e 2500 saleh-e shahanshahi beh revayat-e asnad-e SAVAK,* 1:39.

35. Fakhr Rohani, *Ahram-ha-e soqut-e shah* (Tehran: Nashr-e Tabligh, 1991), 1:108.

36. The quotation of the shah was by Sayyed Mohammad Baqer Najafi, *Shahanshahi va dindari* (Tehran: Nashr-e Radiyo va Televiziyon-e Melli, 1976), 5. The remainder is official commentary provided by the Ministry of Information of the Islamic Republic of Iran. See Markaz-e Barresi-e Asnad-e Tarikhi, *Jashnha-e 2500 saleh-e shahanshahi beh revayat-e asnad-e Savak va darbar: bazm-e Ahriman* (Tehran: Markaz-e Barresi-e Asnad-e Takrikhi-e Vezarat-e Ettelaʿat, 1998), 2:15.

5. *Religious Rituals, Society, and Politics during the Pahlavi Period*

1. Ceremonies were sponsored in the residence of Tabataba'i Diba Na'eb Ra'is Majles (see *Ettelaʿat,* 30 June 1928, ad no. 27), or in Shariʿatmadari's house (*Ettelaʿat,* 23 May 1931, ad no. 409), or by the Azerbaijanis (*Ettelaʿat,* May 1943, ad no. 10629).

2. *Ettelaʿat,* 28 September 1952.

3. For a discussion of this phenomenon, see Mohamad Tavakoli-Targhi, "Anti-Baha'ism and Islamism in Iran, 1941–1955." *Iran Nameh,* vol. 19, nos. 1–2 (2001).

4. *Ettelaʿat,* 12 August 1956, ad no. 11179.

5. Ibid., 20 August 1956, 2.

6. For examples of Borujerdi and Shirazi, see ibid., 6 December 1945, ad nos. 8786 and 8779, respectively. Also, for examples of guilds, see the *senf-e qahvehchiyan* (coffee), in ibid., 25 December 1944, ad no. 7537.

7. For Borujerdi, see ibid., January 1944, ad no. 10664. For Behbahani and Nuri, see ibid., 21 September 1952.

8. Sayyed Hoseyn Mo'tamedi Kashani, *Azadari-e sunnati-e shiʿayan dar boyut-e olama va howzehha-e elmiyyeh va keshvarha-e jahan,* 2 vols. (Qom, Iran: Chapkhaneh-e Eʿtemad, 2000), 2:273.

9. For detailed accounts of the involvement of these ayatollahs in *Moharram* rituals, see ibid., 2:273–95.

10. Ibid., 295.

11. Gustav Thaiss, "Religious Symbolism and Social Change: The Drama of Husain" (dissertation, Washington University, 1973), 123 and 283.

12. *Ettelaʿat,* 13 August 1956, ad no. 11259.

13. Examples include electricians (ibid., 9 August 1956, ad no. 11023); drivers and truckers/transporters (ibid., 8 December 1945, ad no. 8804); the Auto-Shiraz company (ibid., 25 October 1950, ad no. 918); magazine and newspaper distributors (ibid., 23 October 1953, ad no. 8040); and cigarette sellers (ibid., 3 September 1954, ad no. 9211).

14. Ibid., 4 April 1968, ad no. 1059.

15. H. Bahrambeygui, *Tehran: An Urban Analysis* (Tehran: Sahab Books Institute, 1977), 50

16. For data on the Qajar period, see the previous chapter. For data on the Pahlavi period, see *Gozaresh-e Farhangi-e Iran* (Tehran: Showra-e Ali-e Farhang va Honar, 1973–76), 40:85–86 and 87–106.

17. Ibid.

18. Ibid., 40:55 and 56.

19. Bahrambeygui, *Urban Analysis,* 129–31.

20. Kazem Sadat Ashkori, "Amaken-e mazhabi-e Tehran," in *Atlas-e farhangi-e shahr-e Tehran* (Tehran: Showra-e ʿAli-e Farhang va Honar, Markaz-e Melli-e Motaleʿat va Hamahangi-e Farhangi, 1976).

21. Sadeq Homayuni, *Taʿziyeh dar Iran* (Shirazi, Iran: Entesharat-e Navid, 1989), 143–46.

22. Shahrough Akhavi, *Religion and Politics in Contemporary Iran: Clergy-State Relations in the Pahlavi Period* (Albany: State University of New York Press, 1980).

23. *Ettelaʿat,* 4 April 1968, ad nos. 1059 and 909.

24. Thaiss, "Religious Symbolism and Social Change."

25. Ibid., 199–200.

26. *Goftar-e 'Ashura* (Tehran: Sherkat-e Sahami-e Enteshar, 1962), 70–73.

27. Ibid., 85–88.

28. Ibid., 106–7.

29. Ruhollah Khomeini, *Islam and Revolution: Writings and Declarations of Imam Khomeini,* trans. Hamid Algar (Berkeley, Calif.: Mizan Press, 1981), 174–75.

30. Ibid., 177–80.

31. Ali Baqeri, ed., *Khaterat-e 15 khordad: bazar* (Tehran: Howzeh-e Honar-e Sazman-e Tablighat-e Eslami, 1996–97), 1:11. This quote is originally from Ruhollah Khomeini, *Sahifeh-e nur: rahnamudha-e Emam Khomeini* (Tehran: Vezarat-e Ershad-e Eslami, Sazman-e Madarek-e Farhangi-e Enqelab-e Eslami, 1991), 219.

32. For a typical example, see the account of the prominent orator Ali Hojjati Kermani in Baqeri, ed., *Khaterat-e 15 khordad,* 1:44, 46–47.

33. For typical accounts of Khomeini's instructions, see ibid., 3:24, 75–76.

34. For a typical account, see ibid., 5:303–4.

35. Ibid., 3:74. See also 6:30.

36. Ibid., 1:107.

37. Ibid., 3:84–87. Habibollah Shafiq gives a similar account (see also 3:96–97).

38. Ibid., 3:84–87.

39. For typical examples, see ibid., 2:66–68, 123.

40. For further discussion of the *Hey'atha-e Mo'talefeh,* see Vanessa Martin, *Creating an Islamic State: Khomeini and the Making of a New Iran* (London: I. B. Tauris, 2000), 64–69. See also A. Badamchiyan and A. Bana'i, *Hey'atha-e Mo'talefeh* (Tehran: Entesharat-e Owj, 1983).

41. Michael M. J. Fischer, *Iran: From Religious Dispute to Revolution* (Cambridge, Mass.: Harvard University Press, 1980), 101.

42. Baqeri, ed., *Khaterat-e 15 khordad,* 1:176.

43. Ibid., 2:123.

44. Ibid., 3:77. See also 4:31.

45. Ibid., 3:43–48.

46. Ibid., 2:107–8.

47. Ibid., 3:58–59.

48. For a typical account, see ibid., 1:97–99 and 108–9. See also 3:84–87 and 5:25–27, 48–49, 99–100, 113, 125–26, 315–17, and 340–45.

49. Michael Fischer gives a detailed account of the 1975 violence in the Feyziyeh in Fischer, *Religious Dispute,* 124–26.

50. I would like to thank Vanessa Martin for suggesting that I look into the important role Tayyeb Reza'i played in these protests. For several eye-witness accounts of the roles of Tayyeb Reza'i, Esma'il Reza'i, Hajji Nuri, and Sha'ban Ja'fari in the protests, see Baqeri, ed., *Khaterat-e 15 khordad,* 3:43–48, 65, 191, and 199–200, and 6:111–12, 113, and 181–83.

51. Ibid., 6:183.

6. Hoseyn, "The Prince of Martyrs"

1. An earlier version of this material was published in Kamran Aghaie, "The Karbala Narrative in Shi'i Political Discourse in Modern Iran in the 1960s-1970s," *Journal of Islamic Studies* 12, no. 2 (2001): 151–76.

2. The "meta-narrative" is defined here in similar terms to Hayden White's conceptualization of "metahistory" in that it comprises the basic philosophical approach of each of the ideologues under study. See Hayden White, *Metahistory: The Historical Imagination in Nineteenth-Century Europe* (Baltimore, Md.: Johns Hopkins University Press, 1973).

3. For a detailed discussion of how this seminal work was the product of the political environment and circumstances surrounding Kashefi's life, see Abbas Amanat, *"Meadows of the Martyrs:* Kashifi's Persianization of the Shi'i Martyrdom Narrative in Late Timurid Herat," in *Culture and Memory in Medieval Islam: Essays in Honor of Wilfred Madelung*, ed. Farhad Daftary and Josef W. Meri. Institute of Ismaili Studies Series (New York and London: I. B. Tauris, forthcoming).

4. Kashefi refers to such traditional Sunni and Shi'i works as the *Rowzat al-ahbab* and *Ketab-e mabkiyyat* of Imam Waqqar, al-Khwarazmi's *Maqtal nur al-'a'emmeh*, Sa'id al-Din's *Rowzat al-Eslam*, Sheykh Mofid's *Rowzat al-Wa'izin*, Termidhi's *Sunan*, as well as the writings of Yazid Ibn Qa'nab, Basha'er al-Mostafa, Ahmad Ibn Hanbal, and Kamal al-Din Ibn al-Khashshab.

5. Molla Hoseyn Va'ez Kashefi, *Rowzat al-shohada* (Tehran: Chapkhaneh-e Khavar, 1962), 67.

6. Ibid., 15–23.

7. Ibid., 24 25.

8. Ibid., 344–54.

9. Salehi Najafabadi, *Shahid-e javid*, 12th ed. (Tehran: Chap-e Parcham, 1970), 291.

10. Ibid., 324–32.

11. Ervand Abrahamian, *Khomeinism: Essays on the Islamic Republic* (Berkeley and Los Angeles: University of California Press, 1993), 30.

12. Letter titled *Sazman-e Ettela'at va amniyat-e keshvar.* Reprinted in Najafabadi, *Shahid-e javid,* 529.

13. Ibid., 530–31.

14. Lotfollah Safi Golpaygani, *Shahid-e agah* (Tehran: Ketabkhaneh-e Sadr, 1970), 2–3.

15. Ibid., 6. Also see footnote on this page.

16. Ibid., 75–77.

17. Ibid., 42–46.

18. Ibid., 106–7.

19. For a transnational comparison of these Shi'i religious discourses, see Kamran Aghaie, "Reinventing Karbala: Revisionist Interpretations of

the 'Karbala Paradigm'." *Jusur: UCLA Journal of Middle Eastern Studies* 10 (1994): 1–30.

20. Speech by Khomeini in *Ettela'at*, 8 September 1982.

21. Ervand Abrahamian, *The Iranian Mujahidin* (New Haven, Conn.: Yale University Press, 1989), 105–10.

22. Hamid Dabbashi, *Theology of Discontent: The Ideological Foundation of the Islamic Revolution* (New York: New York University Press, 1993), 102. See also Abrahamian, *Iranian Mujahidin*, 103.

23. See 'Ali Shari'ati, *Tashayyo'-e Alavi va tashayyo'-e Safavi*, vol. 9, *Majmu'eh-e asar* (Tehran: Entesharat-e Tashayyo', 1980).

24. 'Ali Shari'ati, *Hoseyn vares-e Adam*, 4th ed. (Tehran: Entesharat-e Qalam, 1991), 112.

25. Ibid., 192.

26. Ibid., 125.

27. Ibid., 178.

28. Ibid., 135.

29. Ibid., 166.

30. Ibid., 160.

31. Ibid., 150 and 189.

32. It was originally titled *Sima-e yek mosalman* (*Portrait of a Muslim*).

33. See the biographical sketch of Reza'i in the preface to the 1976 edition of the same text, which was retitled *Nehzat-e Hoseyni* and was published by Entesharat-e Mojahedin-e Khalq-e Iran in Springfield, Mo.

34. Ahmad Reza'i, *Rah-e Hoseyn* (Tehran: Entesharat-e Mojahedin-e Khalq-e Iran, 1972), page *alef* of the preface.

35. Ibid., 15.

36. Morteza Motahhari, *Hamaseh-e Hoseyni*, vols. 1–3 (Tehran: Sadra Publishers, 1985).

37. Ibid., vol. 2.

38. Ibid., 1:191.

39. Ibid.

7. Fatemeh, Zeynab, and Emerging Discourses on Gender

1. Jalal Al-e Ahmad, *Gharbzadegi* (Tehran: Maqaleh [1961]).

2. Partha Chatterjee, *The Nation and Its Fragments: Colonial and Post-Colonial Histories* (Princeton, N.J.: Princeton University Press, 1993).

3. Ibid., 121.

4. Mehdi Moltaji, *Bozorg banu-e jahan, Zeynab va khotab-e balegheh va ziyarat-e mofajje'eh-e an hazrat* (Tehran: Entesharat-e Ashrafi, 1975), p. "jim." The eight books on Zeynab that Moltaji cites are (1) Mirza Abbasqoli Khan Sepehr's *Toraz al-Mozaffari*, (2) Sheykh Ja'far al-Naqdi's *Hayat-e Zeynab-e kobra*, (3) Nur al-Din Jaza'eri's *Khasa'es-e Zeynabiyeh*, (4) Agha-e

Parvaresh's *Ketab-e nur va zolmat,* (5) Mohammad Haj Hendi's *Sayyedah Zeynab,* (6) Bent al-Shate's *Qahreman-e shirzan-e Karbala,* (7) Javad Fazel's translations of Zeynab's speeches, and, finally, (8) Marhum Mohandes Qomi's *Sharif montaha al-a'mal.*

5. An advertisement for this book appeared in *Ettela'at,* 16 September 1953, 8, ad no. 7872.

6. Mohammad Mohammadi Eshtehardi, *Sugnameh-e al-e Mohammad* (Qom, Iran: Entesharat-e Naser-e Qom, 1997).

7. Ibid., 169–214.

8. See Mohammad Mohammadi Eshtehardi, *Hazrat-e Zeynab, payam resan-e shahidan-e Karbala* (Tehran: Nashr-e Motahhar, 1997), 16.

9. Eshtehardi, *Sugnameh-e al-e Mohammad,* 173–75.

10. Eshtehardi, *Hazrat-e Zeynab,* 15.

11. Ibid., 315–17.

12. Ibid., 283–87.

13. Ibid., 332–70.

14. Ibid., 209–13.

15. Mehdi Moltaji, *Bozorg banu-e jahan, Zeynab va khotab-e balegheh va ziyarat-e mofajje'eh-e an hazrat* (Tehran: Entesharat-e Ashrafi, 1975), 61.

16. "In Islamic law fighting on the battlefield of Jihad is forbidden for women." See ibid., 36.

17. Eshtehardi, *Sugnameh-e al-e Mohammad,* 209–13. For more details, see Qasem's *ta'ziyeh* in Hasan Salehirad, ed., *Majales-e ta'ziyeh* (Tehran: Sorush, 1995), 77–90.

18. Eshtehardi, *Sugnameh-e al-e Mohammad,* 290–93. For Zeynab's willingness to sacrifice her sons, see also 238–39.

19. Bint al-Shati' [Bent al-Shate'], *Zeynab banu-e qahreman-e Karbala (Batalat Karbala),* trans. Habib Chaychiyan and Mehdi Ayatollahzadeh Na'ini (Tehran: Mo'assaseh-e Entesharat-e Amir Kabir, 1979), 61.

20. Ibid., 62–70.

21. Ibid., 157.

22. Mahmud Farshchian, *The Evening of Ashura* (n.p.: Negar Books, 1981).

23. Bint al-Shati' [Bent al-Shate'], *Zeynab,* 139.

24. 'Ali Shari'ati, *Fatemeh Fatemeh ast: Majmu'eh-e asar* (Tehran: Chapkhaneh-e Diba, 1990), 21:3–4.

25. Ibid., 9–10.

26. Eshtehardi, *Hazrat-e Zeynab,* 29.

27. Ibid., 9.

28. Ibid., 11–12.

29. Bint al-Shati' [Bent al-Shate'], *Zeynab,* 99–104.

30. Eshtehardi, *Hazrat-e Zeynab,* 18.

31. Ibid., 21.

32. Ibid., 21–22.
33. Ibid., 21.
34. Ibid., 26–28.

8. The Islamic Republic

1. For a detailed discussion of the role of Islam and secularism in Iranian nationalism, see Kamran Aghaie, "Islam and Nationalist Historiography: Competing Historical Narratives of Iran in the Pahlavi Period," *Studies on Contemporary Islam* 2, no. 2 (2000): 20–46.

2. Michael M. J. Fischer, *Iran: From Religious Dispute to Revolution* (Cambridge, Mass.: Harvard University Press, 1980), 235.

3. See Haggay Ram, *Myth and Mobilization in Revolutionary Iran: The Use of Friday Congregational Sermons* (Washington, D.C.: American University Press, 1994).

4. Sazman-e Chap va Entesharat-e Vezarat-e Farhang va Ershad-e Eslami, *Maktab-e jom'eh: majmu'eh-e khotbehha-e namaz-e Jom'eh-e Tehran. jelde haftom, hafteh-e 211–234*, 9 vols. (Tehran: Sazman-e Chap va Entesharat-e Vezarat-e Farhang va Ershad-e Eslami, 1989–90), 7:144–45.

5. Ibid.

6. Mas'ud Kowsari, ed., *Gozaresh-e Farhangi-e Keshvar, 1377 Majmu'eh-e Amari-e Fa'aliyatha-e Farhangi-e Vezaratha, Sazmanha, va Nahadha* (Tehran: Vezarat-e Farhang va Ershad-e Eslami, 1998–99), 369 and 364, respectively.

7. *Ettela'at*, issue 22446, 19 March 2002, 11.

8. Ibid., issue 21051, 15 May 1997, 7.

9. See, e.g., Jaber Anasori, "Ta'ziyeh, honar-e vaqfi-e Iran," *Miras-e Javidan* 1, no. 3 (1993): 38–41. See also *Ettela'at*, issue 16569, 6 November 1981, 14.

10. For a detailed discussion of how the revolutionary images were related to the traditional genres of Shi'i art, see Hamid Dabbashi and Peter Chelkowski, *Staging a Revolution: The Art of Persuasion in the Islamic Republic of Iran* (New York: New York University Press, 1999).

11. See ibid.

12. *Ettela'at*, issue 20494, 6 June 1995, 3; see also issue 20495, 7 June 1995, 1.

13. Ibid., issue 16014, 28 November 1979, 12.

14. Ibid., issue 16015, 1 December 1979, 2.

15. Mansoor Moaddel, *Class, Politics, and Ideology in the Iranian Revolution* (New York: Columbia University Press, 1993).

16. Sazman-e Chap va Entesharat-e Vezarat-e Farhang va Ershad-e Eslami, *Rahnama-e farhangi-e Tehran* (Tehran: Sazman-e Chap va Entesharat-e Vezarat-e Farhang va Ershad-e Eslami, 1994–95), 7–157. Ali Madanipour points to similar trends in his book, *Tehran: The Making of a Metropolis* (Chichester, Great Britain: John Wiley and Sons, 1998).

17. Eslami, *Rahnama*, 158–67.

18. Madanipour points to similar trends in his *Tehran: Making of a Metropolis.*

19. Sayyed Hoseyn Mo'tamedi Kashani, *Azadari-e sunnati-e shi'ayan dar boyut-e olama va howzehha-e elmiyyeh va keshvarha-e jahan*, 2 vols. (Qom, Iran: Chapkhaneh-e E'temad, 2000), 2:229–32 and 232–36. He is quoting these figures from the *Sazman-e Tablighat-e Eslami-e Tehran* (1997).

20. Markaz-e Motale'at va Hamahangi-e Farhangi Showra-e Ali-e Farhang va Honar, *Gozaresh-e farhangi-e keshvar* (Tehran: Markaz-e Motale'at va Hamahangi-e Farhangi, 1352 [1973–74] and 1363 [1984–85]).

21. Ibid., 1353 (1974–75) and 1354 (1975–76); and Markaz-e Amar-e Iran, *Natayej-e amari-e tarh-e shenasnamehha-e masajed va amaken-e mazhabi-e keshvar* (Tehran: Sazman-e Barnameh va Budjeh-e Jomhuri-e Eslami-e Iran in cooperation with Vezarat-e Farhang va Ershad-e Eslami, 1375 [1996]).

22. Markaz-e Motale'at va Hamahangi-e Farhangi Showra-e Ali-e Farhang va Honar, *Gozaresh-e farhangi-e keshvar,* 1353 (1974–75) and 1354 (1975–76); Markaz-e Amar-e Iran, *Natayej-e amari-e tarh-e shenasnamehha-e masajed va amaken-e mazhabi-e keshvar,* 1375 (1996). For a detailed map showing relative distributions of *takyeh*s, mosques, and *emamzadeh*s (religious tomb shrines), see Bernard Hourcade et al., eds. *Atlas d'iran* (Montpellier, France: La Documentation Française, 1998) 79.

23. Markaz-e Amar-e Iran, *Natayej,* 1377 (1998-99).

24. These data were provided by Dr. Asghar Karimi of the Bonyad-e Da'erat al-Ma'aref-e Eslami and by Eslami, *Rahnama,* 1373 (1994–95).

25. The main *hey'at*s discussed here included two neighborhood *hey'at*s located in central and northern Tehran; the *hey'at* of the Shah Abd al-Azim mosque in the city of Ray (I also accompanied this *hey'at* on its ten-day pilgrimage to Mashhad during *Arba'in,* spending several days with the *hey'at* and staying in the *takyeh* with its members at night); the *Hey'at-i Motavasselin Beh Rasul Allah,* in Shahreza; and the *hey'at*s of the *Masjed-e Karbala'iha* and *Masjed-e Azarbayjaniha* located in the Tehran bazaar. In addition, other *hey'at*s that are referred to include several *hey'at*s in the *Tajrish* bazaar in Tehran and the *hey'at* of Aba al-Fazl in central Tehran.

26. The two main examples referred to here are the mass processions performed in front of the Tehran bazaar on the third day (*sevvom* in 1997) and the mass ritual performed in front of the main entrance to the *haram* in Mashhad on the fortieth day (*Arba'in* in 1997).

27. Two informants in particular said that the government had progressively restricted women's involvement in these rituals over the past two years (i.e., 1995–97).

28. I observed all of these examples of banners while doing research on the day of the *sevvom* in 1997 in the mass ritual in front of the Tehran bazaar.

29. In the mass ritual performed in front of the Tehran bazaar on the *sevvom*, and in front of the main shrine in Mashhad on the occasion of the *arba'in*, Arabs were relatively more active in this portion of the ritual.

30. Javad Mohaddesi, ed., *Farhang-e 'Ashura* (Qom, Iran: Nashr-e Ma'ruf, 1996), 358.

Bibliography

Abedi, Mehdi, and Bary Lengenhausen, eds. *Jihad and Shahadat: Struggle and Martyrdom in Islam.* Houston: Institute of Research and Islamic Studies, 1986.

Abin, Eugène. *La Perse d'aujourd'hui—eran. Mésopotamie—avec une carte en couleur hors texte.* Paris: A. Colin, 1908.

Abrahamian, Ervand. *Iran between Two Revolutions.* Princeton, N.J.: Princeton University Press, 1982.

———. *The Iranian Mujahidin.* New Haven, Conn.: Yale University Press, 1989.

———. *Khomeinism: Essays on the Islamic Republic.* Berkeley and Los Angeles: University of California Press, 1993.

———. *Tortured Confessions: Prisons and Public Recantations in Modern Iran.* Berkeley and Los Angeles: University of California Press, 1999.

Abu al-Hosna, 'Ali (Monzer). *Siyahpushi dar sug-e a'emmeh-e nur: rishehha-e tarikhi, manabe'-e feqhi.* Qom, Iran: Mo'assaseh-e Chap-e al-Hadi, 1996.

Abu Alam, Tawfiq. *Ahl al-bayt.* Cairo: Maktabat al-Anglo al-Misriyya, 1971.

Adelkhah, Fariba. *Being Modern in Iran.* New York: Columbia University Press, 2000.

Al-Adib, 'Adil. *al-A'immah al-Ithna ashariyyah.* Beirut: al-Dar al-Islamiyyah, 1979.

Afary, Janet. *The Iranian Constitutional Revolution, 1906–1911: Grassroots Democracy, Social Democracy, and the Origins of Feminism.* New York: Columbia University Press, 1996.

Aghaie, Kamran. "Husayn and Zaynab: Models for Social and Political Movements in Modern Iran." Dissertation, University of California, 1999.

———. "Islam and Nationalist Historiography: Competing Historical Narratives of Iran in the Pahlavi Period." *Studies on Contemporary Islam* 2, no. 2 (2000): 20–46.

———. "The Karbala Narrative in Shi'i Political Discourse in Modern Iran in the 1960s–1970s." *Journal of Islamic Studies* 12, no. 2 (2001): 151–76.

———. "Muharram Rituals, Social Identities, and Political Relationships under Qajar Rule: 1850s–1930s." Paper presented at the Religion and

Society in Qajar Iran Conference, University of Bristol and British Institute of Persian Studies, Bristol, England, 2000.

———. "Reinventing Karbala: Revisionist Interpretations of the 'Karbala Paradigm'." *Jusur: UCLA Journal of Middle Eastern Studies* 10, (1994): 1–30.

al-e Ahmad, Jalal. *Gharbzadegi.* Tehran: Maqaleh [1961].

Akbari, 'Ali Asghar. *Qahreman nameh-e 'Ashura: zekr-e Mosibat va nowheh khani.* Mashhad, Iran: Mo'assaseh-e Farhangi-e Entesharati-e Gowhar Sayyah, 1996.

Akhavi, Shahrough. *Religion and Politics in Contemporary Iran: Clergy-State Relations in the Pahlavi Period.* Albany: State University of New York Press, 1980.

———. "State Formation and Consolidation in Twentieth-Century Iran: The Reza Shah Period and the Islamic Republic." In *The State, Religion, and Ethnic Politics: Afghanistan, Iran, and Pakistan,* edited by Ali Banuazizi and Myron Weiner, 198–226. Syracuse, N.Y.: Syracuse University Press, 1986.

Algar, Hamid. *Religion and State in Iran, 1785–1906: The Role of the Ulama in the Qajar Period.* Berkeley and Los Angeles: University of California Press, 1969.

Amanat, Abbas. "*Meadows of the Martyrs:* Kashifi's Persianization of the Shi'i Martyrdom Narrative in Late Timurid Herat." In *Culture and Memory in Medieval Islam: Essays in Honor of Wilfred Madelung,* edited by Farhad Daftary and Josef W. Meri. Institute of Ismaili Studies Series. London and New York: I. B. Tauris, forthcoming.

———. *Pivot of the Universe: Nasir al-Din Shah Qajar and the Iranian Monarchy, 1851–1896.* Berkeley and Los Angeles: University of California Press, 1997.

Amin, Cameron Michael. *The Making of the Modern Iranian Woman: Gender, State Policy, and Popular Culture, 1865–1946.* Gainesville: University Press of Florida, 2002.

Amini, 'Allameh. *Fatemeh-e Zahra: umm abiha. goftar-e 'Allameh Amini.* Tehran: Mo'assaseh-e Entesharat-e Amir Kabir, 1983.

Amir-Moezzi, Mohammad Ali. *The Divine Guide in Early Shi'ism: The Sources of Esotericism in Islam.* Translated by David Streight. New York: State University of New York Press, 1994.

Ana'i, Morteza, ed. *Naghmehha-e Karbala.* Qom, Iran: Entesharat-e Sa'id Novin, 1996.

Anasori, Jaber, ed. *Shabih khani, ganjineh-e nemayeshha-e ayini mazhabi.* Tehran: Chapkhaneh-e Ramin, 1993.

———, ed. *Shabih khani, kohan olgu-e nemayeshha-e Irani.* Tehran: Chapkhaneh-e Ramin, 1992.

———. "Ta'ziyeh, honar-e vaqfi-e Iran." *Miras-e Javidan,* vol. 1, no. 3 (1993).

Ansari, Ali. *A History of Modern Iran since 1921: The Pahlavis and After.* Harlow: Longman, 2002.

Ansari, Saraj. *Shi'eh cheh miguyad*. Qom, Iran: Chapkhaneh-e 'elmiyeh-e Qom, AH 1385.

Arjomand, Said Amir, ed. *Authority and Political Culture in Shi'ism*. New York: State University of New York Press, 1988.

———. "Ideological Revolution in Shi'ism." In *Authority and Political Culture in Shi'ism*, edited by Said Amir Arjomand, ed., 178–209. New York: State University of New York Press, 1988.

———. *The Shadow of God and the Hidden Imam*. Chicago: University of Chicago Press, 1984.

———. *The Turban for the Crown: The Islamic Revolution of Iran*. Oxford: Oxford University Press, 1988.

Ashkori, Kazem Sadat. "Amaken-e mazhabi-e Tehran." In *Atlas-e farhangi-e shahr-e Tehran*. Tehran: Showra-e 'Ali-e Farhang va Honar, Markaz-e Melli-e Motale'at va Hamahangi-e Farhangi, 1976.

Ayati, Mohammad Ebrahim. *Barresi-e tarikh-e 'Ashura*. 9th ed. Tehran: Nashr-e Sadduq, 1996.

Ayoub, Mahmoud. *Redemptive Suffering in Islam: A Study of the Devotional Aspects of 'Ashura' in Twelver Shi'ism*. New York: Mouton Publishers, 1978.

"Azadari." *Ettela'at*, 1 June 1931.

Babazadeh, 'Ali Akbar. *Tahlil-e sireh-e Fatemeh al-Zahra*. Qom, Iran: Entesharat-e Ansariyyun, 1995.

Badamchiyan, A., and A. Bana'i. *Hey'atha-e Mo'talefeh*. Tehran: Entesharat-e Owj, 1983.

Bahar, Mohammad Taqi (Malek al-Sho'ara). *Tarikh-e mokhtasar-e ahzab-e siyasi-e Iran*. Vol. 1. Tehran: Chapkhaneh-e Sepehr, 1943.

Bahrambeygui, H. *Tehran: An Urban Analysis*. Tehran: Sahab Books Institute, 1977.

Baktash, Mayel. "'Ta'ziyeh and Its Philosophy." In *Ta'ziyeh: Ritual and Drama in Iran*, edited by Peter Chelkowski, 95–120. New York: New York University Press, 1979.

Baqeri, 'Ali, ed. *Khaterat-e 15 khordad: bazar*. Tehran: Howzeh-e Honar-e Sazman-e Tablighat-e Eslami, 1996–97.

Bayat, Mangol. *Mysticism and Dissent: Socioreligious Thought in Qajar Iran*. Syracuse, N.Y.: Syracuse University Press, 1982.

Baydun, Ibrahim. *Ittijahat al-mu'ariza fi al-Kufa*. Beirut: Ma'had al-Anma al-'Arabi, 1986.

Beeman, William O. "Images of the Great Satan: Representations of the United States in the Iranian Revolution." In *Religion and Politics in Iran*, edited by Nikki R. Keddie, 191–217. New Haven, Conn.: Yale University Press, 1983.

Behnam, Reza. *Cultural Foundations of Iranian Politics*. Salt Lake City: University of Utah Press, 1986.

Behrooz, Maziar. *Rebels with a Cause: The Failure of the Left in Iran*. London: I. B. Tauris, 1999.

Benjamin, Samuel G. W. *Persia and the Persians*. Boston: Ticknor and Company, 1887.

Bill, James A., and John Alden Williams. *Roman Catholics and Shi'i Muslims: Prayer, Passion, and Politics*. Chapel Hill: University of North Carolina Press, 2002.

Black, Max. *Models and Metaphors: Studies in Language and Philosophy*. Ithaca, N.Y.: Cornell University Press, 1962.

Bohrer, Frederick N., ed. *Sevruguin and the Persian Image: Photographs of Iran, 1870–1930*. Seattle: University of Washington Press, 1999.

Bonine, Michael E., and Nikki R. Keddie, eds. *Modern Iran: The Dialectics of Continuity and Change*. Albany: State University of New York Press, 1981.

Bosworth, Edmond, and Carole Hillenbrand, eds. *Qajar Iran: Political, Social, and Cultural Change, 1800–1925*. Edinburgh: Edinburgh University Press, 1983.

Brugsch, Heinrich Karl. *Reise der K. preussischen Gesandtschaft nach Persien 1860 und 1861 (Safarnameh-e ilchi-e Prus dar Iran: safari beh darbar-e soltan sahebqeran 1859–1861)*. Translated by Mohandes Kordbcheh. Tehran: Entesharat-e Ettela'at, 1988.

Brunner, Rainer, and Werner Ende, eds. *The Twelver Shia in Modern Times: Religious Culture and Political Culture*. Leiden: Brill, 2001.

Butehkar, Hasan Elahi. *Zeynab-e Kobra*. Tehran: Mo'assaseh-e Farhangi-e Afarina, 1996.

Calmard, Jean. "Le culte de l'Imam Husayn. Etudes sur la commémoration du Drame de Karbala dans l'Iran pré-safavide." Dissertation, University of Paris III, 1975.

———. "Muharram Ceremonies and Diplomacy (A Preliminary Study)." In *Qajar Iran: Political, Social, and Cultural Change, 1800–1925*, edited by Edmond Bosworth and Carole Hillenbrand, 213–28. Edinburgh: Edinburgh University Press, 1983.

———. "Le Patronage des Ta'ziyeh: Elements pour une Etude Globale." In *Ta'ziyeh: Ritual and Drama in Iran*, edited by Peter Chelkowski, 121–30. New York: New York University Press, 1979.

———. "Shi'i Rituals and Power II. The Consolidation of Safavid Shi'ism: Folklore and Popular Religion." In *Safavid Persia*, edited by Charles Melville, 139–90. London: I. B. Tauris, 1996.

Chatterjee, Partha. *The Nation and Its Fragments: Colonial and Postcolonial Histories*. Princeton, N.J.: Princeton University Press, 1993.

Chehabi, Houchang E. "Ardabil Becomes a Province: Center-Periphery Relations in Iran." *International Journal of Middle Eastern Studies* 29 (1997): 235–53.

———. *Iranian Politics and Religious Modernism: The Liberation Movement of Iran under the Shah and Khomeini*. Ithaca, N.Y.: Cornell University Press, 1990.

————. "Staging the Emperor's Clothes: Dress Codes and Nation-Building under Reza Shah." *Iranian Studies* 26 (1993): 209–29.

Chelkowski, Peter. "Iran: Mourning Becomes Revolution; Annual Rites of Self-Sacrifice, Atonement, and Revenge Precipitated the Toppling of the Shah and the Taking of American Hostages." *ASIA,* 1980, 30–37.

————. "Narrative Painting and Painting Recitation in Qajar Iran." In *Muqarnas: An Annual on Islamic Art and Architecture,* 98–111. Leiden: Leiden Brill Academic Publishers, 1989.

————. "Shia Muslim Processional Performances." *Drama Review* 29, no. 3 (1985): 19–30.

————, ed. *Ta'ziyeh: Ritual and Drama in Iran.* New York: New York University Press, 1979.

Cole, Juan R. I. *The Roots of North Indian Shi'ism in Iran and Iraq: Religion and State in Awadh, 1722–1859.* Berkeley and Los Angeles: University of California Press, 1988.

————. *Sacred Space and Holy War: The Politics and History of Shi'ite Islam.* London: I. B. Tauris, 2002.

Cole, Juan R. I., and Nikki R. Keddie, eds. *Shi'ism and Social Protest.* New Haven, Conn.: Yale University Press, 1986.

Cottam, Richard W. *Nationalism in Iran.* Pittsburg: University of Pittsburg Press, 1964.

Cronin, Stephanie. *The Army and the Creation of the Pahlavi State in Iran, 1910–1926.* London: Tauris Academic Studies, 1997.

Dabbashi, Hamid. *Theology of Discontent: The Ideological Foundation of the Islamic Revolution.* New York: New York University Press, 1993.

————, and Peter Chelkowski. *Staging a Revolution: The Art of Persuasion in the Islamic Republic of Iran.* New York: New York University Press, 1999.

Daniel, Elton. *The History of Iran.* Westport, Conn.: Greenwood Press, 2001.

————, ed. *Society and Culture in Qajar Iran: Studies in Honor of Hafez Farmayan.* Costa Mesa, Calif.: Mazda Publishers, 2002.

Davis, Natalie Zemon. "Women's History in Transition: The European Case." *Feminist Studies,* vol. 3 (1975–76).

De Lorey, Eustache, and Douglas Sladen. *Queer Things about Persia.* London: Evelein Nash, 1907.

De Warzee, Dorothy. *Peeps into Persia.* London: Hurst and Blackett Ltd., 1913.

Douglas, Mary. *Purity and Danger.* New York: Praeger, 1966.

Ekhtiar, Maryam. *Modern Science, Education, and Reform in Qajar Iran: The Dar al-Funun.* Richmond, Va.: Curzon, 2001.

Emadzadeh, Emad al-Din Hosayn Esfahani. *Hazrat-e Zeynab-e Kobra.* Tehran: Nashr-e Mohammad, 1970.

Emanuel, W. V. *The Wild Asses: A Journey through Persia.* London: Jonathan Cape, 1939.

Enayat, Hamid. *Modern Islamic Political Thought.* Austin: University of Texas Press, 1982.

Eshtehardi, Mohammad Mohammadi. *Hazrat-e Zeynab, payam resan-e shahidan-e Karbala.* Tehran: Nashr-e Motahhar, 1997.

———. *Sugnameh-e al-e Mohammad.* Qom, Iran: Entesharat-e Nasir-e Qom, 1997.

Esposito, John, ed. *The Iranian Revolution: Its Global Impact.* Miami: Florida International University Press, 1990.

Ettela'at. Tehran: Mo'assaseh-i Ettela'at, 1941-2002.

Farazmand, Ali. *The State, Bureaucracy, and Revolution in Modern Iran: Agrarian Reforms and Regime Politics.* New York: Praeger, 1989.

Farshchian, Mahmud. *The Evening of Ashura.* N.p.: Negar Books, 1981.

Fernea, Elizabeth Warnock. *Guests of the Sheik: An Ethnography of an Iraqi Village.* New York: Anchor Books Doubleday, 1965.

Fischer, Michael M. J. *Debating Muslims.* Madison: University of Wisconsin Press, 1990.

———. *Iran: From Religious Dispute to Revolution.* Cambridge, Mass.: Harvard University Press, 1980.

Floor, Willem. *Industrialization in Iran, 1900–1941.* Durham, England: University of Durham, 1984.

Foran, John, ed. *A Century of Revolution: Social Movements in Iran.* Minneapolis: University of Minnesota Press, 1994.

Forbes-Leith, Francis. *Checkmate: Fighting Traditions in Central Persia.* New York: Robert McBride and Co., 1927.

Frischler, Kurt. *Emam Hoseyn va Iran.* Translated by Zabihollah Mansuri. Tehran: Sazman-e Entesharat-e Javidan, 1983.

Ghaffary, Farrokh. "Takyehha va talarha-e nemayesh-e Tehran." In *Tehran, paytakht-e devist saleh,* edited by Shahryar Adl and Bernard Hourcade, 159–71. Paris and Tehran: Institut Francais de Recherche en Iran, 1992.

———. "Theatrical Buildings and Performances in Tehran." In *Qajar Iran and the Rise of Reza Khan, 1796–1925,* by Nikki R. Keddie, 94–102. Costa Mesa, Calif.: Mazda Publishers, 1999.

Ghani, Cyrus. *Iran and the Rise of Reza Shah: From Qajar Collapse to Pahlavi Power.* London: I. B. Tauris, 1998.

Gheissari, Ali. *Iranian Intellectuals in the 20th Century.* Austin: University of Texas Press, 1998.

Ghods, Reza M. *Iran in the Twentieth Century: A Political History.* Boulder, Colo.: Lynne Reinner Publishers, 1989.

Gieling, Saskia. *Religion and War in Revolutionary Iran.* London: I. B. Tauris, 1999.

Goftar-e 'Ashura. Tehran: Sherkat-e Sahami-e Enteshar, 1962.

Golpaygani, Lotfollah Safi. *Shahid-e agah.* Tehran: Ketabkhaneh-e Sadr, 1970.

Good, Mary-Jo Delvecchio, and Byron J. Good. "Ritual, the State, and the

Transformation of Emotional Discourse in Iranian Society." *Culture, Medicine and Psychiatry* 12 (1988): 43–63.

Gozaresh-e Farhangi-e Iran. Tehran: Showra-e Ali-e Farhang va Honar, 1973–76.

Gozaresh-e kolli-e faʿaliyatha-e marbut beh jashn-e do hezar va pansadomin sal-e bonyangozari-e Shahanshahi-e Iran dar dakheleh-e keshvar. Tehran: Nashriyeh-e Komiteh-e Omur-e Beyn al-Melali-e Jashn-e Shahanshahi-e Iran [196?].

Hakimi, Mohammad Reza. *Baʾsat, Ghadir, ʿAshura. Mahdi.* N.p.: Fajr Press, 1976.

Halm, Heinz. *Shiʿa Islam: From Religion to Revolution.* Princeton, N.J.: Markus Weiner Publishers, 1997.

Hasan Baygi, Mohammad. *Tehran-e qadim.* Tehran: Entesharat-e Qoqnus, 1988.

Hedin, Sven. *Overland to India.* Vol. 2. London: Macmillan and Co., 1910.

Hegland, Mary Elaine. "Flagellation and Fundamentalism: (Trans)forming Meaning, Identity, and Gender through Pakistani Women's Rituals." *American Ethnologist,* vol. 25 (1998).

———. "The Majales—Shiʿa Women's Rituals of Mourning in Northwest Pakistan." In *A Mixed Blessing: Gender and Religious Fundamentalism Cross Culturally,* edited by Judy Brink and Joan Mencher, 179–96. New York: Routledge, 1997.

———. "The Power Paradox in Muslim Women's *Majales:* North-West Pakistani Mourning Rituals as Sites of Contestation over Religious Politics, Ethnicity, and Gender." *Signs* 23, no. 2 (1998): 391–428.

———. "Shiʿa Women of Northwest Pakistan and Agency through Practice: Ritual, Resistance, Resilience." *Political and Legal Anthropology Review* 18, no. 2 (1995): 65–80.

———. "Two Images of Husain: Accommodation and Revolution in an Iranian Village." In *Religion and Politics in Iran,* edited by Nikki R. Keddie, 218-35. New Haven, Conn.: Yale University Press, 1983.

Homayuni, Sadeq. *Taʿziyeh dar Iran.* Shirazi, Iran: Entesharat-e Navid, 1989.

Hooglund, Eric. *Land and Revolution in Iran, 1960–1980.* Austin: University of Texas Press, 1982.

Hourcade, Bernard, et al., eds. *Atlas d'iran.* Montpellier, France: La Documentation Française, c1998.

Hunt, Lynn. *The Family Romance of the French Revolution.* Berkeley and Los Angeles: University of California Press, 1992.

Hyder, Syed Akbar. "Iqbal and Karbala: Re-reading the Episteme of Martyrdom for Poetics of Appreciation." *Cultural Dynamics* 13, no. 3 (2001): 339–62.

Jafri, S. H. M. *The Origins and Early Development of Shiʿa Islam.* Qom, Iran: Group of Muslims, 1978.

Kaempfer, Engelbert. *Am Hofe des persischen grosskonigs 1684–1685 (Dar dar-bar-e shahanshah-e Iran)*. Translated by Kaykavus Jahandari. Tehran: Ente-sharat-e Anjuman-e Asar Milli, 1971.

Kamrava, Mahran. *The Political History of Modern Iran: From Tribalism to Theocracy*. London: Praeger, 1992.

Karimi, Ahmad. "Imam-e napeyda, ya dastaviz-e tambalan?" *Parcham*, 1943, 2.

Kashani, Sayyed Hoseyn Mo'tamedi. *Azadari-e sunnati-e shiʿayan dar boyut-e olama va howzehha-e elmiyyeh va keshvarha-e jahan*. 2 vols. Qom, Iran: Chapkhaneh-e Eʿtemad, 2000.

Kashefi, Molla Hoseyn Vaʿez. *Rowzat al-shohada*. Tehran: Chapkhaneh-e Khavar, 1962.

al-Kashifulghita, al-Hoseyn. *Asl al-shiʿa wa usuluha*. Beirut: Muntashirat Maktabat al-'Irfan, n.d.

Kasravi, Ahmad. *On Islam and Shiʿism*. Translated by M. R. Ghanoonpar-var. Costa Mesa, Calif.: Mazda Publishers, 1990.

———. *Shiʿehgari*. Tehran: Chapkhaneh-e Peyman, 1943.

Kathir, Ibn. *al-Bidaya wa al-nihaya*. Cairo: Matbaʿah al-Saʿada, AH 1358.

Katouzian, Homa. *State and Society in Iran: The Eclipse of the Qajars and the Emergence of the Pahlavis*. London: I. B. Tauris, 2000.

Kattani, Sulayman. *Fatima al-Zahra*. Beirut: Mu'assasa Wafa, 1983.

Kazemi, Farhad. "The Shiʿi Clergy and the State in Iran: From the Safavids to the Pahlavis." *Journal of the American Institute for the Study of Middle Eastern Civilization* 1, no. 2 (1980): 34–52.

Keddie, Nikki R. *Qajar Iran and the Rise of Reza Khan, 1796–1925*. Costa Mesa, Calif.: Mazda Publishers, 1999.

———, ed. *Religion and Politics in Iran*. New Haven, Conn.: Yale Univer-sity Press, 1983.

———. *Roots of Revolution*. New Haven, Conn.: Yale University Press, 1981.

———, and Juan Cole, eds. *Shiʿism and Social Protest*. New Haven, Conn.: Yale University Press, 1986.

———, and Eric Hooglund. *The Iranian Revolution and the Islamic Republic*. Syracuse, N.Y.: Syracuse University Press, 1986.

Kedourie, Elie, and Sylvia G. Haim, eds. *Towards a Modern Iran: Studies in Thought, Politics, and Society*. Totowa, N.J.: Frank Cass, 1980.

Kermani, Morteza Fahim. *Zan va payam avari*. Tehran: Daftar-e Nashr-e Farhang-e Eslami, 1995.

Khan, Mirza Ebrahim (Navvab Tehrani). *Feyz al-domuʿ*. Tehran: Ente-sharat-e Yasavali Farhangsara, 1984.

Khansari, Molla Aqa. *Kolsum naneh*. Tehran: Entesharat-e Morvarid, n.d.

Kheirabdi, Masoud. *Iranian Cities: Formation and Development*. Syracuse, N.Y.: Syracuse University Press, 2000.

Khomeini, Ruhollah. *Islam and Revolution: Writings and Declarations of Imam Khomeini*. Translated by Hamid Algar. Berkeley, Calif.: Mizan Press, 1981.

————. *Qiyam-e ʿAshura (The Ashura Uprising)*. Tehran: Institute for Compilation and Publication of the Works of Imam Khomeini, 1995.

————. *Sahifeh-e nur: rahnamudha-e Emam Khomeini*. Tehran: Vezarat-e Ershad-e Eslami, Sazman-e Madarek-e Farhangi-e Enqelab-e Eslami, 1991.

————. *Sima-e zan dar kalam-e emam*. Tehran: Entesharat-e Vezarat-e Farhang va Ershad-e Eslami, 1992.

Khoury, Philip, et al., eds. *Modern Middle East Reader*. London: I. B. Tauris, 1993.

Kohlberg, Etgan. *Belief and Law in Imami Shiʿism*. Hampshire, Great Britain: Variorum, 1991.

Kowsari, Masʿud, ed. *Gozaresh-e Farhangi-e Keshvar, 1377 Majmuʿeh-e Amari-e Faʿaliyatha-e Farhangi-e Vezaratha, Sazmanha, va Nahadha*. Tehran: Vezarat-e Farhang va Ershad-e Eslami, 1998–99.

Kramer, Martin, ed. *Shiʿism, Resistance, and Revolution*. Boulder, Colo.: Westview Press, 1987.

Ladjevardi, Habib. *Labor Unions and Autocracy in Iran*. Syracuse, N.Y.: Syracuse University Press, 1985.

Lambton, Ann K.S. *Persian Land Reform, 1962–1966*. Oxford: Clarendon Press, 1969.

————. *Qajar Persia*. Austin: University of Texas Press, 1987.

Lassy, Ivar. "The Muharram Mysteries among the Azerbeijan Turks of Caucasia: An Academical Dissertation." Dissertation, Helsingfors University, 1916.

Lenczowski, George, ed. *Iran under the Pahlavis*. Stanford, Calif.: Hoover Institute Press, 1978.

Lesch, David W. *1979: The Year That Shaped the Modern Middle East*. Boulder, Colo.: Westview Press, 2001.

Ma'tuq, Firidrik. *La representation de la mort de l'imam Hussein a Nabatieh (Liban-Sud)*. Beirut: Université libanaise, Institut des sciences sociales, 1974.

Maatouk, Frederic. *La representation de la mort de l'imam Hussein a Nabatieh*. Beirut: Université libanaise, Institut des sciences sociales, Centre de recherches, 1974.

Madanipour, Ali. *Tehran: The Making of a Metropolis*. Chichester, Great Britain: John Wiley and Sons, 1998.

Mahallati, Sayyed Hashem Rasuli. *Zendegani-e hazrat-e Fatemeh va dokhtaran-e an hazrat*. 3d ed. Tehran: Chapkhaneh-e Daftar-e Nashr-e Farhang-e Eslami, 1996.

Mahmudi, ʿAbbas ʿAli. *Zan dar Eslam*. 5th ed. Tehran: Feyz Kashani, 1995.

Majlesi, Allameh. *Tarikh-e chahardah maʿsum*. Qom, Iran: Entesharat-e Sorur, 1996.

Mansur, Mahmud. *al-Shaqiqan fi Karbala*. Cairo: Dar Nashr al-Thaqafa, 1970.

Markaz-e Amar-e Iran. *Natayej-e amari-e tarh-e shenasnamehha-e masajed va amaken-e mazhabi-e keshvar.* Tehran: Sazman-e Barnameh va Budjeh-e Jomhuri-e Eslami-e Iran in cooperation with Vezarat-e Farhang va Ershad-e Eslami, AH 1375.

Markaz-e Barresi-e Asnad-e Tarikhi. *Jashnha-e 2500 saleh-e shahanshahi beh revayat-e asnad-e Savak va darbar: bazm-e Ahriman.* 2 vols. Tehran: Markaz-e Barresi-e Asnad-e Takrikhi-e Vezarat-e Ettela'at, 1998.

Markaz-e Motale'at va Hamahangi-e Farhangi, Showra-e Ali-e Farhang va Honar. *Gozaresh-e farhangi-e keshvar.* Tehran: Markaz-e Motale'at va Hamahangi-e Farhangi, 2000.

Martin, Vanessa. *Creating an Islamic State: Khomeini and the Making of a New Iran.* London: I. B. Tauris, 2000.

———. *Islam and Modernism: The Iranian Revolution of 1906.* Syracuse, N.Y.: Syracuse University Press, 1989.

Matin-Asgari, Afshin. *Iranian Student Opposition to the Shah.* Costa Mesa, Calif.: Mazda Publishers, 2002.

Mazzaoui, Michel M. "Shi'ism and Ashura in South Lebanon." In *Ta'ziyeh: Ritual and Drama in Iran,* edited by Peter Chelkowski, 228–37. New York: New York University Press, 1979.

Menashri, David. *Education and the Making of Modern Iran.* Ithaca, N.Y.: Cornell University Press, 1992.

Milani, Mohsen, ed. *The Making of Iran's Islamic Revolution: From Monarchy to Islamic Republic.* Boulder, Colo.: Westview Press, 1988.

Miyanji, Sayyed Ebrahim. *al-Uyun al-ibra fi maqtal Sayyed al-shohada.* N.p.: Chapkhaneh-e Haydari, 1959.

Mo'meni, 'Abd al-Hoseyn. *Zendegani-e Fatemeh al-Zahra.* Tehran: Sazman-e Entesharat-e Javidan, 1975.

Moaddel, Mansoor. *Class, Politics, and Ideology in the Iranian Revolution.* New York: Columbia University Press, 1993.

Mohaddesi, Javad, ed. *Farhang-e 'Ashura.* Qom, Iran: Nashr-e Ma'ruf, 1996.

Mohajerani, Sayyed Ata'ollah. *Payam avar-e 'Ashura: barresi-e seyr-e zendegi, andisheh, va jahad-e Zeynab-e Kobra.* Tehran: Entesharat-e Ettela'at, 1996.

Moltaji, Mehdi. *Bozorg banu-e jahan, Zeynab va khotab-e balegheh va ziyarat-e mofajje'eh-e an hazrat.* Tehran: Entesharat-e Ashrafi, 1975.

Momen, Moojan. *An Introduction to Shi'i Islam.* New Haven, Conn.: Yale University Press, 1985.

Monfarid, 'Ali Nazari. *Qesseh-e Karbala: beh zamimeh-e qesseh-e enteqam.* Qom, Iran: Entesharat-e Sorur, 1997.

Moqaddam, 'Abd al-'Ali Adeb al-Molk. *Safarnameh-e Adib al-Molk beh 'atabat (dalil al-za'erin).* Tehran: Entesharat-e Dadju, 1985.

Morton, Rosalie Slaughter. *A Doctor's Holiday in Iran.* New York: Funk and Wagnalls Co., 1940.

Moslem, Mehdi. *Factional Politics in Post-Khomeini Iran.* Syracuse, N.Y.: Syracuse University Press, 2002.

Mostowfi, Abdollah. *The Administrative and Social History of the Qajar Period.* Translated by Nayer Mostofi Glenn. Vol. 1. Costa Mesa, Calif.: Mazda Publishers, 1997.

Mostowi, Abdollah. *Sharh-e Zendegani-e man: ya tarikh-e ejtemaʿi va edari-e dowreh-e Qajar.* Tehran: Ketabforushi-e Zavvar, 1946.

Motahhari, Morteza. *Hamaseh-e Hoseyni.* Vols. 1–3. Tehran: Sadra Publishers, 1985.

Mottahedeh, Roy. *The Mantle of the Prophet.* New York: Simon and Schuster, 1985.

Mounsey, Augustus H. *A Journey through the Caucasus and the Interior of Persia.* London: Smith, Elder, and Co., 1872.

al-Mughniyya, Shaykh Mohammad Jawad. *al-Shiʿa fi al-mizan.* Cairo: Dar al-Shuruq, n.d.

———. *al-Shiʿa wa al-hakimun.* Beirut: Manshurat al-Maktabah al-Ahliya, n.d.

Muson, Henry. *Islam and Revolution in the Middle East.* New Haven, Conn.: Yale University Press, 1988.

Muzaffar, Mohammad Riza. *Beliefs of the Shiʿite School.* Translated by S. M. S. Hyder. Karachi, Pakistan: Islamic Seminary Publications, 1985.

Najafabadi, Salehi. *Shahid-e javid.* 12th ed. Tehran: Chap-e Parcham, 1970.

Najafi, Sayyed Mohammad Baqer. *Shahanshahi va dindari.* Tehran: Nashr-e Radiyo va Televiziyon-e Melli, 1976.

Najmabadi, Afsaneh. *Land Reform and Social Change in Iran.* Salt Lake City: University of Utah Press, 1987.

Najmi, Naser. *Dar al-khalafeh-e Tehran.* Tehran: Entesharat-e Zavvar, 1977.

———. *Tehran-e ahd-e Naseri.* 2d ed. Tehran: Entesharat-e Attar, 1988.

Nakash, Yitzhak. *The Shiʿis of Iraq.* Princeton, N.J.: Princeton University Press, 1994.

Naqvi, Ali Naqi. *Azadari.* Karachi, Pakistan: Peer Mohammad Ibrahim Trust, n.d.

Naysaburi, Zayn al-Muhaddithin Mohammad Ibn al-Fattal. *Rawzat al-waʿizin.* Beirut: Muʾassasat al-Aʿlami li al-Matbuʿat, 1986.

Norton, Augustus Richard. *Amal and the Shiʿa: Struggle for the Soul of Lebanon.* Austin, Tex.: University of Texas Press, 1987.

———. *Shiʿism and the Ashura Ritual in Lebanon.* New York: Al-Saqi, 2003.

Nur al-Din, Hasan. *ʿAshura fi al-adab al-amili al-muʾasir.* Beirut: al-Dar al-Islamiya, 1988.

Nurbakhsh, Masʿud. *Musaferan-e tarikh: moruri bar tarikhcheh-e safar va siyahatgari dar Iran.* Translated by Masʾud Nurbakhsh. Tehran: Entesharat-e Tus, 1985.

Nweeya, Samuel K. *Persia: The Land of the Magi, or Home of the Wise Men.* Philadelphia: Press of the John C. Winston Co., 1910.

Parvinchi, Mirza Hadi. *Aʿzam al-masaʾeb.* N.p.: Chapkhaneh-e Payam, 1994.

Parviz, Nazanin. *Complete Pictorial Guide to Tehran Historical Monuments.* Tehran: A. Zand Publishers, 2000.

Pelly, Sir Lewis. *The Miracle Play of Hasan and Husayn.* London: Wm. H. Allen and Co., 1879.

Pepper, Stephen. *World Hypotheses.* Los Angeles and Berkeley: University of California Press, 1942.

Peterson, Samuel, ed. *Ta'ziyeh: Ritual and Popular Beliefs in Iran.* Hartford, Conn.: Trinity College, 1988.

Pinault, David. *The Horse of Karbala: Muslim Devotional Life in India.* New York: Palgrave, 2001.

————. *The Shi'ites, Ritual, and Popular Piety in a Muslim Community.* New York: St. Martin's Press, 1992.

Qazvini, al-Sayyid Riza. *Tazallum al-Zahra min ihraq dima' al al-'aba.* 3d ed. Qom, Iran: Manshurat al-Riza, 1965.

Qazwini, al-Sayyid Mohammad Kazim. *Fatima al-Zahra: min al-mahd ila al-'ahd.* 1st ed. Beirut: Mu'assasa Wafa, 1977.

Qomi, Abbas b. Mohammad b. Reza. *Romuz al-shahada: tarjomeh-e kamel-e nafas al-mahmum.* Translated by Ayatollah Kamareh'i. Tehran: Chapkhaneh-e Aftab, 1984.

Raby, Julian. *Qajar Portraits.* London: I. B. Tauris, 1999.

Rahnema, Ali, and Farhad Nomani. *The Secular Miracle: Religion, Politics, and Economic Policy in Iran.* London: Zed Books Ltd., 1990.

Rahnema, Zeyn al-Abedin. *Zendegani-e Emam Hosayn.* 15th ed. Vols. 1–2. N.p.: Ketabforushi-e Zavvar, 1986.

Ram, Haggay. *Myth and Mobilization in Revolutionary Iran: The Use of Friday Congregational Sermons.* Washington, D.C.: American University Press, 1994.

————. "Mythology of Rage: Representations of the 'Self' and the 'Other' in Revolutionary Iran." *History and Memory* 8, no. 1 (1996): 68–87.

Ramazani, R. K., ed. *Iran's Revolution: The Search for Consensus.* Bloomington: Indiana University Press, 1990.

Ravandi, Morteza. *Zendegi-e Iraniyan dar khelal-e ruzgaran.* Tehran: Chap-e Ramin, 1984.

Reza'i, Ahmad. *Rah-e Hoseyn.* Tehran: Entesharat-e Mojahedin-e Khalq-e Iran, 1972.

Reza'i, Aniseh Sheykh, and Shahla Azari, eds. *Gozareshha-e nazmiyeh-e mahallat-e Tehran.* N.p.: Entesharat-e Sazman-e Asnad-e Melli-e Iran, 1998.

Richard, Yann. *Shi'ite Islam: Polity, Ideology, and Creed.* Translated by Antonia Nevill. Oxford: Blackwell, 1995.

Richards, Fred. *A Persian Journey: Being an Etcher's Impressions of the Middle East.* London: Jonathan Cape, 1931.

Ringer, Monica M. *Education, Religion, and the Discourses of Cultural Reform in Qajar Iran.* Costa Mesa, Calif.: Mazda Publishers, 2001.

Rizvi, Athar Abbas. *A Socio-Intellectual History of the Isna 'Ashari Shi'is in India*. Canberra, Australia: Ma'rifat Publishing House, 1986.

Rohani, Fakhr. *Ahram-ha-e soqut-e shah*. Vol. 1. Tehran: Nashr-e Tabligh, 1991.

Sa'dvandiyan, Sirus, and Mansureh Ettehadiyeh, eds. *Amar-e Dar al-Khalafeh-e Tehran: asnadi az tarikh-e ejtema'i-e Tehran dar asr-e Qajar*. Tehran: Nashr-e Tarikh-e Iran, 1989.

Sachedina, Abdulaziz Abdulhussein. *The Just Ruler in Shi'ite Islam: The Comparative Authority of the Jurist in Imamite Jurisprudence*. New York: Oxford University Press, 1988.

Sadeqi, Sayyed Rasul, ed. *Naghmeh-e 'Ashura*. Tehran: Entesharat-e Yasin, 1997.

Sadiqipur, A. R., ed. *Collection of Speeches by the Late Majesty Reza Shah the Great*. Tehran: Javidan Publishers, 1968.

Sadr, Hasan. *Hoquq-e zan dar Eslam va Orupa*. 7th ed. Tehran: Chapkhaneh-e Mohammad Hasan Elmi, 1977.

Salehirad, Hasan, ed. *Majales-e ta'ziyeh*. Tehran: Sorush, 1995.

Sanders, Paula. *Ritual, Politics, and the City in Fatimid Cairo*. Albany: State University of New York Press, 1994.

Sarvar Mowla'i, Mohammad, ed. *Qiyam-e Sayyed al-shohada Hosayn Ebn-e Ali va khunkhahi-e Mokhtar*. Tehran: Entesharat-e Bonyad-e Farhang-e Iran, 1980.

Sazman-e Chap va Entesharat-e Vezarat-e Farhang va Ershad-e Eslami. *Maktab-e jom'eh: majmu'eh-e khotbehha-e namaz-e Jom'eh-e Tehran. jeld-e haftom, hafteh-e 211–34*. 9 vols. Vol 7. Tehran: Sazman-e Chap va Entesharat-e Vezarat-e Farhang va Ershad-e Eslami, 1989–90.

———. *Rahnama-e farhangi-e Tehran*. Tehran: Sazman-e Chap va Entesharat-e Vezarat-e Farhang va Ershad-e Eslami, 1994–95.

Schubel, Vernon James. *Religious Performance in Contemporary Islam: Shi'i Devotional Rituals in South Asia*. Columbia: University of South Carolina Press, 1993.

Scott, Joan Wallach. *Gender and the Politics of History*. New York: Columbia University Press, 1988.

Sepehr, Mirza Mohammad Taqi. *Nasekh al-tavarikh*. Tehran: Entesharat-e Ketabforushi-e Eslamiyeh, 1973.

———. *Nasekh al-tavarikh: dar zekr-e faza'el botul al-'ozra ensiyyeh al-howra Fatemeh al-Zahra*. 2d ed. Tehran: Entesharate Ketabforushi-e Eslamiyeh, 1966.

Shah, Naser al-Din. *Safarnameh-e Araq-e Ajam (belad-e markazi-e Iran)*. Tehran: Tirajheh, 1983.

Shahidi, Enayatollah, and Ali Bolukbashi, *Pazhuheshi dar ta'ziyeh va ta'ziyeh khani az aghaz ta payan-e dowreh-e Qajar dar Tehran*. Tehran: Daftar-e Pazhuheshha-e Farhangi, Komisiyon-e Melli-e Yunesko dar Iran, 2001.

Shahidi, Sayyed Ja'far. *Zendegani-e Fatemeh Zahra*. 22d ed. Vol. 3, *Ashna'i ba zendegani-e ma'suman*. Tehran: Daftar-e Nashr-e Farhang-e Eslami, n.d.

Shahri, Ja'far. *Tarikh-e ejtima'i-e Tehran dar qarn-e sizdahom.* Vol. 5. Tehran: Entesharat-e Esma'iliyan, 1988–89.

———. *Tehran-e qadim.* Tehran: Entesharat-e Mo'in, 1990.

Shararah, Waddah. *Transformations d'une manifestation religieuse dans un village du Liban-Sud (Asura).* Beirut: al-Jami'ah al-Lubnaniyyah, Ma'had al-'Ulum al-Ijtima'iyah, 1968.

Shari'ati, 'Ali. *Fatemeh Fatemeh ast: Majmu'eh-e asar.* Vol. 21. Tehran: Chapkhaneh-e Diba, 1990.

———. *Hoseyn vares-e Adam.* 4th ed. Tehran: Entesharat-e Qalam, 1991.

———. *Shahadat va pas az shahadat.* Tehran: Sazman-e Entsharat-e Hosayniyeh-e Ershad, 1972.

———. *Shi'eh: Majmu'eh-e asar.* Vol. 7. Tehran: Sazman-e Entesharat, 1980.

———. *Tashayyo'-e Alavi va tashayyo'-e Safavi.* Vol. 9, *Majmu'eh-e asar.* Tehran: Entesharat-e Tashayyo', 1980.

———. *Zan, Majmu'eh-e asar.* Tehran: Entesharat-e Tashayyo', 1980.

al-Shati', Bint [Bent al-Shate']. *Zeynab banu-e qahreman-e Karbala (Batalat Karbala).* Translated by Habib Chaychiyan and Mehdi Ayatollahzadeh Na'ini. Tehran: Mo'assaseh-e Entesharat-e Amir Kabir, 1979.

Sheil, Lady. *Glimpses of Life and Manners in Persia.* London: John Murray, 1856.

Sheykh al-Eslami, Sayyed Hosayn. *Qiyam-e salar-e shahidan.* Qom, Iran: Daftar-e Entesharat-e Eslami, 1996.

Sheykholeslami, Ali Reza. "From Religious Accommodation to Religious Revolution: The Transformation of Shi'ism in Iran." In *The State, Religion, and Ethnic Politics: Afghanistan, Iran, and Pakistan,* edited by Ali Banuazizi and Myron Weiner, 227–55. Syracuse, N.Y.: Syracuse University Press, 1986.

Shirazi, Vaqqar. *Ashareh-e kameleh.* Tehran: Entesharat-e Foruzangeh, 1981.

Sotudeh, Manuchehr. *Joghrafiya-e tarikhi-e Shemiran.* Vols. 1–2. Tehran: Mo'assaseh-e Motale'at va Tahqiqat-e Farhangi, 1992.

Sreberny-Mohammadi, Annabelle, and Ali Mohammadi. *Small Media, Big Revolution.* Minneapolis: University of Minnesota Press, 1994.

al-Suyuti, al-Hafiz Jalal al-Din 'Abd al-Rahman ibn Abi Bakr. *Musnad Fatima al-Zahra.* Haydarabad, India: Tab' bil-Matba'a al-'aziziyya, 1986.

Sykes, Ella. *Persia and Its People.* London: Methuen and Co., Ltd., 1910.

Tabataba'i, Allameh Mohammad Hosayn. *Amuzesh-e din.* Qom, Iran: Jahanara Press, 1977.

———. *Shi'eh dar Islam.* N.p.: Chapkhaneh-e Ziba, 1970.

———. *Universality of Islam.* Translated by S. M. S. Hyder. Karachi, Pakistan: Islamic Seminary Publications, 1985.

Taqiyan, Laleh. *Ta'ziyeh va te'atr dar Iran.* Tehran: Nashr-e Markaz, 1995.

Tavakoli-Targhi, Mohamad. "Anti-Baha'ism and Islamism in Iran, 1941–1955." *Iran Nameh* 19, nos. 1–2 (2001).

———. *Refashioning Iran: Orientalism, Occidentalism, and Historiography.* New York: Palgrave, 2001.

Thaiss, Gustav. "Religious Symbolism and Social Change: The Drama of Husain." Dissertation, Washington University, 1973.

———. "Religious Symbolism and Social Change: The Drama of Husain." In *Scholars, Saints, and Sufis: Muslim Religious Institutions since 1500*, edited by Nikki R. Keddie, 349–66. Berkeley and Los Angeles: University of California Press, 1972.

———. "Unity and Discord: The Symbol of Husayn in Iran." In *Iranian Civilization and Culture: Essays in Honor of the 2,500th Anniversary of the Founding of the Persian Empire*, edited by Charles J. Adams, 111–20. Montreal: McGill University, 1973.

Torab, Azam. "Piety as Gendered Agency: A Study of Jalaseh Ritual Discourse in an Urban Neighbourhood in Iran." *Journal of the Royal Anthropological Institute*, vol. 2, no. 2 (1996).

Turner, Victor. *Dramas, Fields, and Metaphors*. Ithaca, N.Y.: Cornell University Press, 1974.

Tusturi, Ja'far. *al-Khasa'is al-Husayniyya*. Tehran: Mo'assaseh-e Matbu'ati-e Dar al-Ketab, n.d.

Vahdat, Fazin. *God and Juggernaut: Iran's Intellectual Encounter with Modernity*. Syracuse, N.Y.: Syracuse University Press, 2002.

Van Den Bos, Mathijs. *Mystic Regimes: Sufism and the State in Iran, from the Late Qajar Era to the Islamic Republic*. Leiden, the Netherlands: Brill, 2002.

Walbridge, Linda S., ed. *The Most Learned of the Shi'a: The Institution of the Marja' Taqlid*. Oxford: Oxford University Press, 2001.

———. *Without Forgetting the Imam: Lebanese Shi'ism in an American Community*. Detroit: Wayne State University Press, 1997.

White, Hayden. *Metahistory: The Historical Imagination in Nineteenth-Century Europe*. Baltimore, Md.: Johns Hopkins University Press, 1973.

Wills, Charles James. *In the Land of the Lion and Sun, or Modern Persia*. London: Macmillan and Co., 1883.

Winter, H. G. *Persian Miniature*. Garden City, N.J.: Doubleday Page and Co., 1917.

Yazdi, Mohammad. *Biyayid Hoseyn Ebn-e Ali ra behtar beshnasim*. Qom, Iran: Chapkhaneh-e elmiyyeh-e Qom, 1967.

Yazdi, Sayyed Mohammad Najafi. *Asrar-e 'Ashura*. 4th ed. Tehran: Chapkhaneh-e Daftar-e Entesharat-e Eslami, 1996.

Yunisiyan, Husayn, ed. *Wadi'at al-rasul*. 3d ed. Tehran: Entesharat-e Borhan, 1995.

al-Zanjani, Ibrahim al-Musawi. *Aqa'id al-imamiyya al-ithna ashariyya*. Beirut: Mu'assasat al-A'lami li l-Matbu'at, 1973.

Zarrinkub, Abd al-Hosayn. *Do qarn-e sokut. chap-e 2, ba tajdid-e nazar va ezafat va-tashihat*. Tehran: Amir Kabir, 1957.

al-Zayn, Mohammad Hoseyn. *al-Shi'a fi al-tarikh*. Beirut: Dar al-Athar, 1979.

Index

gender *(continued)*
 discourses, 113–30
 and Eshtehardi's narrative
  of Zeynab, 125–30
 and gender-coded symbols, 115,
  116, 123, 158
 gender-neutral themes in narratives, 118
 modernist vs. traditionalist
  conceptions of, 114–17,
 Reza Shah's policies related
  to, 113–14
 symbolism in graveyards,
  136–37
 wives of Qasem and Vahb, 120
 women as captives at Karbala,
  121
 women associated with mourning and crying, 121–22
 women in Kashefi's narrative,
  93, 116
 See also A'esheh; Fatemeh;
  Zeynab
Ghadir Khom (and Eyd-e Ghadir),
 4, 10, 58, 135
Golpaygani, Lotfollah Safi, 84,
 96–99

Habib Ebn-e Mazaher, 118
Hakimi, Mohammad Reza, 99
Hamdanids of Syria, 6
Hasan, son of Ali Ebn-e Abi Taleb,
 4, 37, 124, 126
Hejazi, Fakhr al-Din, 73
hey'at, 51, 69–71, 79–83, 139, 142–
 51, 160–61
Hey'atha-e Mo'talefeh, 80, 82
hijab, 52, 64, 120–21, 125–26, 130,
 134
Hojjat, Sayyed Ali Akbar, 96
Hoseyn, son of Ali Ebn-e Abi
 Taleb
 early history of, and Karbala,
  4, 7–13
 symbols and rituals of, xi, 27, 53,
  58, 73–75, 80–81, 87–112,
  118–40, 146–52

hoseyniyeh, 18, 69–72, 136–37,
 142–47
Hoseyniyeh-e Ershad, 72, 100, 102,
 108, 124, 135

imamate, 4–5, 7–8
Iran-Iraq war, 106, 138
Isfahani, Mohammad Shari'at, 99
Islamic Republic, xi, 53–55, 67, 115,
 131–61 passim
Isma'ilis, 7
Ithna Ashari Shi'is, 7

Ja'fari, Mohammad Taqi, 99
Ja'fari, Sha'ban, 85
Jafri, Seyyed Hosayn, 99
jahad-e sazandegi, 132, 139
jihad, 75, 88, 103–4, 129, 132–40,
 156

kafan push (burial shroud), 140
Kamareh'i, Ayatollah Mirza Khalil,
 69
Karbala narrative
 core-narrative and meta-narrative, 88–89
 gendered narratives, 113–30
 Golpaygani's interpretations
  of, 96–97
 Kashefi's narrative and interpretations, 12–13, 87–112
 Motahhari's interpretations
  of, 109
 Najafabadi's interpretations
  of, 95–96
 Reza'i's interpretations of, 106
 Shari'ati's interpretations of,
  103–5
 soteriological dimensions of, 88
Karbala paradigm
 definition of, x, 8–9, 163n1
 oppositional interpretations and
  discourses, 86–112, 133, 141,
  161
 state's use of, xi, xii, xiii, 132–41
 See also Karbala narrative
Kashani, Ayatollah, 68

Kashani, Sayyed Hasan, 42–45
Kashefi, Hoseyn Va'ez, 12, 89–93, 103–4, 108, 117, 123
Kasravi, Ahmad, 25–26, 57–58, 101
Kazem, Musa, 7
Khadijeh, wife of Mohammad, 126
Khamenei, Ayatollah, 53, 134, 140, 152
Khansari, Ayatollah Sayyed Ahmad, 41–42, 69
Khomeini, Ayatollah, 53, 63
  death and shrine, 138
  and Islamic Republic, 131–32, 135–40, 152, 156, 158
  and 1963 protests, 76–87
  opposed Pahlavi regime, 76–87, 93, 96, 99–100, 105, 108,
Khwarazmi, al-. *See* Al-Khwarazmi

Majles. *See* Moharram rituals and symbols
Majlesi, Baqer, 3
martyrdom, 9, 11, 19, 87–88
  after Islamic Revolution, 133, 136–40, 151, 156
  gender issues related to, 9, 118–26
  Golpaygani's interpretations of, 96–97
  Kashefi's interpretations of, 92
  Motahhari's interpretations of, 109
  Najafabadi's interpretations of, 95–96
  Reza'i's interpretations of, 106
  Shari'ati's interpretations of, 103–5
meydans, 138
Miyanji, Sayyed Ebrahim, 90
Mo'aviyeh, first Umayyad Caliph, 7, 74, 87, 110
Mo'ezz al-Dowleh, Buyid ruler, 10
Mohammad, Prophet of Islam
  crisis of succession, 3–11
  family of, 9–11, 27, 39, 61, 121
  in gendered narratives, 117–18, 121, 123

in Karbala narratives, 91–93, 97, 103, 106, 110
  symbolism of, 17, 23, 36, 53–54, 74, 77, 135, 137, 151
Moharram processions
  after Islamic Revolution, 137–40, 148–50, 155
  during Safavid and Qajar periods, 16–17, 22–24, 31–38, 50–51
  during Pahlavi period, 54, 57, 60, 63
  early history, 10–12
  and political protests, 60, 63, 79–86
Moharram rituals and symbols
  group contributions to support rituals, 28
  in radio and television programs, 135
  Iranian elites critical of, 25–26, 53–58, 68
  modern changes in patterns of speakers and sermons, 72
  non Shi'is participation in, 14
  number and distribution of performances in Qajar Tehran, 31–33
  patronage outside the court and government, 30, 55
  praise and prayers for patrons and the Shah, 27, 68
  reversal of patron-client relationship, 26, 28
  and rituals used in ulama rivalries and political debates, 43–46
  social status and charity at, 26–27
  violence and clashes involving processions, 37–38
Mohtaj, Mirza Mohammad Ali, 18
Mojahedin-e Khalq, 100–101, 105–8
Moltaji, Mehdi, 117
Montazeri, Ayatollah Hoseyn, 95–96, 99

Reza'i, Esma'il, 85
Reza'i, Tayyeb, 83–85
rowzeh khan (Moharram preachers),
21, 32, 90
rowzeh khani (ritualized sermon)
after Islamic Revolution, 135–36
in Pahlavi period, 55, 59–60, 73
in Qajar period, 31, 43, 67, 154
origins from Kashefi's text,
12–13, 89
and Qajar patronage, 16, 20, 27
Reza Khan participated in, 50
sponsored by ulama, 18, 19
women and, 40, 42, 146

Safavids, 11–12, 14–15, 60, 103
Saheb Ebn-e Abbad, 11
Sa'id al-Din, 89
sayyeds, 26, 34, 155
Sepehr, Mirza Mohammad Taqi,
89
shabih khani, 13, 17–18, 20, 22, 31,
150
shahadat, 103–4. *See also* martyrdom
Shahbakhti, Governor-General of
Azerbaijan, 60
Shahrestani, Sayyed Ahmad, 69
Shamsabadi, Hojjat al-Eslam, 96
Shamsiddin, Sayyid Mahdi, 99
Shari'ati, Ali, 72, 83, 100–109, 117,
122–25, 158
Shari'ati, Mohammad Taqi, 73
Shemr, 9, 11, 22, 92, 111, 128
Shi'ism
conversion of Iran to, in Safavid
era, 3
and crisis of succession after
death of Mohammad, 4–5
early Shi'i states, 7–10
formative period and hetero-
doxy, 3–10
geographic concentrations
of Sunnis and Shi'is, 3
roots of Shi'i-Sunni schism, 3
shi'at Ali (partisans of Ali), 5
Twelver, 3, 7
Shi'i symbols and rituals
financial aspects of rituals dur-

ing Qajar period, 20–21
in early rebellions, 10
pervasive in Iranian society, xi
popular participation in rituals
during Qajar period, 20
soteriological aspects of, 91–93
Shirazi, Vaqqar, 89
sineh zani (ritual beating of the
chest), 37, 51, 139
sofreh (ritual dinner), 40, 146
sugvari, 72

Tabataba'i, Allameh Mohammad
Hoseyn, 99
Tabataba'i, Sayyed Ziya, 49
takyeh
as part of rituals, 81
during Qajar period, 16, 51, 154
funding and financing of,
10–21, 33–35
gendered space and women,
38–42
hey'ats, hoseynehs, and, in
Tehran and Iran, 31–34,
68–71, 142–50
societal groups and, 34–36, 51,
152, 160–61
Sven Hedin's account of, in
Tebbes, 19
Takyeh Dowlat, 20–24, 30–31,
40–41, 55
Taleqani, Sayyed Mahmud, 74–
76, 83
ta'ziyeh
Europeans in audience of, 20,
24–25
in Qajar period, 13–14, 21–22, 31
perceived decline and preservation of, 13, 71, 136
professional performers in, 21
Qajar patronage of, 16, 20, 27
Ulama rulings on, 17–18
women patrons of, 40–41
tollab, 26, 96
Tow'eh, 118
Tudeh Party, 101
Twelvers, 3, 7–8, 11, 16. *See also*
Shi'ism

ulama
  and Islamic Revolution, 133,
    139, 148
  and Mohammad Reza Shah,
    77–82
  and Reza Shah, 49, 51–55, 59
  debates about Karbala narra-
    tives, 95, 99–108
  and *Moharram* rituals, 18–19, 31,
    60, 72–73
  ruling regarding permissibility
    of rituals, 14, 17–19, 53–55
  sermons on social and political
    issues, 43–45
  sponsored rituals in their
    homes, 18–19, 67, 69
  views of Qajars and Westerners,
    16–17, 24–25, 49, 65
  views regarding women in
    rituals, 42
Umayyad Caliphate, 6–7

velayat-e faqih, 131

westernization, 43, 47, 64, 65, 86,
  114, 124–25, 141
women
  as characters at the Battle
    of Karbala, 9
  as characters played by male
    actors, 38–39

involvement in Moharram
  rituals, 22–24, 38–43
lecturing at ritual gatherings,
  72
as patrons of rituals, 40–41

Yazdi, Ha'eri, Marja' al-Taqlid,
  17–18
Yazdi, Mohammad, 90
Yazid
  at Battle of Karbala, 7–9
  symbolism of, xi, 38–39, 73–
    74, 80, 87–111, 121–22, 129,
    132–34

zanjir zani, 139
Zarribaf, Sayyed Esma'il, 79–80
Zarrinkub, Abd al-Hoseyn, 56–
  57
Zaydis, 7
Zeynab, sister of Hoseyn
  at Battle of Karbala, 9, 118,
    136–37
  discourses and symbolism asso-
    ciated with, 113–30 passim,
    136–37, 158
Zeyn al-Abedin, Ali, 9, 119, 121,
  128, 151
Zu al-Feqar, 92
Zu al-Jenah, 92
zurkhaneh, 27